Writing Together/Writing Apart

Writing Together

Writing Apart

Collaboration
in
Western American Literature

Linda K. Karell

UNIVERSITY OF NEBRASKA PRESS
LINCOLN AND LONDON

An earlier version of chapter 3 appeared in
American Indian Quarterly 19.4 (1995): 451–65.
Copyright © 1995 by the University of Nebraska
Press. Reprinted by permission of the University
of Nebraska Press. An earlier version of chapter 4
appeared in *Exploring the Lost Borders*, ed.
Melody Graulich and Betsy Klimasmith (Reno:
U of Nevada P, 1999): 167–82.

Design and composition by Melissa Ehn at
Wilsted & Taylor Publishing Services

Library of Congress Cataloging-in-Publication Data

Karell, Linda K., 1960–
    Writing together/writing apart : collaboration in
    Western American literature / Linda K. Karell.
       p. cm.
    Includes bibliographical references and index.
    ISBN 0-8032-2749-3 (cloth : alk. paper)
    ISBN 978-0-8032-1834-5 (paper : alk. paper)
    1. American literature—West (U.S.)—History and
criticism. 2. West (U.S.)—Intellectual life. 3. West
(U.S.)—In literature. 4. Authorship—Collaboration.
I. Title.

PS271 .K37 2002
801.9'3278—dc21
                                    2002024716

To my mother,

Claudia J. Swanson

◆

CONTENTS

ACKNOWLEDGMENTS

If there is one point I hope to make in this book, it is that no one writes alone. Although my name appears as the singular author of this study (because, as Michael Dorris once put it, "separate bylines work"), I am under no illusions that I am without my own collaborators or that this text is my singularly unique creation. This fact does not seem like a loss to me, whether of power, of prestige, of identity, or of authority. Quite the opposite: it reminds me of the constant and complex web of relationships in which any act of writing is embedded. Individuals, institutions, and many other texts infiltrated my consciousness, prodded me to new insights, kept me company, and in various ways provided essential support throughout the months and years this study has been under way.

My life has been enriched by many fine teachers who, in ways subtle and dramatic, have supported and encouraged me: years ago, when I was an undergraduate at Montana State University (MSU), Alanna Kathleen Brown taught me to risk beginning with what I didn't know, rather than what I did, and write from there. Joe Bourque, also an outstanding teacher of mine when I was an undergraduate, was the first to suggest that my work might be of interest to others. When I was in graduate school at the University of Rochester, Tom Hahn's intellectual enthusiasm and open-door office policy literally kept me going, and Mary Cappello's keen mind and fascinating questions led me in new directions and gave me the confidence to pursue unexpected answers.

Support from my colleagues and students also has been vital: Melody Graulich, editor of *Western American Literature*, has been pivotal in my career several times already. She has been unfailingly supportive and has been enormously generous with that rare commodity in a highly successful academic's life, her time. Her respect, enthusiasm, and insightful critiques demonstrate the highest levels of collegial support. Sara Jayne Steen, formerly my teacher and now my colleague, has been enthusiastic about my project from its start and has given me expert advice and direction. As MSU department chair of English during the six years this study has been under way, she has also fielded more than one anxious phone call; to these calls (usually to her home, on a weekend), she invariably responded with patience, confidence in whatever I was proposing, and laughter—a reassuring combination. Bette London provided important early research leads when I was beginning this project, and Lisa Logan read the entire manuscript and gave detailed, honest, and challenging feedback. I am deeply indebted to my reviewers for the University of Nebraska Press, Melody Graulich and Nancy Cook, whose suggestions for revision combined expertise with generosity. They have contributed directly to the strengths in this study. I am also grateful to the students in my spring 2000 senior capstone course, who entertained my ideas about collaboration and western American literature with skepticism and curiosity, forcing me to clarify my thinking and ultimately helping me produce a finer argument. In particular, my thanks go to Ken Courtney, whose comments on an earlier draft of chapter 6 helped bring focus to key points. The graduate students in my fall 2001 course "Authorship and Literary Authority" deserve thanks as well. Their intermittent but passionate resistance as well as their persistent enthusiasm taught me firsthand how high the stakes are when attempting to view authorship as other than self-evident and individually assumed.

This project has also benefited enormously from institutional support. Specifically, I want to thank Montana State University for a substantial Vice President for Research and Creativity Grant in 1999 that funded a research trip and a summer of writing; Dean James McMillan and the College of Letters and Science at MSU for a research grant and a course release in 1998; and the Department of English for funding a semester of full-time research in 1997. I also wish to thank the Huntington Library and its staff, particularly Sue Hodson, for providing me with assistance during two visits to read drafts of Mary Austin's autobiography and related material and Mary Hallock Foote's letters and for permission to quote from Austin's letters. Not least, English Department administrative assistants Carolyn Steele and Teresa Klusmann have been critical to my day-to-day work life; I give special thanks to Carolyn for getting travel and research reimbursements back to me with near-lightning speed, double-checking everything I give her, and helping me celebrate my fortieth birthday in decadent style.

In my personal life, I am deeply grateful for Kenda Minter, who brings me joy, perspective, and chocolate. W. E., now gone, provided comfort and a steadying presence during tumultuous years. Finally, loving thanks go to my mother, Claudia Swanson, who scraped up money from nowhere to buy me books and eyeglasses all through childhood, and to whom this book is dedicated. At a crucial moment in college, she said to study what would make me happy and everything else would follow. Those words changed everything. Thank you.

Introduction

Collaborative Endeavors/Collaborative Texts

Our debt to tradition through reading and conversation
is so massive, our protest or private addition so rare and
insignificant,—and this commonly on the ground of other
reading, or hearing—that, in a large sense, one would say there
is no pure originality. All minds quote. Old and new make the
warp and woof of every moment. There is no thread that is not
a twist of these two strands. By necessity, by proclivity and by
delight, we all quote.

R. W. EMERSON, "QUOTATION AND ORIGINALITY"

For those who privilege the notion of the solitary author,
literature characteristically provides vicarious pleasure even
while distancing the writer from the reader; literature provides
voyeuristic seeing, possessive knowing, or teasing seduction.
For those who interest themselves in collaborative writing,
literature is reimagined as a place where people meet, where
they must negotiate their differences, where they may contest
each other's powers, and where, while retaining bodily borders,
they may momentarily, ecstatically merge.

HOLLY A. LAIRD, *WOMEN COAUTHORS*

Perhaps the nature of culture is collaboration.

M. THOMAS INGE, "COLLABORATION AND CONCEPTS OF AUTHORSHIP"

TWO EVENTS from my life illuminate my interest in collaboration. Somewhere around 1996, after I had taken my first faculty position at a land-grant institution following a short stint as an administrator at a private university, I found myself living in a deteriorating, cramped apartment. Our notoriously tight-fisted state legislature appeared determined to keep university salaries in Montana hovering only slightly above the bottom nationally, while a moneyed influx into newly trendy Bozeman drove housing prices breathtakingly high. These realities, coupled with student loans demanding repayment, meant that I was living in an apartment considerably shabbier than I had at any time during my student life. One day, though, I had a textbook moment of transcendence while alone in my apartment, writing. I no longer remember what I was writing, but the scene and the feelings it evoked are still sharp in my memory: snow fell gently outside, my cat lay curled at my feet, a candle burned fragrantly on the library table I had "rescued" from the private university's used-furniture graveyard, the apartment building was uncharacteristically quiet, and the words came easily. I was filled with a sense of bliss; it was a palpable feeling, one of consummate happiness. For an hour or so—before the neighbors returned to their stereos, the cat threw up, and the soft snow ushered in a cold wind that tested the heating system—my experience of writing overlapped with our culture's indelible portrait of the solitary, creative artist penning words of brilliance in a tiny garret.

The second event also occurred during that first year in Bozeman, when I began working on Wallace Stegner's 1971 Pulitzer Prize–winning novel, *Angle of Repose*. This event, however, refused to accommodate itself to cherished scenes of literary inspiration and individual creativity that I could play out, or imagine played out, in isolation. Instead, it confounded them. In *Angle of Repose*, Wallace Stegner "borrowed"—to use his word—heavily from western writer and artist Mary Hallock Foote's personal correspondence to a friend back East, using Foote's letters as the basis for characterizing his fictional protagonist's grandmother Susan Ward. However, Stegner's "borrowings" take what I initially felt was a peculiarly plagiaristic form: many of Foote's letters appear in the novel virtually unchanged or only slightly edited, and the title, numerous characters and scenes, and the major action of the novel can be traced directly to Foote's letters and other writings. I felt frustrated in my attempts to describe the complexities of that novel within a critical language that privileged individual authorship: how to discuss "Stegner's novel" when in some blatant ways it was not *his* novel at all, at least not his alone. Frustration gave way to fascination when the composition process of *Angle of Repose*, recurrent themes within the narrative, and the critical debates about attribution that eventually followed the novel's publication all led me to see that the difference I was struggling to identify was that the novel performed collaboratively.[1] While most critical analysis of *Angle of Repose* focused on the protagonist, Lyman Ward, and his efforts to re-create a family history from his grandmother's letters, I was more drawn to Lyman Ward's fictionalized reading of his grandmother's letters as a collaboration that mirrored the collaborative process that Stegner embarked upon when incorporating Foote's correspondence and other writings into his fictional work. I saw there a way in which to discuss Stegner's use of Foote's material in terms that were more historically resonant and less myopically moralistic, to shift the question from whether or not he plagiarized her writings to how the novel performed collaboratively and what that performance might tell us about authorship, authority, and western American literature.

Although these two events happened during more or less the same period of my life, they do not constitute a moment of origin for my project. Indeed, there is in this project's past nothing so grand as a singular (or in this case, dual) moment of genesis. These events do, however, reveal something of my temperament, which includes a fascination for inscrutable, overdetermined literary cases and an occasional nostalgic indulgence in the myth of solitary authorship (a myth that, for women writers, may continue to be valuable as a strategic deployment). Throughout this study, I take advantage of that fascination in order to acknowledge, comprehend, and finally dispense with the nostalgia, if not the myth, surrounding solitary authorship and the reign of the author.[2]

In keeping with a skeptical approach to origins, it seems important to note that mine is hardly the first critical voice to utilize contemporary theories to make comprehensible the tensions and contradictions of collaborative authorship. Collaboration (or, in sometimes subtly different definitions, "multiple authorship," "coauthorship," or "writing together") has until recently been largely ignored or pointedly avoided as a topic worthy of critical interest and investigation. In their influential and groundbreaking 1979 feminist study of women writers, *The Madwoman in the Attic: The Woman Writer and the Nineteenth-Century Literary Imagination*, Sandra Gilbert and Susan Gubar implicitly focus on a form of collaborative writing with their metaphor of the "madwoman in the attic," the shadow-self with whom the nineteenth-century female writer inevitably struggled—and collaborated—in the process of literary production. Not coincidentally, recent feminist studies of collaboration and coauthorship cite Gilbert and Gubar prominently as collaborators who simultaneously coauthor a text and claim the merits of individual authorship. As Bette London, a contemporary critic on women's literary collaborations, points out in her 1999 study, *Writing Double: Women's Literary Partnerships*, Gilbert and Gubar's collaborative partnership seems to defy exactly the possibility of mutuality their book's construction employed. Although their own successful collaborative composing process has proven enormously influential in ushering in and legitimating feminism as a method of analysis, authorship is, in their account, a singular enterprise (1). Despite their focus on internal or metaphorical collaborations between female writers and their dark doubles, rather than on collaboration as an explicit subject meriting investigation, Gilbert and Gubar's decision to write together ensures that their critical work is irrevocably linked with collaboration as a subject of inquiry and debate.

More recently, other critics have begun explicitly focusing on collaboration and coauthorship. Early scholars in this area explored primarily nonliterary forms of collaboration. Composition theory specialists Andrea Lunsford and Lisa Ede's 1990 work, *Singular Texts/Plural Authors: Perspectives on Collaborative Writing*, was a pioneer in legitimating the study of collaborative writing. Although Lunsford and Ede insist on the mutually collaborative nature of their text—the cover alternates their names, so that neither Lunsford nor Ede can be pegged as the text's first or primary writer—their focus is largely on the pervasiveness of multiple authorship, much of it outside the study of literature. Ede and Lunsford are tireless in their ability to challenge our perceptions of authorship, and their most recent work, particularly their essay "Collaboration and Concepts of Authorship," takes on the academy and deftly argues for a recognition of the "widening of scholarly possibilities" offered by collaboration. They urge us to "address related professional standards and practices" and to investigate what "subtle but entrenched conventions (such as the use of *et al.*) do to erase the work of those who already engage in collaborative practices" ("Collaboration" 364). Editors Whitney Chadwick and Isabelle de Courtivron's 1993 collection of essays, *Significant Others: Creativity and Intimate Partnership*, looks at creative couples and focuses on the artistic impact made by the absent or neglected member of the intimate partnership. Martha Woodmansee and Peter Jaszi's study *The Construction of Authorship: Textual Appropriation in Law and Literature* (1994), discusses collaboration in the context of a more explicit focus on the development and cultural and legal impact of current definitions of authorship.

In literary studies, collaborative writing relationships between men have received the most attention, although to significantly different critical ends. Wayne Koestenbaum's 1989 study of collaborative writing relationships between men, *Double Talk: The Erotics of Male Collaboration*, figures writing as an erotic activity, with the male partners engaging in "metaphorical sexual intercourse" (3). Using an approach drawn from queer and feminist theorizing, Koestenbaum looks specifically at generally well-known pairs of male writers, including Freud and Breuer, Coleridge and Wordsworth, Pound and Eliot, and John Addington Symonds and Havelock Ellis, in order to examine the ways in which male collaborations transgress sexual and literary boundaries. In *Multiple Authorship and the Myth of Solitary Genius* (1991), Jack Stillinger convincingly argues against the possibility of solitary genius by examining notable male writers and their close personal and professional relationships with other male writers who in various ways contributed to the final form their texts took. Like Koestenbaum's, Stillinger's focus is primarily on male writers whose literary partnerships, often buried or displaced by terms such as "editor," produced the work often linked to a single individual by a single authorial signature. And yet, as others have noted, Stillinger is at times careful to maintain "the myth of solitary genius" when it comes to particular (male) writers such as Keats.

Taking Shakespeare as a key, although by no means singular, figure for analysis in *Textual Intercourse: Collaboration, Authorship, and Sexualities in Renaissance Drama* (1997), Jeffrey Masten attempts to trace "the correspondences between . . . models and rhetorics of sexual relations, intercourse, and reproduction and . . . notions of textual production and property" (4). Masten finds collaboration prevalent not only in Renaissance theatre but also throughout Renaissance culture. Notably, he also expands on the definition of collaboration. For Masten, the "collaborative texts produced before the emergence of authorship are of a different kind . . . from collaborations produced within the regime of the author" (21). Masten is not looking at two people working together; rather, he is investigating what Renaissance collaboration means within a historical moment when to author a text included multiple relationships we might now consider peripheral: editors, players, other playwrights, the audience reviewing the play, the publisher.

More recently, women writers have become the focus for critics interested in collaboration. Bette London's study *Writing Double* focuses largely on "flesh and blood" female writing pairs while closely examining how specific meanings came to be attached to collaborative writing in the nineteenth and twentieth centuries (2). Even more radically, London's study situates female mediumship as a collaborative practice of authorship that "destabilizes certain cherished assumptions about authorial activity." For London, if we "take seriously that collaboration poses a challenge to traditional views of authorship, we should not be surprised to see that challenge materialized in practices that do not look the same as those of the solitary author" (23). Holly Laird's special double issue of *Tulsa Studies in Women's Literature*, dedicated to a discussion of collaboration, focuses on the potential to women of collaborative writing. In her new book, *Women Coauthors* (2000), Laird redirects our focus away from historical or personal relationships between the women (and men) themselves and toward the implications of women's collaborative writing for our theoretical understandings of writing and authorship. More interested in "the stories collaborators have told about their collaborations and the stories of collaboration enacted in selected works" ("A Hand Spills" 351), Laird's study emphasizes collaborations across differences of gender, race, ethnicity, and traditional writing practices. As even this brief overview of current work in collaboration amply demonstrates, the term *collaboration* is subject to multiple and sometimes radical interpretations.[3] The meanings of the terms *collaboration* and *collaborative writing* are being debated, expanded, and refined; no final decision is in sight. For some critics, such as Stillinger, Ede and Lunsford, and Laird, collaboration is a form of "writing together" or "multiple authorship" and refers to acts of writing in which two or more individuals consciously work together to produce a common text. In this definition, for example, a writer-editor relationship may be considered collaborative, particularly in cases where the editor takes on a role in the formative stages of the work. A spousal, partner, or other companionate or intimate relationship may be collaborative. Even if only one person literally "writes" the text, another person contributing ideas has an effect on the final text that justifies calling both the relationship and the text it produces collaborative. For other critics, such as Masten, London, and myself, collaboration includes these situations and also expands to include acts of writing in which one or even all of the writing subjects may not be aware of other writers, being separated by distance, era, or even death. Throughout this study, I take up the claim that all literary writing is inevitably collaborative, both *regardless* of the circumstances of its authorship (that only one individual literally "wrote" a text, for example) and *because* of the circumstances of its authorship (that authorship is actually a form of production that invariably reveals the presence of others). I also argue that approaching writing, all writing, as collaborative renders its circumstances of authorship ever more complexly revealing, particularly in terms of what it makes visible about how power circulates in specific historical moments and circumstances.

There are problems with this inclusive, everything-is-collaboration approach. In her contribution to *PMLA*'s recent series of essays on collaboration, Heather Hirschfeld points up one of the most serious ones. Although her study focuses on the early modern period, her concern applies widely: "The term *collaboration* has been used by critics to describe a host of associations that enabled literary production . . . not simply two or more writers working on one fictional text . . . to use the term for any of the multiple activities and people that make possible a literary endeavor, or to insist that literary work is by its nature collaborative—risks evacuating the term of analytic meaning" (619). It is a risk I am willing to take. Although Hirschfeld goes on to suggest several remedies, including coining a new critical term to describe shared writing in order to distinguish it from the range of collaborative activities described above, I see considerable value, at least at this historical moment, in employing the term *collaboration* in its widest definition. For example, many of the activities I would designate as collaboration, such as a writer's reliance on a previous text or a passing conversation, have typically been described as "influence" or even "inspiration." The difference? Terms such as "influence" and "inspiration" keep the myth of individual authorship and creativity enshrined, a perspective that becomes apparent when we begin to call such relationships collaborative. "Influence" and "inspiration" and their underlying assumptions regarding authorship work to preempt our recognition of the intricate involvement of often unnamed, unacknowledged participants in the process of literary production.

The largest challenge collaboration poses is to our traditional understanding and practical experience of the author as an individual genius who creates original works of art in isolation. From a collaborative point of view, what was a fairly direct cause and effect scenario (individual author + inspiration = original literary masterpiece) becomes something much less clear: individual authors are always located within a shifting context of texts from which they draw to produce, often with substantial and varied support in the form of other writers, editors, spouses or partners, and institutions, a text that, depending on the degree to which it meets certain established expectations of literary greatness, will be termed "great" and "original." A focus on collaboration insists on recognizing this oft-hidden context of others as an important component of meaning, something our traditional understanding of the author persists in ignoring or displacing. In various ways, deconstruction, new historicism, feminism, and other theoretical approaches to literature all emphasize the importance of context in determining the meaning or meanings of a particular piece of literature, but those insights are rarely taken to their logical conclusion in regard to our understanding of the author in the way a focus on collaboration does. By understanding "author" in Foucault's formulation—as a site of cultural power rather than as a particular individual—my approach to collaboration is consonant with theories that argue for the contextualization and examination of our most cherished ideas.

This historicized definition of the author is particularly useful in today's rapidly moving technological world. As individual authorship falls from view in some instances—film and television productions, for example—the author as a site of power in the form of a conglomerate force seems increasingly common and familiar. As such technologies as the Internet and other forms of "cyber-publication" continue to flourish, what it means to "author" a "text" will be called into question continually. Plagiarism is already a hugely difficult concept to define, legislate, and punish, and this daunting problem will grow even more complicated as the multicultural base of literary studies expands to more fully include those traditions that fail to revere the seemingly natural status of the individual author as sole originator of specific words to which that author has a legal claim. Legal questions will be asked; legal battles will be fought. Understanding collaboration's pervasiveness and its resulting challenges to individual authorship can help us as we negotiate the many decisions that will need to be made regarding these particular texts.[4]

Despite my insistence that collaboration challenges our ideas of authorship, I want to emphasize that as I have been describing it, collaboration does not destroy authorship or even argue for its demise; rather, it emphasizes that the "author" defined, the author's meaning determined and tellable, is a composite figure whose singularity is always a fiction. Nonetheless, nominal authorship—in the form of recognizable bylines and attribution—is ubiquitous and may be an economical, a psychological, and a practical necessity in some cases. In his book *Multiple Authorship and the Myth of Solitary Genius*, Jack Stillinger emphasizes the practical realities of authorship:

> For practical purposes, perhaps the single most important aspect of authorship is simply the vaguely apprehended *presence* of human creativity, personality, and (sometimes) voice that nominal authorship seems to provide. Just as it would be unthinkable for a visitor to an art museum to admire a roomful of paintings without knowing the names of the individual painters and for a concertgoer to sit through a program of symphonies and concertos without knowing the names of the individual composers, so it is impossible to imagine

any presentation of writings (even of writings in which Barthes and Foucault contest the existence of authors!) that does not prominently refer to authorship. Readers must have authors' names on jackets, spines, and title pages of the books they read. (186)

Of course, many ideas once "unthinkable" seem inevitable now, including the idea of the individual author as sole creator of the text. Current studies in the status of authorship in the early modern period, for example, suggest that theatergoers may well have attended plays without knowing who their writers were.[5] We do not need authors because any other possibility is essentially impossible; we need them because any other possibility is still too threatening, too dangerous, to contemplate. Even when we know and acknowledge authorship's complex and collaborative status, critics, students, and general readers require authors because we have virtually no experience with alternatives (even "anonymous" points to an individual author whose identity, while unknown, is nonetheless experienced by the reader as unitary). The material circumstances of textual production and consumption also work to entrench the myth of the individual author. From an economic perspective, authorship is in no danger of disappearing. Authors in the form of particular names that link perceived personalities to specific texts sell books. Who hasn't awaited "the new Louise Erdrich" or "the latest Stephen King"? In our practical reality, we purchase authors as much as we purchase texts. Any serious attempt to alter that approach is guaranteed to bring down a chorus of corporate protests about the sheer "unthinkability" of revising our ideas of authorship to admit the ongoing presence of collaboration.

Authorship is also important when we consider the relationship of a text's historical context to its range of possible meanings. J. E. Gracia writes, "Texts do need historical authors, for texts without authors are texts without history, and texts without history are texts without meaning, that is, they are not texts" (252). Recognizing the presence of collaboration, even when it challenges our traditional convention of naming an individual writer as the creative genesis (as the "author") of a text, does not necessarily conflict with the political call for "history," particularly when we remember that acknowledging collaboration changes rather than destroys authorship. Collaboration is inextricably "about" authorship in fundamental and, I would argue, vital ways. To revisit authorship from a collaborative perspective is not to lose history but instead to regain it in more fullness and complexity. When we begin to view texts as collaborations, we begin to view history from a new perspective as well. Where once a single autonomous individual stood in the coveted position of author, we may see an individual whose subjectivity is multiply constituted, whose autonomy is contested, and whose agency, while real, is very much embedded in and constrained by governing ideologies; we may see many such individuals, some of whom we can identify, some of whom we must speculate; or we may see many social institutions, all of which bear on the finished text. We may see some or all of these new versions of the collaborative writer, all working together in ways specific to their historical moment. An investigation of collaboration can help us see that, while we may train our desires for authorship on particular individuals, we are always leaving something, perhaps many things, out. Collaboration is interested in looking at those things and determining their impact on a particular text. Collaboration gives us *more* history, not less.

In bringing a focus on collaboration to a study of western American literature, I am attempting to examine two complex concepts, neither of which has an agreed-upon definition or canon. My study is not an attempt to provide that definition or to delineate that canon. My term requires some definition, however, since like "collaboration," what we mean by "western American literature" is still being debated and contested. What we mean by "the West" has been neither fully nor convincingly defined, and even less has its emblematic literature been satisfactorily identified or reliably canonized.[6] Is the West a place? And if so, what determines which place or places it is? Do lines on the earth or borders between states determine the West, as Frederick Jackson Turner claimed in his now-famous essay "The Significance of the Frontier in American History"? Is it designated by geographical conditions such as aridity, as Wallace Stegner claimed, or perhaps by land formations or animal habitat? Perhaps, as Turner, Stegner, and many others have also suggested, the West is best understood as a concept, a cultural idea. If so, whose narrative of the West as concept should reign, and whose interests are served by such a decision? Is the West adequately represented by the classic "Western" in fiction and film, with its dual codes of good and evil, masculinity and femininity, white and Native American? Does the West possess a "legacy of conquest," as historian Patricia Limerick has argued? Is the West a place of rugged individualism or governmental dependence and, if both, when should we emphasize one and when the other? If we could (should we wish to do so, about which I will have more to say later) adequately define the West, what about its canon of representative texts? What makes writing western? That it uses the West as a theme, that it is somehow "about" the West? Or perhaps that it is produced by writers living in the West, that it is "authored" by a Westerner? Under what conditions does one achieve Westerner status?[7]

Obviously, the above paragraph is an elaborated rhetorical exercise in which the questions far outnumber the available answers.[8] Yet I am not advocating that we eschew definitions altogether—only that we recognize, even celebrate, their provisional nature. In the case of western American literature, the provisional definitions we must necessarily work with at this historical moment are intellectually and politically useful. They give us an opportunity to examine the assumptions beneath our definitions and to revise them when necessary or useful. To argue, for instance, that western American literature includes books about western themes regardless of the writers' places of origin can provide us with a helpful frame of reference from which further insights may come. On the basis of this definition, for example, Willa Cather's *Death Comes for the Archbishop* is western American literature because of its New Mexican setting and its investigation of Catholic assimilation of Mexican-American and Native American populations—despite Cather's Virginia birth.

Yet the key word here is "provisional": such definitions are always provisional. They are valuable because definitions invariably work to assimilate and exclude. We can see that, while we may be hard-pressed to state exactly what the West is in any essentialized way, the range of definitions attached to the term reveals much about its ideological importance as a historical—and historically changing—concept. The most popular and enduring stories about the West stress independence, isolation, and singularity rather than interconnection and collaboration. Given America's history of westward expansionism and settlement, national goals upheld by ideologies of individualistic and capitalistic superiority, the West's landscape and its relationship to identity have been especially important to writers. Historically, the West has been constructed as America's Promised Land both in literature and in the popular press. A beckoning escape of limitless opportunity from the problems of the East, the West—as both a geographical location and a psychic landscape—replaced the role that the New World once played for European colonists with a variety of religious, economic, and colonizing incentives for coming to America. Touted as an Edenic landscape in which "man" can discover his true identity unfettered by the claustrophobic confines of the increasingly polluted and overpopulated eastern city, the West promised unheralded freedoms and a new, fertile future with endless natural resources to replace the failed past represented by the increasingly industrialist East. Limiting in both its physical architecture and its social constraints, America's nineteenth-century urban landscape was understood to squelch "man's" seemingly natural strength, curiosity, and individual freedom. Away from this cityscape and, not coincidentally, the feminine presence most typically associated with it, the open land of the "Wild West" offered endless opportunity for the individual man to prove himself and flourish.

Yet this opportunity was never as glorious in actual fact as it was in promotional tracts aimed at urging white settlers westward. From the beginning of a significant European presence in America during the seventeenth and eighteenth centuries, a national identity and the related sense of cultural superiority that both helped to create and to maintain it have been tenuous and contested. Eighteenth- and nineteenth-century American literature records this search for national identity in our literature.[9] Newly proclaimed "American" writers in the nineteenth century desired a literature different from the English tradition in which many were schooled, but one that would also be suited to the greatness of the "newly" settled American continent.[10] At home in the American West for thousands of years and in large numbers, Native American tribes struggled to maintain their diverse tribal identities in the face of a steady and violent European invasion. Those new settlers, on the other hand, sought to create regional identities both by defining themselves against the increasingly urban culture they had left behind and in opposition to what they understood as the "savagery" of the native peoples they encountered. Turner's essay forwards just such a thesis with his assertion that American identity and democracy developed as a result of such clashes between the westward advancing colonists and the wilderness they encountered; ironically, these representations of identity were intimately connected to the European models of individualistic selfhood and civilization that settlers were attempting to escape.

In the literary arena, narratives *of* collaboration as well as narrative *as* collaboration have been ignored, pressed to the margins of our western literary canon in favor of the literary version of the myth of individual creativity. If American literature has frequently been defined as American on the basis of its consonance with mythologies of freedom and opportunity for deserving individuals, narratives deemed western are doubly pressured to uphold this dominating mythology. The formula Western, with its lone gunman dispensing an apparently necessary vigilante violence, its polarized constructions of good and evil, and its refusal to admit the gender and sexual confusions that underlie the repeating male sidekick motif littering film and book Westerns, is the most common example.[11] Despite the preponderance of the myth of the individual white male conquering the West—the explorer, the cowboy, the gunslinger, the cattle baron—recent cultural histories and rereadings of historical documents tell us many more stories of collective achievement, governmental dependence, and group rather than individual domination. The Mormon settlement of Salt Lake City is an example of an economically successful community collaboration; railroad building and mining operations, while embodying all of the coerciveness of capitalism, were always the accomplishments of diverse groups of people, not individuals, and the founding and organizing of towns brought people together for achievements of common goals. That these goals included the economic disempowerment of Native Americans, Chinese, and other ethnic minority groups reveals their investments in stories of European American superiority and progress. Even exploration expeditions such as Lewis and Clark's were sanctioned and funded by the government and accomplished with Native American guidance. The image of the lone individual dominating a western landscape partakes in a romanticized nostalgia—more a vision of a desired past than of an actual one.

Yet, because the West has for so long been seen as America's backyard, an adolescent fantasy of escape from a problematic past into a utopian future, the implications of a cultural desire for a defined American identity have played out in western settings since the West's settlement by European Americans. Now, places in the West that were long seen as a virtual haven for the independent and self-made individual are having to face a distressing series of challenges to the tenets of a western identity derived from ideas of European selfhood and independence. Environmentalists and others concerned with shortsighted and dangerous land and animal (ab)use policies erode a traditional sense of entitlement;

governmental regulations, often emphasizing national rather than local interests, dictate land, water, and animal regulations, diluting a sense of self-government; and huge sums of capital allow real estate transactions in figures beyond the comprehension of many citizens, assaulting the western illusion that sustained economic prosperity is the predictable, assured result of an individual's focused labor. William Kittredge sums up this kind of disorientation and disappointment as the logical result of believing too long in a faulty story: "Our old pilgrims believed stories in which the West was a promise, a place where decent people could escape the wreckage of failed lives and start over. Come along, the dream whispered, and you can have another chance. We still listen to promises in the wind. This time, we think, we'll get it right" (234).

The Western Literature Association (WLA) is the national organization through which many of these debates concerning the West and its literature are being waged. The WLA began with a hardy band of secessionists when it split off from the Modern Language Association, and the journal *Western American Literature* was begun in 1966 in an attempt to bring more scholarly attention to western American literature. Yet having an organization—or a journal—of one's own does not by any means delineate the range of literature that somehow "counts" as western. A glance at any recent WLA conference program amply demonstrates that western American literature has been functionally defined to include fiction and nonfiction, novels, short stories, memoirs, biographies, autobiographies, dramatic works including plays and film, poetry, ethnography, and nature writing by male and female writers with a variety of ethnic identifications and political affiliations. Most working definitions of western American literature also challenge traditional standards of literature by including that which is not written: oral storytelling traditions of Native American tribes (re)located in the geographic West. While it might make us feel quite settled intellectually to draw, define, and defend precise and limiting categories of western American literature, we may gain more by leaving the questions open, even as they lead us to more questions and further uncertainties. To refuse a final definition of western American literature does not leave us suspended in a never-never land of no meaning; rather, it requires that we examine the assumptions buried in the range of meanings possible. To foreclose possibilities of interpretation at this early stage of investigation into western American literature, which narrowly focused definitions would do, is premature.

Members of WLA live across the United States, are independent scholars, graduate students, and faculty members, and have a wide range scholarly interests. Members consciously employ a range of theoretical positions, from those whose research areas are literary theory to those who eschew theory altogether, claiming their own ignorance or theory's irrelevance. This, of course, is precisely the point: western American literature's "westernness" is still contested, still variable, still being challenged. At some point in the future, I expect we will speak about western American literature as we now talk about feminisms, as a pluralistic, polyvocal endeavor with sometimes incompatible or competing visions, and all the more exciting and promising for that internal questioning and contentiousness. I look forward to that day because it will signal that significant intellectual and critical growth has taken place in a field that sometimes has been hobbled by unexamined antitheoretical assumptions and a dated, uncritical nostalgia. Unlike Blake Allmendinger, I don't see the field of western American literature as "languishing" (3), nor do I believe, as does Allmendinger, that graduate students, themselves excellent barometers of critical tendencies in a tight job market, perceive the field to be dead (6). To be sure, western American literature still suffers from the pejorative associations of regionalism in a way that southern American literature, for instance, does not. But the field of western American literature promises to be even more provocative and widely useful as more varied approaches are introduced, studied, and debated.

In these ways, the current tensions surrounding definitions of western American literature resemble ongoing debates about collaboration: although suggestive of vast theoretical and practical challenges to our understanding of authorship, collaboration—when it is recognized at all—is usually seen in its simplest, least threatening guise as two or more individual authors consciously working together to produce a text. Likewise, western American literature is often regarded in the most reductive terms: as narrowly regionalist literature of interest only to those with a preexisting fascination with the West. Moreover, western American literature suffers from a historical sense of inadequacy about its "regionalism" and sometimes displays open hostility toward eastern literary centers over real and perceived slights. Yet, like collaboration, western American literature, when subjected to the same critical and theoretical scrutiny other literature receives, has much to tell us about national anxieties and desires, about the pervasiveness of region and its role in all literature, and about the temptation to reject or rewrite history. From another perspective, western American literature is collaborative in that it has always been working to define itself, its parameters, and its representative writers while at the same time being deeply enmeshed with the eastern valuations of literature it has tried to define itself against.

In the variety of definitions of western American literature, one assumption has remained largely unquestioned: the existence of the individual and autonomous author. In this regard, western American literature enacts its own metaphorical stance as an escape from the abstract intellectualism often situated in/as the East. In other words, western American literature, as well as the literary criticism of it, has been nearly untouched by the theoretical insights that question the author as an autonomous being who, in the privileged act of putting pen to paper, transfers his unique genius onto the page. In her essay "Letting Go Our Grand Obsessions: Notes toward a New Literary History of the American Frontiers," Annette Kolodny urges a redefinition of "frontier" "as a locus of first cultural contact, circumscribed by a particular physical terrain in the process of change *because of* the forms that contact takes, all of it inscribed by the collisions and interpenetration of language" (3). Using similar terminology, Mary Louise Pratt defines "contact zones" as "social spaces where cultures meet, clash, and grapple with each other, often in contexts of highly asymmetrical relations of power, such as colonialism, slavery, or their aftermaths as they are lived out in many parts of the world today" (34). Western American literature is itself a contact zone, where important meetings are occurring, where clashes we can learn from are taking place. By examining specific instances of collaboration throughout this book, I hope to show that we have much to learn about literature from our assumptions of western authorship and much to learn about western authorship from our assumptions about literature.

Although the writers I discuss here all have in common writing about some aspect of the West, and all have the experience of living in the western places about which they write, I am not suggesting that they are therefore representative or paradigmatic western writers or that theirs are the only versions of the West that could or should exist. These writers are intriguing to me because they demonstrate unusual examples of collaboration, thereby allowing me—sometimes requiring me—to see newly. What initially intrigued me about this particular group of writers was less my ability to somehow define them (and their subsequent collaborations) as western than it was the curious, sometimes ethically or psychologically troubling, and always downright fascinating processes of collaboration each engaged in at some point in their writing career. That they all wrote about and lived in the West was initially little more than a happy coincidence to me. Nonetheless, the specifically western aspects of their writing became important to me because the writers made it so. Western American literary writers still struggle mightily to shrug off their functionally derogatory label as "regional" and therefore narrowly limited writers; as I continued reading and researching, I came to see that collaboration is one writing strategy these writers use to explore identity and the effect region has on it. Used in this way, collaboration tends to make multiple claims of authority, in which one writer (or in Mary Austin's case, one persona) could provide what the other could not, whether that was information, remembered stories, literary connection, or simply creative stamina, highlighting the fact that writers occupy distinct subject positions but then refuting their limitations via their collaboration.

Although the term *collaboration* usually works to signify the process of individual writers deliberately coming together to compose a text, the forthcoming chapters present collaboration more complexly. As I hope is already apparent, I do not define collaboration as a kind of doubled example of individual authorship. Instead, I argue that absolute individual authority is ultimately impossible; in its stead, we have collaboration—a multivoiced, multilayered process intrinsic to the writing virtually all writers do regardless of their conscious intentions or aspirations. In linking collaboration to western American literature, this study differs from those preceding it in that I claim the crucial importance of landscape and region as a discourse that, when seen from a perspective that denaturalizes our contemporary ideas of single authorship and thus recognizes collaboration, has much to tell us about our constructions of a western ethos and identity.

My opening chapter situates collaboration in a historical context by tracing the development of our contemporary understanding of authorship and sets forth important theoretical challenges to the sovereignty of the author as individual genius. Because in the humanities, at least, collaboration is often viewed as an inferior form of literary production at best (talented writers and scholars should make their reputations individually before taking part in a collaborative effort, in which the best one can expect is to receive half the credit) and an inherently suspicious, even unethical process haunted by whiffs of plagiarism at worst (talented writers and scholars should do their own work), I investigate the role of plagiarism in upholding conventional ideas of authorship. At one level, the concept of plagiarism has historically specific roles in response to changing ideas of authorship, ownership, and intellectual property; in many ways, our understanding of plagiarism works to protect individual writing subjects in the economically vital world of intellectual property. At the same time, our ideas about plagiarism render nearly invisible nagging questions about individual authorship. Because we have learned to think about plagiarism as morally reprehensible and creatively empty, the term functions with unparalleled effectiveness to deflect far more challenging questions about unitary identities composing uniquely inspired masterpieces. When plagiarism is investigated in relationship to collaboration, both terms shed some of their conventional associations and become more self-consciously situated in the political arena.

Following this discussion, the remaining chapters examine what I have designated collaborative writers or collaborative events. In chapter 2, I examine the financially and creatively successful collaborations between writers Louise Erdrich and Michael Dorris. In numerous interviews, this husband-and-wife team consistently attributed much of their individual literary renown to their collaborative writing process. For many years, Dorris and Erdrich together achieved a deliberately collaborative writing relationship that defied critics' expectations and helped redefine what it is to "write together." I avoid the temptation to read Dorris's eventual suicide as a direct commentary on this collaborative relationship, but the sheer energy Erdrich and Dorris devoted to the construction of a richly intertwined collaborative identity is telling of their mutual desire to simultaneously undermine traditional notions of individual genius while constructing an elaborate—and perhaps equally fictitious—alternative cojoined identity. I investigate that double move by looking closely at the ways in which collaborations represented within Erdrich's and Dorris's fictional narratives comment on difficult and destabilizing aspects of collaboration often ignored or deflected in their statements on the subject. In particular, I look closely at the writers' only cosigned novel, *The Crown of Columbus*, which takes the figure of Columbus as the epitome of the solitary writer in a collaborative universe. In a playful, genre-bending search for the "real" Columbus among the many potential Columbuses valorized by various groups, the novel enacts a collaborative approach even as its characters frequently resist their own fateful collaborations. The fascinating and highly criticized novel reveals that collaboration is a staple in the world of literary and academic writing, making the everyday occurrence of collaboration visible.

In chapter 3, I examine what initially appears to be a rather "straightforward" example of collaboration between two mutually consenting collaborators. Native American writer Mourning Dove produced the 1927 novel *Cogewea, the Half-Blood* via her collaboration with her white male mentor, Lucullus McWhorter. Yet their collaboration, although well intentioned and historically significant, illuminates many of the difficulties successful collaborations are assumed to avoid: racial and gender inequities leave traces in their text; differences between European and Native American conceptions of literary authority are apparent and divisive within the narrative; and a persistent contemporary desire to separate the collaborative parts into its writers' separate voices or achievements haunts critical assessments of *Cogewea*. I argue that although specific historical events such as the Indian Removal policies and the First World War, as well as Mourning Dove's and McWhorter's own cultural positioning, prevented either individual from achieving an act of independent authorship, the "work" of the collaboration, as well as the cultural work performed by the resulting text, challenges the very notion of singular authorship, anticipating later poststructuralist theoretical insights. At the same time, it is important to understand that this particular collaboration is not "the same as" the collaboration, across seasons and generations, that produces Native American oral literature. In *Cogewea*, our traditional understandings of literary authorship as an individual, isolated activity derived from European standards for written literature, and of literary authority as cultural power gained by dint of artistic inspiration, are challenged by these collaborators' combined presentation of oral storytelling techniques and highly politicized critiques of the national treatment of Native Americans within a conventional western plot. The very fractures and disjunctions in plot and voicing in *Cogewea* are evidence of its collaborative nature; moreover, the collaborative status of the novel gives a unique relational perspective on both a writing process and a particular historical period usually regarded as unilaterally assimilationist.

In chapter 4, I take up a particularly unusual example of collaborative writing. In her 1932 autobiography, *Earth Horizon*, southwestern writer Mary Austin posits the existence of distinct selves comprising her personality beginning in her childhood. These selves, in conjunction with narrative shifts between first and third person, create in Austin's autobiography a collaborative form of writing that subverts and reframes more conventional models of autobiographical utterance. In addition, Austin openly declares her indebtedness to Native American spiritual beliefs as contributing to her writing. I argue that Austin's desire for a "prior text," be it an alternative self or an alternative literary form, underlies her concept of identity and the subsequent claims she makes for authorship. In these senses, Austin's autobiographical writing (her autobiography proper and her autobiographically influenced short stories) assists us in a necessary process of reexamining collaborative writing. In Austin's *Earth Horizon*, the very real historical difficulties encountered when a woman attempts to claim literary authority via autobiographical writing are present, but the significance of those difficulties is enlarged by Austin's collaboration between multiple personae as well as her claims to prior texts for psychological and authorial legitimacy. More than any other example I pursue here, Austin's rejection of the bedrock concept of authorship—individual subjectivity—reveals that all writing is always collaborative.

Also in the autobiographical genre, in chapter 5 I look at the role collaboration plays in three western writers' memoirs, Ivan

Doig's *This House of Sky: Landscapes of a Western Mind* and *Heart Earth*, Mary Clearman Blew's *All But the Waltz* and *Balsamroot*, and William Kittredge's *Hole in the Sky*. Doig, Blew, and Kittredge each use collaborative strategies to investigate the construction of a western identity. Doig and Blew each work with remembered stories and others' letters or diaries in order to compose their memoirs and, in a fascinating collaborative layering, each writer's second memoir collaborates with the first by using others' writing to change and complicate the prior narrative. Kittredge's memoir emphasizes storytelling and its collaborative nature as he argues for our cultural need to remember certain stories in order to survive. When we read these narratives together, they collaborate in yet another way, making visible elements of class, privilege, and nostalgic mythmaking that are otherwise difficult to see.

In chapter 6, I turn to the text that first piqued my interest in collaboration in western American literature: *Angle of Repose*. Wallace Stegner and Mary Hallock Foote did not elect to work together, a fact that has caused specific and lasting debates surrounding the originality and literary value of *Angle of Repose* and forces us to examine the possible relationship between gender and the privileged status of authorship. Their collaboration, and the fictional Lyman Ward's collaboration with his grandmother that parallels the text's production and major themes, emphasizes the ways in which literary history is itself a collaborative construct, one continually re-created by writers and their readers.

Throughout this study, I argue that collaborations are overdetermined events. They take place at specific historical moments that are never fully recoverable, between sometimes, but not always, identifiable individuals about whom information—itself another indeterminate text—may be sketchy at best. Moreover, these individuals are writing as raced, gendered subjects within a culture where ideological and economic forces affect not only the circumstances of their writing but also their experience of reality. Further, readers who encounter the collaborative event and ex-

pand it by their own participation—from editors to audience—
are also shaped in various ways by these forces. Yet, before I write
myself out of the possibility of coherent discussion about collaboration, it is important to remember that complexity does not pre-
clude efforts at analysis and understanding, even if these efforts
are doomed to fall short of complete illumination and final certainty (in traditional academic parlance, "to fail"). While the
very theories I draw upon in this book to make a case for the unacknowledged frequency and importance of collaborative writing—new historicism, deconstruction, feminism—insist that final, unambiguous meaning is an illusion, they certainly do not
suggest that meaning is absent, impossible to achieve, or irrelevant. Meaning is, however, always a construct, a product of place
and time, of reader and writer, of pressure and resistance. Meaning is not something we find (as in finding "the truth"); rather, it
is something we struggle for and over. It is something we create.
As our creation, meaning is also something for which we are responsible. Viewed from that perspective, collaboration as I discuss it can also be seen as a way to recognize our responsibility for
the interpretations we create and the often far-reaching implications of those interpretations.

It is true that collaboration exacerbates problems of meaning
by introducing yet another layer of mingling texts and evident
gaps. For example, Mary Austin claims that she is writing an autobiography and then expresses frustration that the writing process did not proceed with the linear smoothness she expected, requiring instead considerable editing, rearranging, and the flat-out
omission of key events. Austin expected linearity and certainty;
what she got instead was her mystical (and preferred) earth horizon. In another example, Wallace Stegner argues that he is writing fiction rather than biography and then expresses frustration
when his critics and Foote's descendants fail to see the distinction
between them as clearly as he, thus setting in place a repeating
motif of defensive discussions of his literary intentions. Collaboration reiterates what scholars in biography and autobiography

have long argued: that these particular forms of literature are highly stylized variations of fiction, replete with rules that guide and direct the genre and its readers. As a fictional reconstruction, literary history is likewise challenged by collaboration. Collaboration reveals that fiction, autobiography, memoir, and literary history are endless screens of layered, intertwined exchanges of power rather than a grand parade of definitive, truthful moments.

I also saw that as a strategy, collaboration is of profound use to women. If "intellectual property is about masculine creation," as Debora Halbert argues (113), then women writers are definitionally excluded from even the illusion of individual creation of literature. If, as some critics have suggested, a move west challenged some gender codes while strengthening others, writing as an occupation for women continued to be fraught with difficulties when the female writers were displaced westward. In this context, collaboration could be seen as a survival strategy, albeit a sometimes desperate one. From another angle, such male writers as Stegner and Doig also use collaboration as a type of survival strategy, this time to preserve female narratives that otherwise surely would have been lost. In any case, we would be remiss if we believed that these narratives remain somehow untouched or unaltered by ideological and historical forces or even by the collaborative process itself. These beliefs erase the contributions of many others who also collaborate in the production of a text, and they situate power as existing solely within the being of the (male) author, obscuring the reality that power is shifting, multiple, and available in unexpected ways. What I have come to see, and what I attempt to argue throughout this study, is that collaboration is always more than two people "writing together." Even when individual writers sit down to create a text together, with a conscious awareness of that intention, they bring with them narratives that are already collaborations and intentions beyond those they can identify or articulate. By insisting on interrogating the gaps of fiction, literary history, memoir, and autobiography, collaboration swings its attention to the margins, those places typically occupied by women, people of color, and other frequently disenfranchised peoples. The reader, bringing to the experience a host of expectations regarding literature and authorship, in fact becomes yet another collaborator in the meaning(s) of a text. The effects of gender, race, and sexuality on the text become substantially more visible when reading with collaboration in mind.

The writers I have chosen to include here do not coalesce into a cohesive group of emblematic "western" writers—nor should they. Ivan Doig's poetic nostalgia, for instance, represents a different West than does the antinostalgic, sometimes piercingly anguished narratives of Blew and Kittredge. Erdrich's and Dorris's collaboration was inordinately structured, publicized, and successful; to many critics, it was also inordinately distressing. Mary Austin's critiques of subjectivity via her multiple personae are strikingly contemporary, and her appropriations of Native American literary and spiritual forms are very different from McWhorter's responses to Mourning Dove. Mourning Dove and McWhorter, in turn, are situated very differently than contemporary writers Erdrich and Dorris. In fact, I chose these writers, who are very different from one another, in order to demonstrate the persistence of collaboration across a wide variety of writing and composing situations. Although these writers are not representative of western writers as a whole or of western American literature, their collaborative strategies, in all their variety, are representative of the collaborative nature of the literature that surrounds us. Whether collaboration takes place between multiple writers or between multiple aspects of one writing situation, it is an irreducible component of the writing process and poses specific challenges to our traditional understandings of authorship.

For some readers, it may seem as if I am arguing that there is no way out of collaboration. I am. But far differently than seeing collaboration as a monolithic trap that has already been sprung, I see collaboration *as* the way out: out of the dominance of the author and the illusion that he (it is usually he) creates alone. When we understand collaboration as the common, even inescapable process by which an intricate interplay of competing desires etches itself across a text, we can glimpse a richness and depth in our literature that is often ignored or denied. If, as the humanists argue, we go to literature to learn about ourselves, the fragmented selves collaboration reflects back to us are also more faceted.

Writing Together/Writing Apart

1

Writing Together/Writing Apart

The Politics of Collaboration in
Western American Literature

*The coming into being of the notion of "author" constituted the
privileged moment of individualization in the history of ideas,
knowledge, literature, philosophy, and the sciences. Even today,
when we reconstruct the history of a concept, literary genre,
or school of philosophy, such categories seem relatively weak,
secondary, and superimposed scansions in comparison with
the solid and fundamental unit of the author and the work.*
MICHEL FOUCAULT, "WHAT IS AN AUTHOR?"

*To what extent is a text itself not something passively
attributable, as effect is to cause, to a person? To what extent
is a text so discontinuous a series of subtexts or pretexts or
paratexts or surtexts as to beggar the idea of the author as
simple producer?*
EDWARD W. SAID, *BEGINNINGS*

Collaborative writing is a fact of life.
LISA EDE AND ANDREA LUNSFORD, *SINGULAR TEXTS/PLURAL AUTHORS*

FOR MORE THAN thirty years now, the idea of the author has
been a focal point of literary critical theory; in predictably re
peating cycles, the author has been dissected and deconstructed,
rejected and reclaimed. The author has been pronounced dead
and subsequently resurrected until it seems only Elvis has had
more sightings. Indeed, the status of the author has been just
about everything but decided, as the current interest in collaboration attests. Yet, despite the repeating focus on the author as a

fundamentally unstable (although surprisingly durable) constellation of meanings, we in literary studies willfully ignore the implications that instability has for our ideas of individual authorship. Even if we momentarily accept the traditional, seemingly straightforward definition of collaboration as the creation of a text by two or more individuals working together, a definition that leaves our underlying belief in the unique creativity of the individual author intact, the landscapes of both American and British literature are lush with examples of collaboration that, if taken seriously, confound our beliefs in the "masterwork" as a unified and original example of individual genius. The early modern period in Britain, for instance, offers nearly endless opportunities for critical investigations of collaboration.[1] However, even the occasional reader has no doubt encountered writers and texts for which the role collaboration plays in textual production is either well known or the subject of extensive research and debate: the early modern dramas of Beaumont and Fletcher; many of the plays we attribute to Shakespeare; Gilbert and Sullivan's work; Coleridge's "The Ancient Mariner," with Wordsworth; Wordsworth's lyric poetry with his sister, Dorothy Wordsworth; Mary Shelley's "help" from husband Percy Shelley in *Frankenstein*; T. S. Eliot's "The Waste Land," with Ezra Pound; H.D.'s literary relationship with Ezra Pound, who created her nom de plume from her initials; the blatantly collaborative American novel *The Whole Family*, by William Dean Howells, Henry James, and ten other writers; James Joyce's tangles with the censors and their effect upon *Dubliners*; Nathaniel Hawthorne's habitual reliance on his female family members for literary assistance; and Sylvia Plath's relationship with husband Ted Hughes, who posthumously destroyed some of her writing and then rearranged and edited much of her poetry for publication; for just a brief glance.[2]

Of course, the above examples refer to well-known writers, many of whom are canonical figures of British and American literature, and they do not begin to address the intricacies presented by collaboration in literature not based in European understandings of individual authorship and intellectual property. Native American oral literatures and African folk tales, for example, rely upon cultural acts of storytelling, with stories being passed from teller to hearer, from generation to generation. Many of the current technologies we rely upon are also collaboratively based: literary web sites, hypertext, and publishing venues on the Internet all may involve readers and writers in the construction of meaning in a myriad of ways that are no longer dependent on the concepts of the individually composed text or the isolated author, while "fanzines," underground literary publications, subvert mainstream publishing avenues and mores. Even in the face of these marginalized, but still generally well known, examples of collaboration, the fact of collaboration—and its theoretical challenges to longstanding ideas of individual creativity and intellectual property—is only very rarely acknowledged as an important component of our discussions about these works and writers. Most often, the complex landscape of literary production I am calling collaboration is passively ignored or blatantly denied.

Throughout this study, I use the term *collaboration* to mean something different than joint or multiple authorship. The terms *joint authorship* and *multiple authorship* usually refer to two or more authors, each regarded as an individual, coherent identity, who put their respective unique contributions side by side to create what is then called a collaborative text. Another commonly used term, *composite text*, refers to the product of such a yoking of individual contributions. Yet the terms *joint authorship* and *composite text* safeguard the traditional beliefs in authorial individuality and genius that *collaboration* subverts. As Jeffrey Masten claims in *Textual Intercourse*, "Collaboration is a dispersal of author/ity, rather than a mere doubling of it; to revise the aphorism, two heads are different than one" (19). Traditional criticism, implicitly or explicitly, has seen collaboration "as a mere subset or aberrant kind of authorship, the collusion of two unique authors whom subsequent readers could discern and separate out by examining the traces of individuality and personality . . . left in the collaborative text" (16). Although, as the case of Louise Erdrich and Michael Dorris suggests, discerning those traces of individuality is anything but reliable, we tend to behave as if it is. Rather than maintaining the concept of author as unique and individual, collaboration as I discuss it focuses on "the author" as a historically changeable concept, a repository of meanings about the process of making meaning. I am not arguing that collaborative writing is something we should do more of or that it offers new or dramatically different ways to write, although in some forms this may be so. Rather, I am arguing that collaboration is something we already do, always, when we write "alone" or with others and when we read others' writing, as Masten notes when he says, "If we accept that language is a socially produced (and producing) system, then collaboration is more the condition of discourse than its exception. Interpreting from a collaborative perspective acknowledges language as a process of exchange; rather than policing discourse off into agents, origins, and intentions, a collaborative focus elaborates the social mechanism of language, discourse as intercourse" (20). In short, I am arguing for an awareness of the implications of the collaborative process in which all literary experience is drenched.

Since a studied ignorance of the persistent presence of collaboration—like the persistent presence of Native Americans, African Americans, or even women in literature—requires a great deal of energy to maintain, it follows that there must be some substantial benefits or pleasures associated with what I see as our largely collective, even willful, blindness regarding collaboration. If we look closely at those "theoretical challenges," for example, we crash headlong into questions that cannot be answered easily or definitively. The historical persons named Beaumont, Fletcher, and Shakespeare, for instance, all wrote during the early modern period in Britain, when literature, particularly drama, was routinely conceived of as a collaborative process that in itself renders our contemporary obsession for the sole author of particular words peculiar, even incomprehensible. Are we therefore under any historical imperative to view early modern literature as intrinsically collaborative because of the historical circumstances of its production? If so, what (if any) difference does a work of literature's historical context make to our understanding of these canonical figures as "authors"? Did Coleridge and Eliot rely on Wordsworth and Pound, respectively, as editors and commentators, or were their contributions significant enough to merit joint authorship? Should we, as Stillinger implies, refer to the epic modernist poem as *Pound*'s "Waste Land" (121)? Are spousal or partner relationships collaborative, particularly when much of the "work" centers on talk and encouragement? Is there, as Wayne Koestenbaum, Jeffrey Masten, Holly Laird, and Susan Leonardi and Rebecca Pope suggest in their studies of collaboration, an erotic element to collaboration that must become a visible aspect of its theorization?[3] To what degree is the editing process of African and African American slave narratives by more culturally powerful and privileged white editors also a form of collaboration? Is an editor—often unseen and unacknowledged—a collaborator in a literary text?[4]

Although I take these questions very seriously, I also present them in the spirit of intellectual play. As they reveal, literary collaboration is an expansive, entangled area whose key tensions inevitably center on problems with the definition of an author and with unexamined assumptions about the nature of language and the process of making meaning. At the deepest level, nothing less than our ideological claims to fixed identity and stable meaning are at stake in a careful investigation of collaboration. Put another way, when we question longstanding definitions of authorship as a singular, isolated, and inspired enterprise, we risk altering our understanding of the world and our place in the center of it. Not incidentally, many people experience such decentering as an attack on the pleasure of the reading process and the competency of the reader, both important aspects of perceived mastery, the sense of one's self commandingly in the center of the text. However, as C. Jan Swearingen shows, this is hardly a novel risk because multiculturalism in its various forms has been launching such a revisioning of European-based understandings of authorship for half a century now: "Comprising not only multicultural curricula, but growing numbers of multicultural students, today's colleges and universities serve students who enter the college classroom believing that truth, wisdom, and cultural artifacts such as art and literature are cultural community property, the result of years of accumulated wisdom transmitted by venerated leaders and by oral traditions, many of them religious" (19). Narrow conceptions of literature as the product of individual genius are being questioned in and out of the classroom; revisionist challenges to the literary canons are producing new knowledge, increasing classroom vitality, and emphasizing the pertinence of literature to our daily lives in ways that a purely aesthetic approach grounded in textual "mastery" cannot. Nonetheless, we are sometimes at a loss for a theoretically sophisticated and effective language to account for the challenges multiculturalism brings to a discussion of authorship. Put another way, we've heard this before: the author has been challenged, proclaimed dead, and then resurrected— again and again. Yet a fundamental belief in individual authorship, despite its effective dismantling by poststructuralist, feminist, and colonialist perspectives, persists with stunning consistency. Turning to a theory of collaboration is one way both to explain that persistence and to intervene in it.

In part because what we mean by collaboration, as well as what collaboration means to our understanding and evaluation of literature, is anything but clear and agreed upon, we generally persist in ignoring it altogether in the humanities. For instance, in the sciences within the academy—where knowledge is commonly understood as a group endeavor built upon prior knowledges and tested by scientific methods—jointly authored articles, one example of collaboration, are the norm.[5] Yet when it comes to literature or scholarly research in the humanities, the idea of the insulated, individual author still reigns despite persuasive and influential theories of language and meaning construction of the last several decades. In the humanities, collaborative writing is re-garded warily; it is often tainted by whiffs of plagiarism, hidden from view by claims of innocent "borrowing" from one individ-ual author by another, and rarely investigated from a theoretical vantage point. One goal of this book is to address these suspicions by placing collaborative writing in a theoretical context that will allow us to examine it more fully and self-consciously. But I be-lieve that there are other reasons for collaboration's near invisibil-ity in the humanities, reasons that can be located in the history of the development of a concept of authorship as an isolated, iso-lating activity and in the humanities' subsequent devotion to the idea of the singly authored text—its own history of denial of the constructed, culturally influenced reality of our ideas of author-ship. Despite theoretical challenges that have otherwise met with enthusiastic if sometimes contentious debate, the belief that the vast majority of literary texts are singly authored, coherent, and contained masterpieces has assumed a naturalness that passes for truth. Although this definition of authorship appears as both in-evitable and commonsensical, it is not. Authorship is a histori-cally produced construct with significant political stakes attached to maintaining the stance of inevitability and naturalness. As re-cent historical studies have shown, the very meaning of author-ship, of what it means to write a text, and of which individuals are recognized as contributing substantially or wholly to that text's creation has changed enormously over the years in response to ad-vances in available printing apparatus, legal protections such as copyright laws, and philosophically, the privileging of individual selfhood and the shifting value of originality.[6] These studies re-veal that, far from being natural or inevitable, authorship is a con-structed concept, responsive to the cultural context in which it exists and therefore changeable as cultural needs regarding au-thorship change.

For example, during the Middle Ages, when "the reverence for authority, the reliance on scriptoria for copies of manuscripts, and the development of such rhetorical arts as the *ars dictaminis*, manuals for letter writing that, at their most elaborate, provided countless formulas and models for imitation," authorship had little or no connection to a concept of originality (Lunsford and Ede, *Singular Texts/Plural Authors* 77). Decoration or embellishment might take place but with the understanding, on the part of the writer or the audience, that the material was not changed in any artistically original way: "The medieval writer wrote 'in order to praise and extend his object, not to express himself or to enhance his personal reputation.'"[7] Martha Woodmansee notes that "from the Middle Ages right down through the Renaissance new writing derived its value and authority from its affiliation with the texts that preceded it, its derivation rather than its deviation from prior texts" (281). What we would today call plagiarism was the accepted method of composition in the Middle Ages, and without a concept of literary property, plagiarism did not exist as a meaningful concept (Lunsford and Ede 78). Furthermore, during the Middle Ages, the writer was one of many skilled artisans who contributed to the production of a text, but he was no more valuable than, say, the papermaker, the typesetter, the proofreader, or the bookbinder, to suggest just some of the craftspeople who collaboratively created a finished product.

Collaboration as the cornerstone of literary production continued throughout the early modern period, particularly in the dramatic arts.[8] In England, it was the theater's dominant mode of production (Masten 14). To return to my earlier mention of Beaumont, Fletcher, and Shakespeare, without a concept of literary property, dramatic works were understood as collaborative productions with no sacred connection to the writer or to the writer's intention: "The idea of the sacredness of an individual author's text was as yet unacknowledged, and nothing in either law or sentiment stood in the way of adapting, cutting, rearranging, and even massive rewriting in the interest of spectacle, story and entertainment" (Stillinger 164). Masten argues that, within the Renaissance theater company, "the construction of meaning was polyvocal—often beginning with a collaborative manuscript, which was then revised, cut, rearranged, and augmented by book-holders, copyists, and other writers, elaborated and improvised by actors in performance, accompanied by music and songs that may or may not have originated in a completely different context" (14). The widespread filmic adaptation of plays attributed to Shakespeare, which continues today, is a contemporary display of the collaborative nature of drama existing even during the time of their composition. What is different today is the way in which our belief in an individual author doggedly reappears nevertheless: even in its trendy, pounding, and relentlessly visual Southern California setting, the 1996 film *William Shakespeare's Romeo + Juliet* gets its primary cachet from its association not with its producer, director, screenplay writers, or even its popular youthful stars but with its "author"—Shakespeare. Behind the shifts in time, nationality, cultural context, and conflicting information regarding the historical personage named William Shakespeare lies the belief that we can locate the sole author, the genius of the text, intact and uncontaminated. And alone.

The emergence of the concept of intellectual property forged the link between collaboration and the potential for plagiarism and became an important step in the development of authorship as we now understand it. Equally important in the gradually changing status of authorship were developments in philosophy that led toward the privileging of the individual self. Queen Anne's Act of 1710 was the first legal recognition of the writer rather than the bookseller as copyright holder. Lunsford and Ede note that "the protection afforded by copyright laws that contemporary writers take for granted was once a hotly contested issue—one with no preordained or inevitable outcome" (*Singular Texts/Plural Authors* 81). As copyright law gradually became accepted and the philosophy grounded in individual selfhood became widely assumed, an enduring link was forged between the individual self and the privileged creator of a text in the term *author*. Authorship also became increasingly professionalized with the advent of printing presses, which, when combined with ownership of copyright, created sweeping conceptual changes in the concept of authorship as an individual enterprise: "Although it is by no means the only factor responsible for the development of the concept of authorship, the ability to profit from one's writing—an ability eventually guaranteed by copyright laws—did in fact play a crucial role in establishing not only the profession of letters but equally important notions of originality and the ownership of texts" (Lunsford and Ede, *Singular Texts/Plural Authors* 81). In Britain and America, the Romantic movement, and particularly Wordsworth's 1815 "Essay, Supplementary to the Preface," further redefined writing as an inspired, original, and necessarily solitary act and the writer as a genius whose very unique creativity requires his isolation: "Of genius the only proof is, the act of doing well what is worthy to be done, and what was never done before: . . . widening the sphere of human sensibility for the delight, honor, and benefit of human nature. Genius is the introduction of a new element into the intellectual universe" (Wordsworth 82). The construction of authorship thus changes from a structurally collaborative event wherein neither writing nor authorship is essentially linked to originality to one in which originality resides in the privileged individual self whose very uniqueness establishes, tautologically, his originality and thus his identity as author.

As Ede and Lunsford point out, a belief in an "organic" connection between the writer and his ideas helped to further establish this new view of solitary authorship and of literature as a privileged activity: "For if texts express an author's individual genius, how can a single text manifest the essential being of more than one person? The organic connection between writer and text—a connection so strong that the text in some sense represents or embodies the author—would be broken. Thus the same theoretical move that elevated certain kinds of poetry and prose to 'literature' and guaranteed writers the ability to earn a living from their writing also inevitably defined the activity by which they did so as essentially isolating, even alienating" (*Singular*

Texts/Plural Authors 85). As authorship became a more privileged act in the culture, it simultaneously became a more specifically gendered act, a move that became increasingly effective in preventing women from claiming the status of author, while shifting ideas toward literary production began to identify it as intellectual property, eventually leading to copyright legislation. Additionally, there was a cultural belief in an organic connection between writing and masculinity and, correspondingly, between inspiration (the muse, or Nature, for example) and femininity.

Although certainly women have entered the changing arenas of authorship across time, their presence there is frequently vexed by gendered expectations surrounding authorship. In nineteenth-century America, socially constructed and accepted ideals regarding femininity placed women's interests in the domestic realm. Writing was considered not just a masculine activity but a distraction from those things that truly required women's attention: home and family. To write, then, was not just to challenge a set of vague expectations about what women should be doing; it was to risk betraying one's femininity, to risk denying one's identity as a woman and suitability as a mother. Nonetheless, many women did write, publish, and sell their works. American women writers' domestic novels were extremely popular, for example. Susan Warner's *Wide, Wide World* was widely read, and Harriet Beecher Stowe's *Uncle Tom's Cabin* was second in sales only to the Bible. Columnist Fanny Fern, prompted to public writing as a way to support her family after the death of her husband, was enormously popular and, for the time, well paid. But the ideal of woman-as-inspiration, rather than as author, was still important. Friedrich Kitler argues that "Nature, love, and women—the terms were synonymous in the 1800 discourse network" (73). As some of America's most notable male writers crusaded to identify a specifically American literature, women became more fully the muse rather than the representative American author. In her classic essay "Melodramas of Beset Manhood: How Theories of American Fiction Exclude Women Authors," Nina Baym argues that women are so seldom recognized as authors because "what critics have done is to assume . . . that the women writers invariably represented the consensus, rather than the criticism of it; to assume that their gender made them part of the consensus in a way that prevented them from partaking in the criticism. The presence of these women and their works is acknowledged in literary theory and history as an impediment and obstacle, that which the essential American literature had to criticize as its chief task" (69). In *West of Everything: The Inner Life of Westerns* (1992), Jane Tompkins claims that the classic literary Western developed in response to the nineteenth-century sentimental novel's popularity in the eastern United States. In American literature, writing became inextricably linked to masculinity as American writers became obsessed with issues of paternity, with fathering a tradition that would stand as distinct from a now-rejected European one: "Certainly, this idea involves the question of authority, and 'authority' is a notion related to that of 'the author.' And there is some gender-specific significance involved since authority in most cultures that we know tends to be invested in adult males. But the theory has built from these useful and true observations to a restriction of literary creation to a sort of therapeutic act that can only be performed by men. If literature is an attempt to *father* oneself by the author, then every act of writing by a women is both perverse and absurd. And, of course, it is bound to fail" (Baym 78). Although nineteenth-century women were not likely to achieve status as enduring canonical authors, they were celebrated as muse and inspiration. Women viewed thusly were important, even crucial, to literary production; they might at times even be writers, but they were not authors. American literature, in other words, defined itself *as* American in part by denying the literary collaboration that took place between its (male) authors and the women who stood in as muse. Because authorship was considered an individual act of creative genius, relegating women to the margins did not lessen their participation as collaborators.

It did, however, rid the so-called individual authors of any need to identify their influences—who they collaborated with or appropriated from—because in the mythology of individual genius, inspiration is a gift given freely to the deserving.

We can see from even this brief description how much our ideas of authorship, while seemingly self-evident, are actually fluid, changeable, and gendered. For philosopher and theorist Michel Foucault, authorship is never more—or less—than its ideological function within a particular historical moment. Yet we should not underestimate the power of authorship's ideological function or the resistance encountered when we subject it to analysis rather than reverence. For example, Peter Jaszi demonstrates how this "ideology of authorship" is linked to "the formation of particular doctrinal structures in the law of copyright" (31). For Jaszi, "the persistent notion of 'authorship' in American copyright law makes it difficult for any new legal synthesis, which would focus on the reality of collective creativity to emerge" (31). Jaszi continues: "That Romantic 'authorship' is alive and well in the late twentieth-century American legal culture has consequences for the law's engagement with (or failure to engage) the realities of contemporary polyvocal writing practice—which increasingly is collective, corporate, and collaborative. . . . The law is not so much systematically hostile to works that do not fit the individualistic model of Romantic 'authorship' as it is uncomprehending of them. Such works are marginalized or become literally invisible within the prevailing ideological discourse in copyright—even to the point of literal invisibility" (38). Marginality and invisibility are hardly new obstacles to consider when interpreting literature. Feminist and gender theories, poststructuralist theories, Marxist theories, and post-Colonial theories all debate how we construct meaning and knowledge when faced with literature by marginalized writers: non-Europeans, women, people of color, and gays and lesbians. But even in these situations, while scholarship often traces strategies of literary resistance, refusal, or subversion of patriarchal, capitalistic, or heterosexist norms, it rarely questions the status of the solitary author from the vantage point offered by collaboration.

As legal and cultural constructs simultaneously embodied and protected the concept of the individual author, literary theorists have for many years doubted or outrightly rejected that concept as powerful but illusory. The most familiar and frequently cited discussions are probably Roland Barthes's essay "The Death of the Author," Michel Foucault's essay "What Is an Author?," and Mikhail Bakhtin's idea of "heteroglossia," in which each writer decenters the traditional author as an embodiment of stability, genius, and originary meaning, reconstructing in his stead other possibilities of meaning creation. In his now very famous 1977 essay "The Death of the Author," Barthes insists that the reign of the author must cease and advocates returning the reader to a privileged position in the construction of meaning: "Classic criticism has never paid any attention to the reader; for it, the writer is the only person in literature. . . . To give writing its future, it is necessary to overthrow the myth: the birth of the reader must be at the cost of the death of the Author" (148). Of course, Barthes is speaking metaphorically. His goal is to shift the privilege of meaning making to the reader; it is with the reader, and the reader alone, that authority, and thus meaning, resides.

Although Barthes has been criticized for merely substituting the reign of the author with that of the reader, his theory has important implications for collaboration. In one sense, Barthes substitutes another author (the reader) for the now-dead "Author" and, to use the language of paternity Barthes employs, another collaboration is born. Yet the reader-as-author carries little of the cultural mythology attached to the individual writing author; after all, Barthes writes the essay because readers are ignored or undervalued, not because they have a status of genius akin to that attributed to the author. If we assume that readers exist in cultural and historical contexts as much as authors do, that readers are shaped by ideological values and assumptions concerning literary

meaning, that they occupy gendered, raced, classed subject positions and, further, that they share reactions and interpretations,
argue over characters, read book reviews, and ask their friends
for suggestions, then the process of meaning making is itself
complexly, contextually collaborative. Meaning (or "truth"), no
longer believed to reside passively in the text until an alert reader
uncovers it, is also no longer created through any simple, recoverable exchange between reader and text. From this reader-centered
view, collaboration is an intricate, culturally influenced process
that can always result only in provisional meaning.

In response to Barthes, Foucault is more skeptical that the author can be so readily dispensed with. For Foucault, the author is
so intricately connected to unexamined assumptions and unin-
vestigated avenues of power that he will not readily disappear or
be displaced by proclamations of his death: "The author is not an
indefinite source of significations which fill a work; the author
does not precede the works, he is a certain functional principle by
which, in our culture, one limits, excludes, and chooses; in short,
by which one impedes the free circulation, the free manipulation,
the free composition, decomposition, and recomposition of fiction" (159). The "author function," Foucault's designation for
the meanings attributed to the word *author* in terms of the cultural work it performs during particular historical moments, is
still very strongly with us. Questioning the very nature of the traditional, autonomous, coherent subject, Foucault argues for a
radical shift that Lunsford and Ede identify as "one that would
view texts as contested sites in a complex, situated world of political, cultural, economic, ideological, or other forces" (*Singular Texts/Plural Authors* 88). The result would be a drastically
changed definition of authorship:

> We would no longer hear the questions that have been rehashed so
> long: "Who really spoke? Is it really he and not someone else? With
> what authenticity or originality? And what part of his deepest self
> did he express in his discourse?" Instead, there would be other ques-
> tions, like these: "What are the modes of existence of this discourse?

Where has it been used, how can it circulate, and who can appropriate it for himself? What are the places in it where there is room for possible subjects? Who can assume these various subject-functions?" And behind all these questions we would hear hardly anything but the stirring of an indifference: "What difference does it make who is speaking?" (160)

Foucault resituates the very nature of both self and author, and with him we begin to see an opening for a different consideration of collaboration. If the author is "the ideological figure by which one marks the manner in which we fear the proliferation of meaning" (Foucault 159), if the self is no longer the coherent whole that, filtered through a personality, consciously expresses genius in a text but rather is an always fragmentary self written upon by various, inescapable social forces, which are, in turn, traceable in the text produced, then the idea of multiply authored (or multivoiced) text becomes not just viable but as seemingly inevitable as the Romantic concept of author currently seems.

Russian Marxist Mikhail Bakhtin's dialogic theory of language is equally suggestive of a notion of collaborative textual production. For Bakhtin, both text and self are composed of multiple, shifting voices that depend upon social contexts and their relationship to other utterances for their meaning. This conception of shifting values, which Bakhtin calls "heteroglossia," means that, in essence, any text is collaborative; the socially constructed nature of language and the interactive ways in which meaning is made require a conception of collaboration from a structural standpoint. For Bakhtin, however, collaboration is rendered inescapable by the very nature of language, in which "language is heteroglot from top to bottom: it represents the co-existence of socio-ideological contradictions between the present and the past, between differing epochs of the past, between different socio-ideological groups in the present, between tendencies, schools, circles and so forth, all given a bodily form. These 'languages' of heteroglossia intersect each other in a variety of ways, forming new socially typifying 'languages'" (291). For Bakhtin, the intricate web of heteroglossia ensures that all languages are intrinsically collaborative. Thus, to claim a text, and the words within it, as one's own is highly problematic. Bakhtin writes that "the word in language is half someone else's" and that "it becomes 'one's own' only when the speaker populates it with his own intention, his own accent, when he appropriates the word" (293). But language often works against such an appropriation, and "many words stubbornly resist, others remain alien, sound foreign in the mouth of the one who appropriated them and who now speaks them; they cannot be assimilated into his context and fall out of it; it is as if they put themselves in quotations marks against the will of the speaker. Language is not a neutral medium that passes freely and easily into the private property of the speaker's intentions; it is populated—overpopulated—with the intentions of others. Expropriating it, forcing it to submit to one's own intentions and accents, is a difficult and complicated process" (294). Despite a backlash against poststructuralist theories as jargon laden, elitist, or themselves heavily invested in the patriarchal privilege they appear to condemn, poststructuralist theories denaturalize the apparently inevitable, letting us recognize and account for the deployments of power or the unacknowledged investments that make the individual author so durable. These theories offer a crucial critique of the notion of the individual self and the singly authored text and thereby provide us the best lens through which to examine the complicated process of collaboration and its implications.

However, for all the revolutionary promise of these contemporary poststructuralist theories, there are problems, most notably as the theories address—or fail to address—the practical difference made by race, gender, sexuality, or other categories currently dense with meaning and rife with discernible power in American culture. Finally, particularly because poststructuralist theories relentlessly decenter meaning and authority, questions arise about agency. If authorship, and thus authority, is always located somewhere else, not here, how can responsibility for acts of appropria-

tion be assigned? Does textual appropriation, what we call plagiarism, even exist in this seemingly "loose" redefinition of authorship, or is Mark Twain correct when he sputters, "As if there
were much of anything in any human utterance, oral or written,
except plagiarism!"[9] I would suggest here that, while these theoretical approaches can be interpreted as ignoring the importance
of agency, poststructuralist theory does not *inevitably* do away
with culpability, any more than it does away with meaning. However, as is true when we evaluate meaning from a poststructural
perspective, responsibility for one's actions in the collaborative
event must also take into account the potentially complex cultural context in which the collaboration occurs as well as the one
in which it is read. For this reason, there are no "bad guys" in my
account of collaboration in western American literature, despite
the emotionally compelling quality of that emblematic Western
dichotomy. However, I do identify choices made, both freely and
compelled, that situate collaborative writers in more or less subversive contexts, choices whose implications reinscribe the privilege of the writer's authorial (or gendered or raced) position to a
greater or lesser degree.

Feminist criticism, which has both utilized and challenged de-
constructive critiques of selfhood and language that decenter traditional humanistic understandings, also argues that, under specific circumstances, we must go even further in our critiques in
order to understand the roles that categories of difference play in
constructions of meaning and power. Although collaboration has
only begun to be studied and theorized, feminist approaches tend
to see collaboration as a method of textual production that challenges the patriarchal structure inherent in the ideas of "genius,"
"masterpiece," and "autonomous self." From this point of view,
particularly given women's historical definition as "other" to
man's "self," collaboration is often identified as an act of resistance, an ideal subversive act. Nonetheless, it is important to keep
in mind that, as an act, collaboration is still embedded within the
patriarchal culture in which it takes place; it is practiced by indi-

viduals whose gendered, sexed, raced, and classed identities are constructed within that culture. Collaboration therefore is neither inherently benign nor politically subversive. As Lunsford and Ede astutely point out, "Collaborative writing itself constitutes a technology of power, one we are only beginning to explore" (*Singular Texts/Plural Authors* 120). Even when collaboration does challenge traditional power relations, it does not inevitably destroy them, and it always simultaneously creates other equally pervasive and context-driven power relations.

The practical applications of my theoretical assertion that collaboration is always the state of writing reinforce my belief that it is well nigh time to theorize collaboration. As Lunsford and Ede have shown, even if we have not considered collaboration per se, we make assumptions about it in our personal and professional lives every day, and "writing teachers err if, in envisioning students' professional lives upon graduation, they imagine them seated alone, writing in isolation, misplaced Romantic spirits still struggling in a professional garret to express themselves. Although some of our students will commit themselves to professions, such as creative writing, where solitary writing is the norm, most will work in situations where they are at least as likely to participate in a group brainstorming session for a proposal or edit a collaboratively written report on-line as they are to sit alone in their offices, pen (or computer keyboard) in hand" (*Singular Texts/Plural Authors* 72). Lunsford and Ede's primary concern here is to dispel the notion that students or the subsequent employees they become benefit from the humanities' enduring belief in our traditional conception of the author as a solitary genius producing his (or, less frequently but admittedly possible, her) masterwork. Yet even Lunsford and Ede acknowledge that in some professions "such as creative writing . . . solitary writing is the norm." A subtle reading reminds us that "solitary writing" is not necessarily *single authorship*, nor do Lunsford and Ede claim that it is.[10] But they do risk reinscribing the notion—at this point a rather nostalgic and fruitless one given the range and rigor of theoretical challenges to the concept of individual authorship—that creative writing is a one-person job. In other words, they imply that, at least sometimes and perhaps often, creative writing —the production of literature—is individually authored and produces a text that is not collaborative. In her discussion of plagiarism, Rebecca Moore Howard sums up the current tension between composition studies and collaboration: "Although contemporary critical theory asserts that all writing is collaborative, composition scholarship's treatments of collaboration characteristically assume the possibility of an autonomous writer and depict collaboration as an option that the autonomous subject may elect. More tellingly, almost all composition scholarship requires the student to function autonomously when interacting with written texts. Collaboration, in other words, occurs between writers or between one writer and another or between writer and reader—but it must not occur between writer and text" (88). The tenacity with which a fundamental belief in the image of the individual author lives on in our imagination, even within the one area of scholarship that has begun thoughtfully studying collaboration, attests less to its reality than to its political usefulness in the complex landscape in which literary production takes place.

And indeed, such a stance may be politically useful: the traditional literary canon, contemporary categories of literary merit, and even tenure decisions in the humanities rest upon a belief in the individual author. What is actually a deeply held belief in the individual author as autonomous creator comes to appear, over time, as a self-evident, natural, and inevitable "truth" about authors and their relation to creativity. Many people benefit from this perspective on authorship; publishers, editors, specific individuals whose names are appended to the text, and others who produce texts that are then sold to the public, often at substantial profit, all benefit from the marketing of an individual name as the "author" of a text. Professors seeking tenure or promotion routinely list "their" articles, reviews, and books as evidence of their individual contributions to the discipline; to fail (or refuse) to do so is tantamount to admitting one is naive at best and deadwood at worst. In the writing classroom, a focus on uncovering an individual voice or polishing a distinctive style presumes that sole authorship is both possible and expected. In the literature classroom, with such relatively few exceptions as traditional Native American tales and poetry, discussion of literary works overwhelmingly centers on "the author" of the text, whether we're reading Milton or Morrison. Even the proliferating numbers of web sites offering student papers on a host of subjects (already written or written to order!) hinge on a belief in individual authorship; their niche is substituting one author (the unknown author of the essay) for another (the student purchasing it in order to present it as his or her own paper). In short, a belief in individual authorship simplifies what can be the overdetermined and unstable world of collaboration and thus helps us to navigate the areas of marketing, teaching, learning, and reading in multiple ways. Moreover, as feminist theory has shown, claiming individual genius is a politically astute, even necessary, move at times, particularly for women and minority writers. If the world—from publisher to audience—agrees that authoring is inherently individual, to emphasize collaboration is, effectively, to become silent, even invisible. Staking a claim to individual authorship is effective in large part because it doesn't *appear* political; although a fiction, individual authorship is a fiction that circulates as uncomplicated "truth." My claim that even when we investigate singly authored texts we can readily find traces of collaborations unsuccessfully hidden within or curiously enacted by those texts threatens to displace our current, largely authoritative systems of knowledge at virtually every level. Ultimately, locating those traces of collaboration is both a politically subversive and an avowedly political act.

This discussion highlights the intractable presence of power relationships behind every assumption we make about what constitutes authorship. In one sense, I am advocating recognizing the collaborative aspects of all texts and the constructed nature of our concept of authorship. But that does not necessarily mean jetti-soning the strategic identity politics employed by claiming indi-vidual authorship. Rather, we will likely always have *authors*. But what we *mean* when we talk about authors will no longer evoke the romantic image of the isolated genius or, alternatively, the marginalized writer successfully wielding the master's tools.

One of the key ways in which a study of collaboration chal-lenges traditional power relations is evident when we discuss pla-giarism. Although, as we have seen, plagiarism is a constructed concept, one that in medieval times would have been irrelevant or even incomprehensible, in the twenty-first century, plagiarism does not exist any the less for its constructed nature. Plagiarism often becomes evident as an anxiety or even as a threat when col-laboration is occurring; for that reason, we must grapple with it, all the time realizing that plagiarism is, in fact, a historically de-rived definition rather than a specific, unchanging act. As a defi-nition or series of definitions, it points to specific acts and ascribes them political import. In this way, a contemporary charge of pla-giarism is a politically situated way (only one of many potential ways) to alleviate anxieties surrounding the complex process of authorship.

Curiously, of the writers I discuss in the following chapters, only Wallace Stegner has been pointedly accused of plagiarism, an accusation he rightly recognized as "an attack." Why have none of the other writers I discuss been similarly "attacked" by critics or readers, even when at times their collaboration with oth-ers was hidden or denied? Part of the reason, which I discuss at more length in chapter 6, concerns the power relations not only between Stegner and his source, Mary Hallock Foote, but be-tween Stegner and his readers, many of whom identify Stegner as the West's most promising claim to original genius—the last, best author. The other writers I examine here either possess less ex-alted literary reputations or have been both more forthcoming and less defensive about their collaborators, even if they do not use that term. For example, Louise Erdrich and Michael Dorris have been insistent to the point of annoying their interviewers about their collaborative relationships; they leave no space for charges of plagiarism because they so readily admit, even celebrate, the ways in which they rely upon each other during the writing process. Mary Austin has been accused of appropriating Native American belief systems, but she visibly and enthusiastically credits that culture with returning her ability to write to her. Moreover, Austin's appropriations, if they exist, are not of words from paper, not of legally recognized intellectual property, which is the only kind of theft a charge of plagiarism accurately addresses. Unlike those of any of the other writers I discuss, Wallace Stegner's reputation as a "great" western author hinges on several contradictions: he is simultaneously western and universal, male and universal, unique and universal. Not only is an accusation of plagiarism more initially damaging because previously unthinkable concerning our "great" authors—remember, authorship itself has come to mean individual genius—but precisely that insistence on originality and isolation leaves no alternative ways of understanding Stegner's actions regarding Foote's work other than plagiarism. In the language of authorship available to us, Stegner is *either* one of the West's stellar authors *or* he plagiarized.

A second instance of power relations involves collaboration's highly sexualized connotations. Pejoratively, the term *collaboration* conjures images of dishonor on the battlefield, where one cooperates with an enemy rather than resists, subverts, or even dies with honor. As Laird points out, "It may be no accident that collaboration is still strongly associated with the meaning it acquired during the Nazi occupation of France, where to collaborate was to collude with the enemy. Collaboration has played the villain's role in modern liberation movements ('solidarity' gets to be the good guy), and the term *collaboration* has thus become sedimented in a highly political, unstable binary between free individualism and enslaving totalitarianism" (*Women Coauthors* 6). This is the emphasis of the term *sleeping with the enemy*, which suggests an intimate as well as an intricate relationship with a person or an institution opposed to one's best interests. The sexual metaphor here asserts self-betrayal, treason, and even masochistic victimization; at the very least, the collaborative relationship is understood as clouding the collaborator's perception of "truth." In this interpretation, collaborators carry with them the potential for destruction, a potential that must be monitored but may also be mined for its subversive power.

As a subversive act, however, the sexual connotations of collaboration can indicate a desire not for victimization but for the erotic possibilities collaboration offers.[11] Because writing has long been linked to the sexual, collaborative writing lends itself both to (hetero)sexual parallels, such as intercourse and the joint production of the resulting text as child, and to a marginalized form of libidinal pleasure that Leonardi and Pope call "queer": "As a term that assimilates a variety of unconventional practices, desires, and social positions, *queer* seemed to us an apt label for collaborative writing. . . . In the humanities, cowritten texts have been the sturdy spinster aunts and odd bachelor uncles of the traditional discursive family. From this perspective, all collaborative scholars, no matter what their self-identifications and practices, become queer practitioners" (633).[12] However, I want to suggest with Audre Lorde that our definition of the erotic is impoverished if it only signifies the specifically sexual, whether literal (the collaborators are sexually involved or their writing substitutes for a sexual relationship by displacing that desire or both) or metaphorical (the pen equates to the penis/phallus, which signifies authority and which the female writer desires, or the collaborators' text is a substitute child resulting from their collaborative union). Rather, Lorde argues that the erotic teaches excellence and provides "the power which comes from sharing deeply any pursuit with another person" (56).

It is not only a blurring of boundaries or a figurative "union," whether sexual or otherwise, that the erotic component of collaboration can offer. More pragmatic, more potentially revolutionary, and more profoundly threatening is the recognition of difference *that is not subsequently assimilated or suppressed.* Lorde continues, "The sharing of joy, whether physical, emotional, psychic, or intellectual, forms a bridge between the sharers which can be the basis for understanding much of what is not shared between them, and lessens the threat of their difference" (56). Because collaboration is always about negotiating a relationship in some sense—a relationship between writers, between sources of influence, between prior texts and current ones, between literary conventions or expectations—collaboration inevitably encounters a relational difficulty: acknowledging the other, who is commonly the screen onto which the threat of difference is projected. Barbara Johnson approaches the difficulty of addressing difference, the difficulty of the threat it poses, in the feminist community: "Conflicts among feminists require women to pay attention to each other, to take each other's reality seriously, to face each other. . . . It places difference among women rather than exclusively between the sexes. Of course, patriarchy has always played women off against each other and manipulated differences among women for its own purposes. Nevertheless, feminists have to take the risk of confronting and negotiating differences among women if we are ever to transform such difference into positive rather than negative forces in women's lives" (194). The possibility of transforming difference into a positive force, which can occur during the recognition and negotiation of difference, is one of the compelling aspects of collaboration for both writers and readers.

Difference as a valued, potentially positive aspect of identity has long been part of the western mythos and is therefore one of the ways in which the collaborative aspects of western American literature may have lessons to teach us about our national literature and about recurring attempts to assert a unified national identity. The West has long been seen as an escape from the vicissitudes of the East, a site of redemption and transformation. Men especially were encouraged to travel there, to flee the "civilizing" forces represented by the eastern city centers and to redeem and re-create themselves in the untrammeled regions past civilization's reach. In both of these desires—escape and transformation—difference is a key force: the West is geographically, attitudinally, even legally, different than the East and so, therefore, must be its inhabitants; as a site of transformation, the West promises the creation of differences—we become different (and presumably better and happier) than we were prior to our encounters with the West. Such is certainly the thinking displayed in Frederick Jackson Turner's frontier thesis, in which he argues that the American character is literally created by the ongoing clashes of West-venturing men with the wilderness frontier.

Although Blake Allmendinger laments the absence of "the literary equivalent of a frontier hypothesis, a unifying theory that argues that the entire corpus of American literature stems from a fascination with the nation's frontier" to legitimize western American literature in ways similar to the ways in which Turner's frontier thesis has legitimized the study of western American history, western American literature does display an insistent fascination with landscape (2). In western American literature, most of the responsibility for accomplishing the very western changes involved in escape and transformation is assigned to the landscape, which is most often discussed as either nature free from the polluting presence of humankind or, alternatively, nature enhanced and made useful by the industrious presence of humankind. In the first example, a transcendent nature collaborates with humankind's nature in order to produce the salvific, transcendent experience; we go to nature to be purged of the muck of culture and emerge transformed. In the second example, we collaborate with nature in order to create new landscapes and new, usually economically profitable uses for the land; we purge nature of its passive "thereness" and turn it into something that actively works for us.

Few western writers treat the landscape as irrelevant, perhaps because even tentative or provisional definitions of the terms *western writer* and *western American literature* all take as their basis the implicit belief that relationships to the land will be expressed in the writer's work. For instance, Willa Cather, who is not one of the writers I discuss in this study, has what is arguably a dubious relationship to the West: she was born in Virginia, spent most of her childhood in the Midwest (Nebraska), and spent most of her adulthood living and writing in the eastern United States and traveling abroad. Her time west of Nebraska was largely composed of visits and research trips. Yet Cather's enduring status as a western writer hinges largely on her "pioneer novels," such as *O Pioneers* and *My Ántonia*, and on work set in the Southwest, such as *Death Comes for the Archbishop*, all novels that, as numerous critics have noted, often feature the land as an active character.

In western American literature, then, landscape and region play key roles in constructing the differences that become so important to claims of western identity. Yet, as many of the western writers I discuss here demonstrate, there are contradictions at work when attempting to define a western identity based upon region. To begin with, American writers particularly want to avoid being categorized as regionalists. Despite the fact that, for American writers, literature has always been "about" region in explicit ways—what makes American literature "American" rather than "European" or even "British" was a central question for nineteenth-century writers, for example—regionalism also carries with it distinct whiffs of the inconsequential, the minor, the minutely local. Although Mary Austin argues in her essay "Regionalism in American Fiction" that all literature is regional, that rather than "one vast, pale figure of America" there are "several Americas, in many subtle and significant characterizations" (131), the label "regional writer" acts as a death sentence for most writers, western or otherwise.[13] While I share Allmendinger's frustration over how anyone could "come to believe that an introverted poet such as Emily Dickinson, or a resident of tiny Walden Pond, was somehow 'American,' while anyone who took as his or her subject the whole western half of a continent was a regionalist, a local color writer, or a miniature portraitist" (1), the fact remains that the illusion of universality, however false it may be in actuality, is still a powerful criterion of literary merit in the American canon of literature.

The desire for universality—one story, applicable to all, where either difference does not exist or, more frequently, does not matter—is exactly the desire that a focus on collaboration deliberately leaves unmet. Even as it refuses to satisfy a desire for universality, collaboration emphasizes the presence of that desire *as a desire* via its challenges to singularity and its insistence on the ways in which difference always exists and is important to the process of meaning making, even if rendered invisible or stripped of cultural power. In other words, a study of collaboration does not substitute one universal for another, even if my claim that we are always making meaning collaboratively seems to suggest such a substitution. Because collaboration is primarily about negotiating a relationship, inevitable power shifts and inequities prevent satisfying claims of universality. In fact, at times, the only way we can recognize the presence of collaboration is by recognizing the negotiations that surround writing and reading relationships and then using that information first to recognize the presence of collaboration and then to understand that collaboration as a whole. From this perspective, a study of collaboration in western American literature is also a study of the place of difference there, of what we make of it and what we can learn from it.

As an example, let me return to my discussion of Willa Cather. No matter how critics have categorized Cather over the years— and the variations have been enormous—she has never been described as a collaborative writer. Yet a number of Cather's novels directly engage the idea of writing and authorship as a mutual endeavor between the writer and others who give or lend their stories to that individual. *My Ántonia*, for instance, is based on a historical immigrant woman whose life story Cather adapts, embellishes, and through her narrator, Jim Burden, attempts to take artistic control over. *Shadows on the Rock* focuses on the ways in which endlessly circulating stories cohere to form an accepted history. Set in Cather's childhood home of Virginia, *Sapphira and the Slave Girl*, one of Cather's most provocative and least-studied novels, casts itself into the ambivalent space of an "as remembered" story by a young girl Cather claims in the final pages of the novel is herself, frustrating the supposedly clear demarcation between history and fiction, master and slave, writer and character. In each of these instances, collaboration best describes the power relationships circulating in the fictions; the image of Willa Cather as solitary, inspired author is challenged when the novels themselves depict more fraught, interwoven, and collaborative meaning-making scenarios than our critical language has yet acknowledged. Moreover, this brief illustrative discussion does not begin to address the complexities Cather implicitly acknowledges when she points to extraliterary events (her relationship with Isabelle McClung, for instance, for whom she claimed she wrote, or her enduring life partnership with Edith Lewis) as crucial in the production of her novels. Although I do not pursue it in this study, an investigation of Cather as a collaborative writer holds enormous explanatory power to unravel the critical investments in individual authorship that underlie the various categories Cather as author has been placed over the years and to explain why various Cather camps struggle to locate a stable western identity for Cather as, for instance, a great western American nature writer, a conservative patriot, an apolitical aesthete, a defender of diversity (in the form of immigrants to the Midwest or Catholicism to the Southwest), a radical lesbian forced into coded expression, a transsexual adopting male personae, a resisting yet exemplary modernist, and so on.

For western writers, then, the stakes attached to a discussion of collaboration are somewhat larger than we might initially think, in part because western writers still consistently labor under the derisive label of regionalists. Or, if they escape that label (as Cather occasionally does and as Stegner certainly worked to do), it continues to haunt them in the background: at best, a west-

ern writer may be thought of as a regional writer who has tran-
scended the limitations of place in order to—wonder of wonders—create national literature. Yet western American literature
is also an important site from which to discuss collaboration because of its differences—its regional focus, its insistence on the
importance of place—from other genres of American literature.
The western writers I discuss here use collaborative strategies to
directly and decisively investigate identity and its paramount relationship to landscape and region. There is a difference here, and
in this instance I disagree with Foucault in that I am not "indifferent" at all when I ask why it matters who is speaking or at least
who it is we think is speaking: the West is the region of searing
claims of individualism, and yet it is also the place where such
individualism is questioned by these writers' use of collaborative
relationships and collaborative strategies that in turn have the
ability to undermine the cherished models of authorship and authority upon which their writing relies. It is a tangled and difficult
tightrope they walk and is fascinating for exactly that reason.

2

Partners in Collaboration

Louise Erdrich and Michael Dorris

*Columbus, idea if not man, was before us and behind us and
beside us. . . . He was the capital of Ohio, and he was a country
terrorized by drug cartels. He was the excuse for hundreds of
federally funded quincentenary committees from which Indians
and Hispanics and Italians were scrupulously not excluded, and
he was the impetus for yet one more expedition mounted by
officious agents of the National Geographic Society. Who he
really was was at once irrelevant and crucial, an enigma that,
if repeatedly solved, could never be allowed to disappear. He
stands for the question mark of history, the loop of inevitability,
the joker heading the deck of cards. He is Rosebud. He is the
Walrus. He is the pane of glass.*

LOUISE ERDRICH AND MICHAEL DORRIS, *THE CROWN OF COLUMBUS*

*The positivist notion that the past is readily accessible through
the study of documentary and physical evidence has undoubtedly
contributed in no small way to the persistent editorial resistance
to the fact that the only source we possess on the Discovery is not
a fair copy of a primary source, or even a copy of a copy, but a
highly manipulated version of a copy of whatever Columbus may
have written. . . . In suggesting that Las Casas was a ventriloquist
speaking through a Columbus-dummy or, conversely, a faithful
and passive conduit for Columbus's voice, what is ultimately
affirmed is the privilege of the Admiral's testimony and the fiction
that it is available to us in a fundamentally pristine text. Yet in
the final analysis, neither those who vituperate Las Casas nor
those who hold him up as a model of editorial fidelity can ignore
the presence of another's pen in the Columbian "Diario."*

MARGARITA ZAMORA, "READING IN THE MARGINS OF COLUMBUS"

FROM THE TIME of their marriage in October 1981 until Michael Dorris's suicide in April 1997, critically heralded collaborative writers Louise Erdrich and Michael Dorris consistently and publicly point to each other as ideal reader and essential partner in the creation of their best-selling, highly respected literary novels. In individual and joint interviews alike, Erdrich and Dorris present with escalating insistence an ideal of authorship that is collaborative in multiple and complex ways while at the same time retaining a claim to individual creativity and authorship. Their only cosigned novel, *The Crown of Columbus*, delves into this contradictory stance: as a metaphor for the individual, privileged author, Columbus rapidly deconstructs into a variety of Columbuses—one for every season, reason, and politicized agenda—all without losing "his" overwhelming cultural cachet as an enduring emblem of individual discovery whose diary reflects his unique literary achievement. Key characters in the novel work and write collaboratively, revealing the competitions, power inequities, manipulations, utopian desires, and potential rewards of collective creativity. Although *The Crown of Columbus* is Erdrich's and Dorris's most deliberate and visible embodiment of literary collaboration, a conscious positioning of the novel that led some reviewers and critics to view it as an autobiographical commentary on the writers' marriage, it is not their only novel addressing the pleasures and problems of collaboration. Erdrich and Dorris claim in repeated interviews that, regardless of whose name is appended to the title page, their writing process is densely mutual and eventually requires that each agree on every word before publication; at the same time, however, they stop short of claiming full collaboration, insisting that their writing also requires "solitude in order to really fall as deeply into a piece of writing as one must" (Erdrich in Bonetti 82). By refusing to rid themselves completely of the prestige of individual authorship, but also by refusing to wholeheartedly embrace it, Erdrich and Dorris, with their elaborate collaborative process, put our hopes for collaboration, as well as our anxieties about it, into sharp relief.

Erdrich's and Dorris's writing, along with their published discussions of it, emphasize not only the promising and difficult nature of language and writing but also the collaborative nature of each. These emphases occur differently in their interviews than in their fiction, however. Where their interviews repeatedly celebrate collaboration as the positive outgrowth of the heterosexual romance plot organizing their description of their marriage, their texts are considerably more cautious and ambivalent, both about collaboration and about the romance plot itself. Their interviews glory in the creative delights of collaboration and the felicity of love; their novels investigate the hidden hazards and painful struggles of collaboration and the vicissitudes of love. Beginning with the writers' extensive remarks concerning their work, which are surprisingly consistent even in their contradictions, notable are Erdrich's and Dorris's indefatigable efforts to construct their collaboration in opposition to the commonly accepted European model of individual genius and yet to simultaneously retain claims to that traditional model. Erdrich describes this model as "the idea that people have of a writer is someone who goes into a locked room and doesn't come out" (Foster 172), and she and Dorris counter this version of isolated authorship with a very different, collaborative scene: " 'It's sort of a conversational process; we just talk about it all the time,' says Erdrich about their collaboration. 'We take lots of walks around here. It's nice walking. And we talk about ideas for characters, and one of us gets excited about a conversation and starts writing something' " (Caldwell 65). As Erdrich's comment implicitly suggests, talk counts. The authorial process begins well before pen is put to paper (or keystrokes to computer screen); relational interaction and the pleasure of speaking with each other are equally a component of authorship, an understanding of authorship that undermines the explicit privilege accorded written language and an individual writer's implied ownership of it. By asserting that authorship begins much earlier, with conversation, Erdrich and Dorris explicitly challenge traditional ideas of authorship and, from this perspective, insist that the idea of the individual genius is not just untenable but also unnecessary.

At some point in the composing process, however, Erdrich and Dorris do enter the individual genius's isolated room:

> The heart of our collaboration is a commitment to one another's separateness. I certainly respect the solitude and silence it takes for Michael's work, and he does the same for me. The idea of linking brains or even working in the same space—I find that impossible. As would anyone. . . . In a collaboration such as *The Crown of Columbus* we shared in one book the creations of our own selves, but the source itself, that is a well closed except to the free wondering of an individual mind. . . . However, there is no putting aside the sheer volume of sweaty maneuvering it takes to shape books, and we have done so much of that between ourselves that I find it impossible to ever thank Michael enough for his passionate commitment. (Chavkin and Chavkin, "An Interview with Louise Erdrich" 226)

Even in the midst of asserting the solitary creative process, Erdrich refuses to isolate that process as either the only or the most important component of authorship. In addition, although they do emphasize the intense mutuality of the collaborative relationship between them, no doubt in part because it is the topic to which critics and interviewers relentlessly return, Erdrich and Dorris do not hold it up as an easy or conflict-free way to write. By taking such a seemingly self-contradictory stance in regard to their writing process, Dorris's and Erdrich's collaboration obviously unleashes anxieties rooted in deeply held convictions about the proper road to literary greatness. Indeed, Dorris and Erdrich do break the entrenched, apparently inevitable laws of authorship with their collaborative relationship. In numerous interviews, their insistence on collaboration "in all aspects of writing and life" (Bruchac 97) disturbs constructions of authorship that are

firmly based in hierarchical and individualistic models of authority and genius, and the result has been substantial critical puzzlement.

As Dorris and Erdrich describe it over a decade of interviews,
their collaborative process is consistent and, Erdrich insists, "not
very mysterious" (Wong 35). Because authorship begins as a collaborative process long before anything is written, during the
months before a character is actually committed to paper, Erdrich
and Dorris flesh out that character's personality, tastes, even food
preferences (Moyers 139): "We'll start talking about something
a long time in advance of it—the germ of a plot, or a story that
has occurred to us, or an observation that we've seen" (Dorris in
Wong 35). After the writing begins, "whoever is going to be the
primary author of the piece will sit down in isolation, confront
the blank page, and create some words that get passed back. The
other partner goes over them, makes comments about word
changes and even about where the plot will go after this section—
what's missing, or what possibilities are suggested by it" (Dorris
in Huey 125). Dorris and Erdrich negotiate, revise, and redraft together. As we see here, again Erdrich and Dorris do not entirely
relinquish the idea of individual authorship: the person who had
the idea originally, and who does the initial drafting ("in isolation"), is the primary author and has his or her name on the finished text. However, Erdrich and Dorris equally insist that the
other is the single largest influence on the finished product, an influence that is an essential component of authorship. Again and
again, Dorris and Erdrich stress that the work they do goes well
beyond editing each other's material: "I think it's co-conceiving
that differentiates this relationship from an editorial relationship.
I can't think of any example of an editor and a writer who sit
down and have this swell time imagining into a literary novel this
set of characters" (Erdrich in Bonetti 82). Before any book leaves
the house for publication, each writer has agreed on every word,
regardless of whose name is on the book. Dorris describes the
process: "The final say clearly rests with the person who wrote the

piece initially, but we virtually reach consensus on all words before they go out, on a word by word basis. There is not a thing that
has gone out from either one of us that has not been through at
least six rewrites, *major* rewrites" (Wong 35). A feeling of mutual
responsibility for the final published version of a particular text is
apparent in interviews, when Erdrich and Dorris habitually speak
of "our books." Dorris says, "We both have a real proprietary
sense of all the books. We *both* have that sense regardless of
whose name is on them. We take a lot of pride and feel very personal about them and the characters" (Wong 37). At the same
time, by defining a hierarchical division of power where the "primary author" has "the final say," Erdrich and Dorris delineate a
boundary where the contradictions of collaborative creativity are
settled by recourse to traditional understandings of authorship—
the very model of individual genius they reject elsewhere.

To the degree that they insist on a construction of authorship
that rejects the romanticized isolation thought necessary to inspire literary greatness and replaces it with a mutual responsibility for the texts produced, Dorris and Erdrich baffle critics who,
particularly in the early years of their collaboration, expressed
puzzlement and even declared the collaboration doomed. Jack
Beatty, senior editor at the *Atlantic*, says, "The whole thing [writ-
ing fiction] is an exercise in your own creativity, eccentricity, your
own strangeness. I don't know how you can let anybody else in on
that" (Cryer 84). Michael Curtis, editor of several stories published under Erdrich's name, remarks, "I have a hard time believing [the collaboration] can last for long. If it does they will certainly have set a world record for suppressed egos. . . . Some
couples work together and help each other, but none of them insist to such great lengths and in such a firm way on their mutuality" (Cryer 84). If critical response is any measure, a collaborative
relationship that consciously disperses power and authority appears not only unusual but psychologically unnatural, as if Dorris
and Erdrich are breaking the laws of authorship.

Despite Erdrich's insistence that the collaboration is not mysterious, the writers do construct themselves as an enigma when they link their creativity to the heterosexual romance script, in which each individual is made into a whole and complete writer by virtue of ever deepening layers of intimacy that culminate in their marriage. In 1988, Erdrich tells interviewer Kay Bonetti, "I didn't really get anywhere until I went to Dartmouth as a visiting writer. Then Michael and I fell in love, married, and started working together. It was like overdrive, or something. I finally began to really get things together," and she goes on to stress the intensity of their intimacy by claiming that "we can read each other's minds" (81). Interviewer Vince Passaro describes their self-presentation as "insist[ing] on a conception of themselves that is far more romantic and defiant of convention, in which art and marriage are complementary mechanisms. The impression they have promoted is that they are attempting as artists to make themselves, by mutual consent, into one voice, one vision, one language. Theirs is an art, as well as a life, directed toward synthesis and unity" (161). While, as we have seen, Dorris and Erdrich do not completely abandon the privileges of individual genius, they do insist that the product of their collaborative process —whether fiction or nonfiction—hinges on romantic fusion.

For the duration of their collaboration, critics largely refused to go along with the heterosexual romance script Erdrich and Dorris constructed as essential to their collaboration and to their subsequent literary success. For critics, a key component to unraveling the enigma that their collaboration-marriage creates is the possibility of distinguishing each writer from the other. Charles Trueheart demonstrates the most common method of distinguishing between Dorris and Erdrich when he says, "If the books that bear their different names are a reliable measure of individual style, they don't write indistinguishably. Michael's narratives seem carefully invented and then set down, one foot before the other; Louise's stories seem received from the ether, and allowed to pass through her onto the page. Dorris is vernacular, Erdrich is oracular" (118). Passaro also asserts stylistic distinctions between Erdrich's and Dorris's writing in order to resituate them within the traditional definition of author as individual, unique, and above all, distinct from each other: "For those who have read both of them, this [impression of synthesis and unity] remains difficult to accept. So far, Dorris has worked in an entirely realistic style. . . . Erdrich's writing, on the other hand, has been called 'a northern outpost of magical realism' " (161). Apart from the buried gender assumptions here (Dorris creates; Erdrich translates), these critical responses understandably rely upon our shared acceptance of the importance of stylistic distinctions to fix identity and thus to locate authorship. As a result, critics marshal as evidence the very stylistic distinctions Dorris and Erdrich undermine through their collaboration. Such critical responses run aground on the culturally unimaginable: a collaboratively produced text in which the individual writers compose in ways that are deliberately, consciously indistinguishable; in which particular stylistic traits no longer guarantee ownership of the words; and thus where which writer is truly the "author" of a particular text (chapter, paragraph, sentence, or word) is never fully knowable.

Dorris responds to this critical desire for stable distinctions based on a definite, attributable literary style belonging to one individual, emphasizing its uncertainty by, ironically, calling upon an essentialistic notion of voice located not in an individual author but in an individual character: "People made distinctions between our work. . . . Fleur [of Erdrich's *Tracks*] is mythic and so forth and Rayona [of Dorris's *Yellow Raft*] is very contemporary. But they're also different people. . . . I think that Louise could write in the voice of Rayona or Christine or Ida . . . and they would sound very much as they do when I write about them" (Trueheart 118). Dorris challenges one traditional argument with a second traditional argument: the character's voice is the character's own, and either writer could mimic it. None of this is to deny that books that bear Dorris's name have a style that is different than, even distinct from, books that bear Erdrich's. Yet, as we can see in the discussions of their collaborative process, those distinctions in style do not necessarily guarantee certainty in authorial attribution. As Dorris and Erdrich grew familiar with each other's stylistic preferences—Erdrich prefers first-person narration, for instance—it is not only possible but quite likely that they would consciously work in the style of the primary writer of any particular text. With Erdrich and Dorris, stylistic distinctions between writers—the cornerstone tool of literary attribution and the "proof" of individual genius and creativity—are malleable and subject to appropriation.

At its basis, critical arguments about stylistic distinctions are ones with which we are all intimately familiar and with which, because of that familiarity, we tacitly agree. Yet Dorris's and Erdrich's consistent emphasis on their mutual collaboration is not presented only as the romantic fusion critics love to discount; instead, they also speak of it as difficult, laborious, and eminently practical work. They write together because what they produce collaboratively is better than what they produce alone. With this view of authorship in mind, there is no solitary genius, no such thing as "Erdrich's writing." Such possessive descriptions as "Erdrich's writing" or "Dorris's book" break down; while these terms continue to signify particular texts, they no longer designate either Erdrich or Dorris as the traditionally understood "author" of that text. In a 1986 interview, Erdrich comments on how unhelpful such terms turn out to be: " 'But with the novels, it's either I wrote it or Michael wrote. *But*,' she amplified, 'when you're writing it, you're always remembering the characters, the plotting, the talking . . . the very shape of the books' " (Stokes 56). Dorris agrees: " 'When you think, "how did this particular development come about?" you remember that we were out there,' he gestures toward the garden beyond the window, 'talking about it. And of course it comes to your mind while you're writing, too' " (Stokes 56–57).

Although the writers' published discussions of their collaborative process are fascinating, they provide only one angle of vision onto this richly layered collaboration. Connected to the idea of individual greatness and the unreliability of literary attribution is a host of other literary beliefs that Dorris and Erdrich undermine with their insistence on a collaboration that still maintains separateness. In one sense, collaboration offers Erdrich and Dorris, both mixed-blood Native Americans, a familiar and useful way of viewing the world. Erdrich was born in North Dakota; her father was of German ancestry, and her mother was a member of the Turtle Mountain Chippewa tribe. Dorris was born in Kentucky; his father was a member of the Modock tribe, and his mother was white. With mixed ancestry, both consider themselves Native American writers, but it is a mixed Native American–European heritage that creates a liminal identity: "It's partly that once one is a citizen of both nations, it gives you a look at the world that's different. There is an edge of irony. If you have a Native American background, it's also a non-Western background in terms of religion, culture, and all the things that are important in your childhood. There's a certain amount of commitment because when you grow up and see your people living on a tiny pittance of land or living on the edge, surrounded by enormous wealth, you don't see the world as just" (Erdrich in Moyers 144). Although both see Native American oral storytelling traditions as influential in their work, neither Erdrich nor Dorris forgets the ways in which a mixed-blood heritage positions them, not only between western and Native American cultures but between individual tribal cultures as well. Dorris says, "There are 300 different tribes and there's no way we should, or could, be spokespersons for all of them. Plus we're mixed bloods. . . . So it would be presumptuous to pretend to be more than we are. We can only speak for ourselves" (Trueheart 120). In a cultural context in which fractional quantities of bloodlines are used to determine tribal affiliations, collaboration becomes a useful metaphor for understanding the mixing of bloodlines that produces two individuals who experience their identities as multiply constituted.

These complex layers of identity positions and affiliations help create the separateness Dorris and Erdrich require while emphasizing the collaborative relationship. Although many of their interview comments point to their collaboration and their marriage as transcending their individual limitations and corporeal boundaries, other comments just as quickly reassert those limits and boundaries. The range of their speech and writing functions to remind us that a "pure" collaboration, in which all difference is erased, is as fictitious as the dominating idea of individual authorship, in which the author is privileged because of his (or her) originality and difference. As a professional writer, Dorris remained closely associated to academia; Erdrich, while she "love[s] university atmosphere and get[s] along fine there," did not (Chavkin and Chavkin, "An Interview with Louise Erdrich" 227). Ironically, one of the fruits of the collaborative relationship seems to be Dorris's growing emergence as a "primary writer" within the relationship. Early interviewers describe Dorris, who had a humiliating experience writing fiction in college, as rarely, if ever, drafting material. In 1985, Shelby Grantham described Dorris's participation in the collaboration: "Dorris may have his fingers in a good many pies, but Erdrich is the writer. . . . Dorris is easy— perhaps, he feels, easier than Erdrich is—about his remaining in the wings. 'I'm not like a frustrated writer who wishes it were me. I'm glad it's Louise. What I do now may be the best thing I can do literarily. It's such a kick to be more than just a cheerleader. I have no problem with the fact that my name is not on the books. . . . Louise is always careful to give me credit' " (17). By 1993, however, Dorris and Erdrich had published *A Yellow Raft in Blue Water* (1987) and *The Broken Cord* (1989) under his name, and both writers talk about the collaborative process of their books: "It's like having children: The fictional characters belong to both of us, regardless of who's sort of trotting them out at any given time" (Dorris in Schumacher 178).

Apart from the interviews, Erdrich's and Dorris's most deliberate public insistence on the collaborative nature of textual production occurs in their novels' dedications to each other. Without exception until after Dorris's death, novels that bear Erdrich's name are dedicated to Dorris and vice versa.[1] The dedications perform in interrelated, sometimes contradictory cultural ways by allowing the writers to claim the status of individual author inherent in the single byline system of attribution and to construct their creative relationship in the pattern of the heterosexual romance. At the same time, the cumulative effect of all of these dedications is an acknowledgment and celebration of their working relationship that goes beyond the standard acknowledgments of spousal patience and understanding, establishing an intimacy and erotics in their collaboration that disturb the hierarchies of literary merit that Erdrich and Dorris elsewhere put into place with their discussions of "primary" authorship. Knowing that this pattern of dedications continued even after the couple was estranged and no longer living together only heightens each of these cultural performances.[2]

If their dedications keep the collaborative focus of their relationship continually in play, their use of separate bylines simultaneously draws attention to their separateness, to their cultural status as individual authors. Separate bylines, the traditionally accepted guarantees of individual authorship, function in Erdrich's and Dorris's work simultaneously as overt acknowledgments that there are limits to this collaboration, regardless of their published accounts of marital harmony, and as literary conventions the writers find economically useful. Or, as Dorris claims, "Separate bylines work. We don't want to fool with it too much" (Cryer 84). The economic need for separate bylines is complicated by the ways in which their romantic relationship is intertwined in the process of producing and promoting each other's work as ostensibly individual. When asked about the genesis for *Love Medicine*, the story "The World's Greatest Fisherman," Erdrich describes an important initial collaboration. The story "had been written in a very rough draft" (Bonetti 84) and, during the couple's first year of marriage, when "looking for money," they decided to finish the story and submit it to the Nelson Algren competition, with its five-thousand-dollar prize. As Erdrich constructs it, this originary collaborative effort has all the makings of romantic adventure the writers would later capitalize on in their book *The Crown of Columbus*. Erdrich "hadn't really had the guts to do anything with [the story]" and "Michael got ill—he was flat on his back" (Bonetti 85). "I would be writing on the kitchen table with people about to come in at any minute. Michael would read it, make adjustments, and, you know, it was very much the beginning of that kind of process" (Bonetti 85). The story, which won the prize, eventually became the first chapter of *Love Medicine*. Holly Laird ties together the writers' motives when she claims: "If their collaboration began as a romantic mystery of veiled coauthorship or as a real-life romance of working marriage, it also began as a mutually beneficial commercial partnership: Romance proved profitable" (*Women Coauthors* 235). In a second example of profitable romance, again concerning *Love Medicine* and the beginning of the couple's collaborative venture, Dorris describes promoting the book as its agent: "We had an agent . . . and it didn't go anywhere. . . . Finally, we said, 'let's give it a whirl ourselves.' So I went and had stationery printed up with my name on it and claimed to be an agent and sent it out, and two major houses bid on it" (Bonetti 93). The cumulative effect of the writers' discussions of their collaboration is to construct their writing relationship as sufficient unto themselves, a romantic union that leads to commercial success.

Literary collaboration between married couples is not particularly unusual; what makes Erdrich and Dorris stand out is their deliberate efforts to elevate both writers, rather than positioning one as editor or literary helpmeet to the other. In other words, Dorris and Erdrich do not necessarily write differently than other writers; they do, however, consciously rely upon and acknowledge an intrinsically collaborative writing process as few others do. Discussing the extremes into which writers are often pigeonholed, either as two individuals merged seamlessly into one or as "solitary in the garret," Dorris insists, "There's a lot in between that is unacknowledged. I mean, we have writer friends who never do other than, 'I thank my spouse for her or his enduring patience while I worked on the book, or typing the manuscript, taking care of the kids, blah blah blah,' who really worked much more closely together, we know, than is acknowledged" (Foster 172). Erdrich agrees: "Many, many writers have someone who is more than an editor, but it isn't . . . something writers like to talk about" (Foster 172). By acknowledging the presence of collaboration where it is usually denied, Erdrich and Dorris force readers out of their reliance upon unselfconscious categories of distinctions and their associated roles.

One such category of distinction is gender, and the complications are twofold: first, Dorris and Erdrich each conceive and revise together characters of each gender; second, expectations surrounding what constitutes feminist writing make it difficult to know how to "place" Erdrich, who has gained a following as an important Native American feminist writer, when Dorris presumably collaborated with her, agreeing to every word before publication. Erdrich's feminism is regularly celebrated for creating female characters who break stereotyped molds both for women and for Native Americans. What difference does it make to realize that the signature "Erdrich" denotes not the feminist genius of so many critical articles but rather the collaborative result of Erdrich and Dorris discussing, writing, and revising together? In one sense, much of what we call feminist writing is concerned either with challenging prior authoritative scripts ("tales of burning love") for women or with collaborating with those scripts in order to undermine them. Thus, Erdrich's and Dorris's collaboration, while concerned with gender, is not inevitably gendered in any simple or biographical way.[3]

A particularly provocative example of the conflation of the writer's gender with gendered readings occurred when *The Broken Cord*, a nonfiction investigation into the effects of fetal alcohol syndrome (FAS) on Native American children published under Dorris's byline, was severely challenged by Katha Pollit as sexist by laying the blame for FAS at women's feet. Dorris defends his views, which Pollit characterizes as an antifeminist stance in the fetal rights debate, in a 1992 interview with Allan Chavkin and Nancy Feyl Chavkin (205–06). Dorris argues that his position is unrelated to feminism and that he is a feminist: "Nobody has been more supportive of that book's message than female physicians, female health care workers, teachers, psychologists, and so forth, because *women* in those professions traditionally have a much more direct involvement with victims of FAS than men do. FAS is *not* a feminist issue. I consider myself a feminist" (206). While I find Dorris's defense less than entirely convincing, the point I want to raise here is Erdrich's absence. While in interviews Dorris alternately discusses *The Broken Cord* as a mutual production and as "his" book, an approach consonant with the writers' shifting conceptions of collaboration, only Dorris was criticized on the basis of faulty feminism. In this case, the privilege of asserting individual authorship was also a risk, one Dorris took and later took responsibility for. In other words, he also did not invoke Erdrich and her recognized credibility as a feminist writer in order to deflect Pollit's charges. However, if *The Broken Cord* is a collaborative text, as both Erdrich and Dorris assert that it is, Erdrich's absence from the discussion is palpable and reestablishes the primacy of the individual author as one who owns his words and ideas.

A second category of distinction concerns the definition of Native American literature and, subsequently, its relationship to established categories of literary merit. Not only does the writers' collaborative pairing cross tribal affiliations as mixed-blood Native Americans, their writing subverts any attempt at a romantic notion of Native American writing even while it does, at times, encourage a pan-Indian universality.[4] The role of Native American oral traditions in the American literary canon is itself unsettling: Native American literature has not been adequately defined, nor has a Native American literary canon been fully established. Yet the presence of Native American literature inevitably critiques such categories as written literature, linearity, and character development, categories upon which traditional canonical distinctions rely. Discussing the absurdities implicit in defining Native American literature, Dorris says, "I don't know what Native American literature is. . . . Does 'Native American literature' mean literature about Indians? Does it mean a literature by Indians about Indian themes? Does it mean literature by Indians about anything? Is *Gorky Park*, for instance, 'Native American Literature' because Martin Cruz Smith is part Indian?" (Chavkin and Chavkin, "An Interview with Michael Dorris" 212).

Furthermore, there are distinctions between literary writing, academic or scholarly writing, and popular writing that readers may rely upon to evaluate literature without being consciously aware of the distinctions they are making. *The Crown of Columbus*, in a somewhat autobiographical parallel to which I will return later, addresses this issue by combining academic revisionist historicizing, literary poetry and prose, and the more typically designated "low" genre of the adventure romance plot. By choosing to collaborate, Dorris and Erdrich challenge traditional routes of power and recognition, ones that have worked to guide readers' interpretations of literature. One of those challenges is precisely the expectations readers and critics have regarding Native American literature. As Peter Beidler puts it in an early review in *Studies in American Indian Literatures*: "Early critics seemed to believe that for these two Indians to write a best-seller is a little like Indians setting up a casino on reservation land: such behavior, if technically legal, is simply bad form for Indians. We expect more from the descendants of America's aboriginal people" (48).

Yet, if Dorris and Erdrich use collaboration to undermine critical expectations or diminish some conceptions of power, that very collaboration reformulates and redeploys power in alternative ways. As I have argued, collaboration is neither neutral nor benign in terms of power relationships. Collaboration does not always produce a successful writing relationship, despite Erdrich's and Dorris's persistent commentary that it comes close, nor does it lead to the downfall of all our notions of literary merit, although it may challenge them. What we see in a critical commentary needing to establish the individual author of a text, or at least of particular portions of the text, is that collaboration reveals the power relationships beneath what appear to be "natural" tendencies to categorize literature in order to evaluate it. Collaboration keeps in circulation the reality that interpretations hinge on who has the power to control them. The Erdrich-Dorris collaboration, by refusing to invest either partner with "more" or "better" power, ultimately reveals that literature itself, whatever else it is, is a negotiation of power at every level, in which meaning is conferred not despite that negotiation but because of it. In other words, literature *is* collaboration, structured as a particular collaborative event that, when we consider the role of the composing process, the reading process, and so on, in turn fans out to incorporate other layered collaborate events.

To state it another way, collaboration is all around us, is all there is. In Erdrich's and Dorris's interviews, because of the writers' conscious reiteration of the fact of collaboration in their lives, even moments of monologue reveal their collaborative foundation, making it less likely that a reader can become completely absorbed in the illusion of individual genius again. In their published fiction, too, collaboration is important. For example, Dorris and Erdrich challenge the primacy of linear development in the series published under Erdrich's name, requiring readers to perform collaborative readings of the novels. *Love Medicine* is the first novel of the series, published first in 1984; *Beet Queen* was published next, in 1986, followed by *Tracks*, in 1988. Yet chronologically, the books unfold in exactly the opposite order, with *Tracks* developing the pasts of characters first introduced to the reader in *Love Medicine*. Later novels *The Bingo Palace, Tales of Burning Love,* and *The Last Report on the Miracles at Little No Horse* follow chronologically, with some reappearing characters and with shifting perspectives within the novels as characters represent alternate points of view. The novels bearing Dorris's name follow a similar strategy: *A Yellow Raft in Blue Water* was published in 1987 and introduces Rayona, whose paternal ancestry is traced in Dorris's later novel *Cloud Chamber*, published posthumously in 1997.[5]

Collaboration is often a prominent structural component and theme within these novels as well. In *Tracks*, for instance, Nanapush and Pauline tell the story in alternating chapters. Nanapush, a more traditional Native American storyteller who recognizes that the losses faced by his tribe are a result of white settlement, has a very different perspective than Pauline, who was first introduced to readers as the quixotically masochistic Catholic nun Sister Leopolda in *Love Medicine* and who returns in *Tales of Burning Love* and *The Last Report of the Miracles at Little No Horse* as a breathtakingly disturbing blend of visionary Christian piety and festering personal rage and ambition. Pauline, who strives desperately to assimilate into white society by literally veiling her Native American ancestry with her Catholic faith, likewise tells her story from a far different perspective than Nanapush's. Joni Adamson Clarke discusses the importance of the dual narration throughout the text: "Finally, the reader, just as if she were at an actual oral storytelling performance, must listen to both Pauline's and Nanapush's stories and create her own interpretation or theory . . . by carefully weighing what she knows about the two narrators against their interpretations of the story; then the reader must 'hook' parts of each version of the story together to create a 'design' . . . of her own" (41). The effect of the text's collaborative structure prevents the reader from dismissing Pauline as entirely untrustworthy; her story collaborates with Nanapush's and forces the reader to interact with both perspectives, enacting yet another collaboration, this time involving the reader. Whatever meaning the reader draws from *Tracks*, it is an intricate interweaving of two opposing views brought together and made not to cohere but to connect. Nanapush and Pauline remain individuals, yet the story, the "tracks" the reader must follow to create meaning, are left by them both.

A similar collaborative structure appears in later novels. *A Yel-*

low Raft in Blue Water follows the interwoven story of three women: Rayona, a fifteen-year-old part–Native American, part–African American teen; her mother, Christine, a Native American; and Christine's mother, Ida. Throughout the novel, events are told from the different perspectives of daughter, mother, and grandmother, beginning with Rayona and moving "back" in time until we learn Ida's perspective. The novel ends with an image that has threaded itself through the novel, that of braided hair: three strands woven together into one whole, imagistically drawing together the collaborative effect of the novel. In *Tales of Burning Love*, Jack Mauser's former wives collaborate, literally, on "the tales of burning love" in a modern storytelling session while trapped in their vehicle during a snowstorm. Each woman tells her "own" story, whole in itself and yet contributing to the complexity and depth of the other women's stories and of the novel itself. Even after Dorris's death, the theme of collaboration continues in Erdrich's latest novel. *The Last Report on the Miracles at Little No Horse* collaborates with prior novels with its returning characters, including Fleur, Nanapush, Pauline/Sister Leopolda, and others. In addition to having a great deal of fun crossing gender boundaries and reinterpreting yet again events set out in earlier novels, *The Last Report* also requires the reader to incorporate seemingly oppositional viewpoints when Father Damien Modeste is revealed as Agnes Dewitt, who was for a time Sister Cecilia.

Collaboration takes other forms in the fiction as well. In *Love Medicine*, Erdrich and Dorris place prior texts in collaboration with contemporary ones in order to produce meaning, a kind of collaboration I will investigate more closely in my discussion of Mary Austin in chapter 4. *Love Medicine* recasts the Christian symbol of the stigmata by associating it with Sister Leopolda's wounding of Marie with a fork. For readers, Christian authority is simultaneously presented and undercut by Leopolda's religiosity and her crazed reading of the stigmata. These two versions collaborate to create a new, less authoritative religious event. In *The Last Report on the Miracles at Little No Horse*, the uncertainty surrounding the meaning of this event returns during an official investigation of the now-deceased Sister Leopolda's potential candidacy for sainthood. In a parallel event in *Love Medicine*, Lipsha grinds together frozen turkey hearts, rather than the required ones from wild geese, to create the "love medicine" on which Nector Kapshaw chokes and subsequently dies. The collaboration of traditional Indian beliefs with contemporary shortcuts ends in a darkly comic scene of mis/dis/placement. The need to collaborate with a prior text in order to create a contemporary interpretation continues in *The Beet Queen*, in which the interpretation of the "miracle" in the snow changes with each different viewer: is the mark in the snow Karl, Christ, or simply a squashed place? By using collaboration thematically to investigate the complex and often unreliable chain of interpretations, the writers ultimately challenge the status of authorship in the prior text they return to—the Bible. As Christianity's preeminent sacred text, the Bible already has a curious relationship to authorship: it both has a single divine author (it is "God's text") and has no individual authorship at all (it is given divinely through numerous men). If we understand the Bible as divinely inspired and transmitted, then it is an act of unrepeatable, even incomprehensible, authorship; if we see the Bible as a collaborative process of interpreting events significant to Christianity's development, then authorship is again profoundly vexed, multiple, and subject to competing agendas and historical mores—quite the same situation as the reader encounters when faced with the task of interpreting the "stigmata" or the curious image in the ice.

Storytelling from a Native American perspective is itself a form of collaboration Erdrich and Dorris take part in by "retelling," but the writers also allow white literary influences when they write. Throughout the novel, mixed lifestyles—traditional Native American with urban Indian, mixed bloodlines—create new possibilities in life but not without tension, displacement, and loss. Clarke writes that "Erdrich disorders the boundaries between 'high' and 'low' by demonstrating how the oral tradition, which has usually been assigned to the category of 'low' discourse because it is historical, changing, contradictory and unwritten, can live in the 'tracks' of a printed text and serve as the antithesis of all that is hard, unyielding or finished, to every ready-made solution in the sphere of thought and world outlook" (41). In *Tracks*, two worlds collide, interact, and to some degree are destroyed: Nanapush's world dissolves into a white future; Pauline's world descends into the madness of a zealot or the ineffable wisdom of a saint.

We can see all of these collaborative processes at work in Erdrich's and Dorris's collaborative tour de force, *The Crown of Columbus*. This text is their most seamlessly collaborated romp and their most deliberate, focused investigation of collaboration. Tellingly, it is also the text most likely to be dismissed as lacking literary merit. *The Crown of Columbus* has a somewhat spectacular publication history: the five-page "outline is famous for having brought them $1.5 million from Harper & Row, the winning publisher in a brief but intense round of bidding" in 1988 (Trueheart 118). The novel appeared during the 1991 Quincentennial, amid significant Columbus celebrations and protests, something some critics felt was an act of precipitous timing, a calculated move designed to capitalize on the national focus on Columbus's journey. The writers disagreed by making recourse to a definition of authorship that insists on a collaborative prehistory, insisting that they had already begun a conversational collaboration on the Columbus novel a decade before they began writing.

What baffles and disturbs critics most about *The Crown of Columbus*, however, is its seemingly antiliterary, antischolarly stance. Early reviewers of the novel found it more popular than literary and therefore disappointing, something they frequently blamed on the collaboration between Erdrich and Dorris or, more specifically, on Dorris's contribution to the collaboration. As Laird notes, "Their one cosigned novel, despite mixed reviews, paradoxically boosted her individual reputation because critics were wary of its coauthorship and often compared it unfavorably with their noncoauthored works" (*Women Coauthors* 236).[6] For readers familiar with Dorris's and Erdrich's writing, *The Crown of Columbus* is a departure in both style and content, or at least so it initially seems. In part because of the same sprawling and somewhat fantastic plot line that troubles many critics, the novel is difficult to summarize. The main action centers around Vivian Twostar, an untenured, pregnant assistant professor in Native American studies at Dartmouth College, and her stodgy, self-important, tenured colleague Roger Williams, a poet and Columbus scholar. Twostar is overworked, underappreciated, and tired of always being cast as the representative Indian point of view. Pressured by a rapidly approaching tenure review, Twostar has reluctantly agreed to write a piece on Columbus for the alumni magazine. While she is expected and encouraged by her dean to produce the requisite Native revisionist argument, Twostar is angling for a truly original approach, a new take on Columbus. Twostar is somewhat reluctantly in love with the meticulously intellectual Williams, who is simultaneously at work on a dramatic poem about Columbus entitled "Diary of a Lost Man," which he, with characteristic self-assurance, fully expects to be momentous. Twostar is pregnant with Williams's child but has broken off the relationship with him; Williams, in turn, is passively baffled by Twostar's unexpected rejection of him. While trapped overnight in the library, in the early stages of labor and sorting through the few books remaining on the shelves that Williams hasn't garnered for himself, Twostar stumbles upon clues that eventually lead her to previously unknown, possibly authentic pages of Columbus's diary and a strange collection of oyster shells with mysterious writing on them. The diary pages she finds hint at a possible crown given by Columbus to the natives he encountered on his first arrival to "the New World," and the oyster shells will eventually reveal enigmatic clues to finding the crown. Intrigue mounts, and the love story between Twostar and Williams intermeshes when they travel, with Twostar's rebellious teenaged son, Nash, and their newborn daughter, Violet, to the

Bahamian island of Eleuthera to meet Henry Cobb, who has the rest of the diary and is searching for the elusive crown, which he believes is a golden or bejeweled treasure that will restore to him a fortune. Intrigue, betrayal, kidnapping, a close call with a shark, attempted murder, under-the-wire escapes, and a lost—and found—newborn all unfold before the end, when the crown is discovered buried under centuries of bat dung in a remote cave where Williams is washed ashore. Rather than the precious European crown of royalty Cobb hopes for, it is a wooden crown of thorns. This crown, sealed in its seamless crystal casket until Twostar's perfect karate chop destroys the crystal that might have been the actual work of art, reveals that Columbus's intention was to give the native people the treasure of Christianity, a treasure perhaps stolen and then either lost before it could be bestowed or accepted, or rejected by the natives to whom it was given. However, the more significant treasure for a modern world turns out to be Columbus's words: Twostar finds evidence in the newfound diary that Columbus considered the natives sovereign nations, and at the end of the novel she uses this historical information to effect changes in Indian land rights. Now tenured, she eclipses Williams in importance, a turn of events Williams would have found intolerable earlier but now readily accepts and supports, ensuring their implausibly happy home life. The novel's final pages are given to the young Valerie Clock, the Bahamian girl who finds baby Violet after she is set adrift. Having had her own experience of discovery—for which she was not recognized or thanked —Valerie looks to the sea with the sense that everything has changed, that the sea is now something she will cross.

Although the temptation, to which many early critics succumbed, is to evaluate *The Crown of Columbus* as a lesser novel in the couple's collective oeuvre, as a notable lapse in their steady output of serious, literary work, the structure of the novel is an important aspect of its "meaning." For those who demand a reserve of nonacademic, nonintimidating "fun" in their novel reading, *The Crown of Columbus* cooperates, to the chagrin of some critics. Dorris says, "Another thing that I think disturbed some people is that *The Crown of Columbus* was fun to write. We enjoyed it thoroughly—the process of working together and being able to try a big expansive book that was full of information and populated with characters who were well-educated, who had at their disposal the lexicons of several traditions" (Chavkin and Chavkin, "An Interview with Michael Dorris" 209). The interconnection of those many traditions find their parallel in Twostar, whose own mixed-blood heritage helps her identify with Columbus: "We're called marginal, as if we exist anywhere but on the center of the page. . . . 'Caught between two worlds,' is the way we're often characterized, but I'd put it differently. We are the *catch.* I could relate to Columbus, stranger to stranger. . . . An Italian in Iberia. A Jew in Christendom. A *Converso* among the baptized-at-birth. A layman among Franciscans. He spoke all languages with a foreign accent. . . . He didn't completely fit in, anywhere, and that was his engine. He was propelled by alienation, by trying to forge links, to *be* the link, from one human cluster to the next" (*The Crown of Columbus* 124). In an essay that identifies the novel's convoluted adventure romance plot as a valuable component of the challenges it poses to readers, Helmbrecht Breinig writes:

> A particular class of readers is given what it demands and another class of readers, the established critics, in particular those specializing in Native American literature, is antagonised, intentionally, I think. For what is being displayed here is an example of the strength of people's (the characters' and the readers') desire to get carried away. Narrative emplotment, the authors seem to say, distorts reality, and the more it does so, the more we are ready to suspend our belief. . . . The more contrived it is and the better (and the less realistically) all details fit together to form a strong chain of teleological causality, but also the more the plot appeals to our sense of (individual and historical) poetic justice, the more it will satisfy our basic instincts, our Kermodian hunger for closure and purpose. . . . This artificial side of emplotment will not diminish our sense of participatory illusion but rather enhance it. (339–40)

Although he states it differently, Dorris describes the plotting mechanism and structure of the novel as deliberate: "The many genres that are represented in the book are very intentional on our part because what we were attempting to do was reflect the chaos of discovery. It's sometimes melodramatic; it's sometimes surprising; it's sometimes poignant; it's sometimes poetic; it's all of those things wrapped into one. So what we were trying to do was make the form follow the content" (Chavkin and Chavkin, "An Interview with Michael Dorris" 208–09). Both Breinig's and Dorris's comments on the intentional aspects of *The Crown of Columbus* function to deflect criticism of the novel's apparent status as "entertainment" rather than lofty literature. This was deliberate, they assert, thereby arguing for the novel as a self-reflexive example of contemporary literature. More important, I would suggest, are the ways in which the novel is both entertainment and literature at once, the ways in which the quotidian and the lofty collaborate in a single text, eroding the dualisms that many critics employ to dismiss the text. In a parallel to its treatment of its central missing character, Columbus, the text performs several different ways simultaneously: it is a rousing, fun novel; it is a thoughtful revisionist presentation of the Discovery; and it is a complex narrative performance of meaning making in a postmodern universe.

Dorris's comment in particular reminds us that, in addition to the adventure romance plot, other aspects of the novel collaborate to create a larger "whole" that the reader pieces together in yet another collaborative relationship. In *The Crown of Columbus*, as in earlier texts, several voices collaborate to tell the story, each offering the reader a piece rather than the whole. Much of the novel alternates between Twostar and Williams in first person addresses, often describing the same event from their different perspectives. Intervening in those voices are vignettes of young Valerie Clock, the native girl who finds Twostar's and Williams's lost baby, Violet. Twostar's disgruntled teenaged son, Nash, also comments on events, and even Columbus is present, first in the translations of the missing pages Twostar finds and at the end of the novel, in a letter discussing his second voyage. In addition to these multiple perspectives, from which the reader must construct a reading, the collaborative nature of literature is emphasized when Williams's epic poem is incorporated into the novel, which he recites to an audience of bats when lost in the cave containing the crown. Williams's rescue, as unlikely as any in an adventure novel, is also reminiscent of Native American emergence stories, complete with the scatological imagery of the trickster as Williams emerges from the guano-filled cave. The novel hovers between genres, partaking of many: epic poem, epistolary, oral storytelling, adventure romance, revisionist history, futuristic fantasy. Although all of these character perspectives and narrative genres are combined in one text, in which the time frame moves among the distant past of Columbus's voyages, the present, and the future, the overwhelming impression of *The Crown of Columbus* is not competition but collaboration. Yet it is a collaboration in which no one perspective or genre has dominance; at every turn, there is another, equally persuasive (or equally ludicrous) perspective to consider. *The Crown of Columbus* does not so much demand alternative readings from us as it persuades us to take satisfaction from the presence of many simultaneous readings. We can see this when even Columbus's voice enters the text, but only through a series of obscurant, potentially misleading layers. Twostar longs to find the historical Columbus, to dispense with the myth, without which "he's just another man. Not the father of Manifest Destiny. Not the hand of fate. Not the inevitable force. Not some agent of God. Just a man whose good luck was our bad. That's somebody familiar. That's somebody we can handle" (164). Twostar's desire, while propelling her into an adventure of utopian proportions, will not be met. In a move playfully reflective of the complexities of authorship, the pages of Columbus's diary are reproduced in the text. They are handwritten, suggesting authenticity, but we find out that the handwriting is not Columbus's nor even Las Casas's but Twostar's and that the pages themselves were translated—more or less accurately—by Twostar's grandmother. Not incidentally for a novel fascinated by collaborative authorship, even these translated pages bear Twostar's and Williams's handwriting, as they debate possible meanings for the already dubious translation.

Given the multiple turns we have of Columbus's diary, it is clear that one of the central preoccupations of the text is not "Who *was* Columbus?" but rather "Who *is* Columbus?"—with the realization that we cannot recover the historical Columbus. Instead, we can always only struggle to understand the contemporary, metaphorical Columbus, the collaborative construct that circulates throughout a society. Dorris says: "We didn't know and we couldn't figure out who Columbus actually was, so one of the benefits of having two characters, each being a first person narrator, is that they each get to present a strong position that is different, one from the other. Whichever Columbus you believe in, in *The Crown of Columbus*, he is much more complex than most of the simplistic lore about Columbus gives him credit for. He was a complicated individual, and he told so many versions of his life he couldn't be everything he said he was—that's precisely why he is an interesting character for fiction" (Chavkin and Chavkin, "An Interview with Michael Dorris" 207). *The Crown of Columbus* teaches us that, however we wish or need to interpret him, Columbus is always a fiction. Such a realization does not make him less "real," however, since the meanings a culture attaches to the figure of Columbus are more powerful than any historical individual.

From this perspective, the collaborative construct that is Columbus is also a contemporary version of the modern—and collaborative author. Romanticized as an important figure of discovery, Columbus epitomizes the solitary genius. The novel makes great fun of the contemporary version of the solitary genius in the character of Roger Williams. Not coincidentally named after the seventeenth-century Puritan rebel Roger Williams, whose *Key to the Languages* functioned both to acknowledge the inherent value in Native American beliefs and to market

Native Americans to European colonists as unthreatening, the novel's Roger Williams is more complicated—and less tradition bound—than he initially appears. Williams's Columbus poem, "Diary of a Lost Man," is a "mission of paternity. Columbus would be my child, his exegesis my midnight feeding. . . . Content followed form and I bent the acts to my will. Posterity would be thankful for the man I would create" (*The Crown of Columbus* 51). Whereas Twostar's research is initially prompted by tenure requirements, and subsequently driven by a desire for the "real" Columbus and the potential to use him to make cultural and political interventions, Williams's poetry aims to transcend culture and, with it, any mundane requirements for truth or historical accuracy. For Williams, literature is a masculine art, a "fathering," and women are prevented from participating except as muse: "Let graduate students in the coming decades debate my muse —they would never guess Twostar, whose superficial Columbus promised to be mere regurgitation, served up as filler between real estate advertisements and endless columns of class notes" (53). Yet, as the poem's title indicates, the novel plays on the parallels between Williams and his construct of Columbus: while Columbus was literally lost during his voyages, the historical truths surrounding the biographical man have also been lost to history. Like Williams, we now have only the Columbuses we construct. Williams, too, is "lost"—in his academic ambitions, which blind him to personal connections and prevent his growth—and he, too, will become literally lost in a dung-filled cave by the end of the novel. Likewise, just as these men are variously lost, so are their diaries. We no longer have Columbus's original diary, and Twostar's son, Nash, breaks into Williams's house and steals his diary, leading him in poignant and absurd pursuit as Nash lumbers through a series of student dormitories late one night, posting the torn-out pages on various doors, while Williams gives secretive chase, collecting the jumbled pages in an attempt to prove that "what had once been found could be found again" (*The Crown of Columbus* 70).

Neither Twostar nor Williams finds "the real" Columbus, of course; their mutual and sometimes crossed searches reveal the depth and range of the cultural hold the myth of Columbus has on us. But the Columbus we claim to know through the writing attributed to him is as complicated and changeable as any modern theorist could hope to find. Although Columbus's diary continues to be our best source for his voyages, its authorship is divided and debatable: "Columbus's story has come to us in the narration, the paraphrases, and the marginal annotations made to his diary by the Dominican friar Bartolomé de Las Casas and through the biographical materials written by his own son Hernando. . . . The original diary has been lost, but we know that Las Casas worked effectively to make of the mariner the hero he needed to inspire the Christianization of the natives" (Jara and Spadaccini 4). David Henige points out that "the fact that what has survived is not the original document but a copy that is about four-fifths admitted paraphrase has seldom deterred historians from using the *diario* repeatedly and intensively, and not a little boldly" (199). In *The Crown of Columbus*, Henry Cobb emphasizes this point of view when he discusses with Twostar Columbus's two diaries: "One for his crew's consumption, to convince them that they hadn't gone as far as they thought so that they wouldn't want to turn back. And an unexpurgated version for himself and for the king and queen." When Twostar wants to know whether Cobb's diary is the second, "true" version, he replies, "The document in my possession is the single one that survived. That makes it the true one" (197).

The impossibility of full meaning, whether in words or in the experiences they construct, fascinates Dorris and Erdrich, and elsewhere in the novel their play with this postmodern concept continues when characters Williams and Twostar experience a mutual orgasm. Williams insists that "as wonderful as it was, you know, it wasn't simultaneous. *Nothing* is simultaneous," and Twostar acquiesces, noting that at least they had the same experience. Williams disagrees, arguing that "since whatever syntax we do use misrepresents the reality of our respective sensations, we should simply remain mute." Twostar rails against the very problems of representation that plague her in her search for a true Columbus:

> I know words are messy, Roger, full of connotations, old desires and memories. I know no word has the identical meaning to two people. I know there is no way to absolutely describe what just happened to us, but to give up on language, to give up on what we have, no matter what a rag box it is—that is an act of cowardice. I love language, I give it its peculiarities, its old bones, its failings. I love words in my mouth. I love to spill them and I don't really care how every one of them fits. I love the fluidity and ripeness of talk, the forgetfulness of it, the way it vanishes into thin air, or how a sentence sags with meaning, laden like a piece of dry bread, sopping up soup. (248–49)

Like Columbus, the author is always no more, and no less, than the cultural meanings attached to her or him. Behind the chaos, there is no individual genius waiting for authentication. Instead, there are storytellers, readers, writers, editors, institutions, all of whom have various and sometimes competing interests in fixing an identity that cannot be found, an identity they partake of collaboratively. There is no Columbus, but there are many; there is no author, but there are many. The collaborative notion of authorship does not destroy authorship; it resituates it. Twostar's alumni magazine article is eventually finished collaboratively, signed by both Williams and her. We can see Dorris and Erdrich happily playing in another move that skewers notions of authorship and individual genius as well as emphasizing the functional reality of fictional characters when they submitted character Roger Williams's unfinished epic poem, "Diary of a Lost Man," to *Caliban*, where it was accepted. Dorris says, "We were a little jealous because it got a first-submission acceptance" (Chavkin and Chavkin, "An Interview with Michael Dorris" 210). Besides testing the degree to which Williams's Columbus poem meets contemporary standards of "good" poetry—something that is consonant with Williams's character and that also confirms his opinion of himself as, in fact, a talented poet—placing the poem in *Caliban* is also a playful, prescient response to the kind of criticism the book would receive as not literary enough.

That Erdrich and Dorris were willing to take the literary risk of creating a novel about a provocative and highly debated historical figure, a novel overflowing with different points of view and genres, suggests that they were confident in their literary relationship and their belief in the importance of collaboration. In the various ways in which Erdrich and Dorris include or enact a collaborative process in their marriage and across the range of their novels—as a generative writing process, a structural element of many of their novels, and a necessary way of reading—collaboration is usually a positive source of interaction and knowledge. Yet Erdrich and Dorris are also aware of its tensions, conflicts, and costs. For example, in "the unexpurgated, annotated version of Columbus's *Diary*" she eventually publishes, Twostar finds "within the text, material for a plethora of legal approaches under international law, issues of aboriginal claim and sovereignty, of premeditated fraud. The prospects for victories—here, in Brazil, in New Zealand, in Mexico—appear better than anyone would have expected" (*The Crown of Columbus* 375). It is truly a utopian ending but, ironically, one that would require forgetting exactly the complexly collaborative nature of Columbus's *Diary* were it to become a reality. It is unimaginable that any serious attempts to refute the kind of political and economic reorganization that Dorris and Erdrich anticipate in the wake of Twostar's own "discovery" wouldn't win precisely because authorship in this instance is so undecidable. Laird notes that the novel undermines its own ending when "as Roger stays at home with the new baby, Vivian takes her archaeological discovery of the Crown of Columbus and its alternative meanings and disappears with these into the limelight in a simple reversal of traditional male/female roles" (*Women Coauthors* 241–42). The novel ends with Valerie Clock's implicit condemnation of Twostar's colonizing attitudes in failing to recognize the crucial actions of others in saving Violet, and at the same time, Clock looks out to sea in exhilarated anticipation of "discovery."

Throughout Dorris's and Erdrich's ouevre, stories of collaboration are often also stories of competition, which can be dangerous, even deadly. Moreover, in their fiction—unlike in their published tributes to their marriage—love is frequently represented as untrusting, anguished, and punishing. Even in *The Crown of Columbus*, collaboration is sometimes secretive and frequently dangerous. Williams, for instance, is willing to share his wealth of library books on Columbus, but only in the role of full professor in order to help Twostar avoid an embarrassment that would likely spill over onto him. Twostar, too, goes to meet Cobb with hopes of outwitting him, even though it is only together that they have "the whole damned story" (200). She keeps her discovery of the oyster shells, and their cryptic directions to the crown, hidden from Williams, and she is convinced to go on the doomed sailing trip with Cobb because "offshore, Roger couldn't show up and break into the conversation" (272). *Cloud Chamber*, for example, traces out the first-person stories of Rose's ancestry on her father's side and introduces us to a particularly threatening version of collaboration, whose reverberations echo through subsequent generations. The novel opens as Rose, the family matriarch, makes a choice to betray her lover, Gerry, to the Irish resistance in response to his greater betrayal: Gerry has collaborated with the British forces against the Irish resistance. In this instance, layers of collaboration take on ominous and inescapable moral implications, and neutrality is impossible to attain and dangerous to attempt. *The Antelope Wife* is even more menacing about collaboration's negative potential. The novel is structured with headings that reflect a Native American origin myth: twins beading the pattern of the world. Yet these twins are engaged in intense competition, each trying to upset the balance of the world, creating a pattern that "glitters with cruelty" and is checked only by the other twin's complementary competition (73).

By the time Dorris committed suicide in 1997, the couple was estranged and beginning divorce proceedings. Dorris's death, amid painful accusations of child sexual abuse and impending arrest, shattered the collaborative relationship he shared with Erdrich and forever changed how that collaboration would be viewed. Many critics and most students now comb the couple's novels for the single encompassing interpretation; they search for signs of impending doom in a fervent conviction that art foreshadows life and that everything from their fiction's frequent focus on unhappy, unresolved endings to Roger Williams's syllabus "Suicide in Literature" anticipates Dorris's final act. I would suggest, however, that the ways in which Dorris's and Erdrich's texts consistently refuse any single interpretation, favoring instead multiple and collaborative interpretations, teach us that any simplistic biographical reading of their literature as a key to their lives would be woefully inadequate and inaccurate. At the same time, because both Dorris and Erdrich consistently presented their married relationship as paralleling their working relationship—and both as deeply satisfying and productive—their marital estrangement and news of Dorris's ongoing depression and eventual suicide came as a profound shock to their wide circle of readers, critics, and admirers. What we do know is that this particular, consciously crafted collaboration ended abruptly, painfully, and sorrowfully. However, there is still much valuable insight to be gained from closely examining the collaboration they shared. The literary output that Erdrich and Dorris accomplished together—the short stories, the numerous novels, the mountain of interviews—helps us see collaboration for what they claimed it was: a vital, inescapable part of literary production.

3

A Question of Perspectives

Collaboration and Literary Authority
in Mourning Dove's Cogewea

I have just got through going over the book Cogewea *and am*
surprised at the changes that you made. . . . I felt like it was
someone elses [sic] book and not mine at all. In fact the finishing
touches were put there by you, and I have never seen it. . . . Oh
my Big Foot, you surely roasted the Shoapees strong. I think a
little too strong to get their sympathy. I wish we had not gone
too strong now. That is the only thing I am afraid of.
MOURNING DOVE TO LUCULLUS MCWHORTER

There is nothing mysterious or natural about authority.
It is formed, irradiated, disseminated; it is instrumental, it is
persuasive; it has status, it establishes canons of taste and value;
it is virtually indistinguishable from certain ideas it dignifies as
true, and from traditions, perceptions, and judgments it forms,
transmits, reproduces. Above all, authority can, indeed must,
be analyzed.
EDWARD W. SAID, *ORIENTALISM*

FOR MANY READERS and critics, Louise Erdrich's and Michael Dorris's consciously chosen and elaborately presented
collaborative relationship represents the pinnacle of critical accomplishment and financial success in Native American literature over the past two decades. With the range of their collaborative oeuvre, its recognized literary quality, the length of their
collaborative relationship—and, unfortunately, the spectacularly
lurid and troubling nature of its collapse—Erdrich and Dorris
have made Native American literature more recognizable, presti-

gious, and accessible to a wide variety of readers. While their collaboration is certainly the most deliberately undertaken and well known such relationship, collaborative writing relationships occur often in the transition of Native American literature from oral art forms to written ones. Collaborations between Native Americans and white anthropologists, ethnographers, and writers were frequent occurrences in the late nineteenth and early twentieth centuries, as Native American stories were collected, translated, and frequently edited to conform to the literary tastes and expectations of a white reading audience. One important collaboration, between a Native American woman, Mourning Dove, and her white male mentor, Lucullus V. McWhorter, produced a text that remains widely unread, primarily because it leaves intact clear markers of its multidimensional collaborative process of literary production. The wealth of information it offers us regarding collaboration, particularly across gender and racial boundaries, regarding western American literary production and early-twentieth-century conceptions of Native identity is still largely unacknowledged.

In 1927, after more than a decade of rejection, delay, and uncertainty, Christine Quintasket's only novel, *Cogewea, the Half-Blood: A Depiction of the Great Montana Cattle Range*, was published under the name Mourning Dove, the Anglicized version of her Indian name, Hum-ishu-ma.[1] There is conflicting evidence regarding the year of Mourning Dove's birth, but we know that she was born between 1882 and 1888 near Bonner Falls, Idaho. She claimed Native American and Irish or Scots ancestry.[2] During its lengthy passage to print, the original draft of *Cogewea* was extensively revised, amended, expanded, and edited by Mourning Dove's friend and mentor, Lucullus McWhorter, a white amateur ethnographer and activist for Native American rights in the northwestern United States. Mourning Dove had a draft of her novel in 1914, when she met McWhorter at Walla Walla Frontier Days in Washington State. McWhorter's activism on behalf of Indian rights was well known regionally, and their meeting would change both of their lives, prompting a complex collaboration that contained elements of colonialist paternalism, gendered expectations and exploitation, cultural appropriation, lifetime loyalty and mentoring, financial sacrifice, and sincerely felt friendship.

That original draft of *Cogewea* has been lost or destroyed, but a lengthy correspondence between Mourning Dove and McWhorter, and between McWhorter and various individuals concerned about the publication of *Cogewea*, reveals that, besides additions and revisions to the main narrative, McWhorter extensively footnoted *Cogewea*, added literary epigraphs to each chapter, inserted a "biographical sketch" of Mourning Dove, and included her photograph.[3] McWhorter's addition of her photograph and other information identifying her mixed-blood ancestry—a move Mourning Dove resisted because she feared white readers would attribute her literary abilities to "the white part of me"—nonetheless displays the cross-purposes each writer had in mind.[4] Susan Bernardin writes that "McWhorter 'strengthened' Mourning Dove's statements by stamping the text with what it noticeably lacked, the culturally authoritative indices of Indian authenticity" (488). Her photograph "offers the reader proof of her authenticity: headband, braids, beads, and buckskin" (493).[5] The resulting text, dense with such ethnographic information intended to add "authenticity" and to clarify information unfamiliar to a white readership, situates itself uncomfortably at the crossroads of western romance, the sentimental novel, ethnographic autobiography, and anthropological record. By examining the complex collaboration between Mourning Dove and McWhorter, we literally are able to study a textual frontier, a historical moment of meeting, clashing, and cooperating multicultural encounters. The result is a fascinating, disturbing, and illuminating text that reveals the coercive possibilities of collaboration while underscoring their potential for subversion and reappropriation. Equally fascinating—and to critics and readers, even more disturbing—are the ways in which the text documents the writers' self-collaborations. As we will see, the multitude of authorial signatures that mark the text emphasize that neither McWhorter nor Mourning Dove claims a stable identity or a single "voice," and the text itself investigates the impossibility of such an identity in the midst of the assimilationist period during which Mourning Dove and McWhorter wrote. Finally, because *Cogewea* partakes of several different literary genres, each with its own story of Native American and American culture to tell, reading the text entails collaborations between literary genres and between text and reader that in turn highlight cultural expectations about *Cogewea*'s historical moment and the construction of western American literature during the frontier period.

If *Cogewea*'s readers desire unity, whether in the form of a clear demarcation between the text's collaborators, in a harmonizing of multiple histories, or simply in a unified presentation of a single literary genre, those desires are immediately problematized. Even before the narrative proper begins, *Cogewea* announces the cultural work it will perform: to cast the European concept of literary authority granted by single authorship into the much more vexed and undefined literary space of collaboration. What's more, the novel will document, to some degree in contradiction to the desires expressed by both Mourning Dove and Mc-Whorter, a literary relationship both troubling and generative. Evidence of their collaboration is first present in the mingled, even competing, attributions announced on *Cogewea*'s title page: formally titled *Cogewea, the Half-Blood: A Depiction of the Great Montana Cattle Range*, the text is credited primarily to "Hum-ishu-ma," or "Mourning Dove." "Mourning Dove" is the English translation of "Hum-ish-uma," her Indian name, and it provided her with a literary and public identity that allowed her to claim white and Indian authority simultaneously. Mourning Dove's public signature, while Anglicized, conveys to her largely white reading audience that *Cogewea* was written by a Native American. However, the title page indicates that the text is "given through" Sho-pow-tan (Old Wolf), an Indian appellation for Mc-

Whorter. The name "Old Wolf" was given to McWhorter when he was adopted into the Yakima tribe, and its inclusion on the title page establishes McWhorter as a credible cultural translator. It also positions the text in a liminal space between formulaic fiction and the developing social science of ethnography, as do the notes and a biographical sketch of Mourning Dove, which are included in the text and are credited to "Lucullus Virgil McWhorter" on the title page. Thus, by the time readers begin to read the fictional narrative, they have encountered two collaborative writers, each of whom has at least two cited names that indicate both the varied cultural positions (white and Native) each occupies and the challenges to individual identity and, ultimately, to individual authorship, that the novel will take up. That such a range of cited names appears within the space of a single page may give a reader pause, but it parallels the intricacies of Mourning Dove's and McWhorter's enduring friendship and complex literary relationship at a time when the American literary canon was unable to recognize Native American literature as legitimate except in highly translated or altered form as examples of a vanishing race of people.[6]

Reading *Cogewea* requires that the reader take part in a parallel collaborative process. For instance, many readers may be unaware of the cultural beliefs regarding names that Mourning Dove would have held. In a manuscript left unpublished at her death and later published as her autobiography, Mourning Dove directly addresses the importance of naming in Colville tradition: "In ancient times it was customary for a person to have many names, by inheritance and by outstanding deeds. A medicine man might take a name when a spirit requested him to do so in a dream or vision. . . . Before the whites came, we had no surnames. They were given by Jesuits and pioneers for convenience, overcoming the difficulties of pronouncing native words. . . . The sisters at Goodwin Mission also gave out names to students when they enrolled. Often they were given the first name of their father as a family name. In this way I once became Christine Joseph" (96).[7] Naming here does not fix identity. Rather, it implies the range of identities conferred and assumed, and it shows the interwoven spiritual and material power relations traditionally invoked in acts of naming, while Anglicized names inevitably uphold patriarchal ideologies. Mourning Dove makes clear that the "convenience" of naming is experienced by those who have the power to name. Through its variety of names, *Cogewea*'s title page announces that authorship is fluid, composed not so much by a concept of coherent historical individuals as by the varied cultural positions those individuals occupy, or are seen to occupy by an audience with its own expectations regarding "authentic" Native American literature. Furthermore, as a collaboration, *Cogewea* demonstrates Bakhtin's notion of dialogic interplay, or heteroglossia: Kathleen Donovan writes that "*Cogewea*, as polyphonic novel, derives its complexities of language and culture not simply from the fractured modernity of the novel genre, but also from the interplay of voices and textures of the oral tradition with its multiple narrative versions, and the exchange between performer and audience that creates the meaning of an oral performance, while implicitly denying a singular, unified authorship" (119). In his study of cross-cultural readings of Native American texts, *Keeping Slug Woman Alive*, Greg Sarris also refers to heteroglossia as an important component in the reader's response, forming yet another collaborative overlay: "A unit or system of language, say the novel, can be seen as a representative of dialogue and interaction between a number of languages and voices. . . . It is not just a representative of interaction but also the occasion for interaction. A reader's intermingling internal voices hold dialogue with the intermingling voices of the novel" (4–5).

Although early critics of *Cogewea* tended to interpret such intermingling voices as a mishmash of entangled perspectives and agendas, a point I will return to later, Mary Louise Pratt's discussion of what she calls the "*autoethnographic* text" can help us better understand how a novel such as *Cogewea* emerges and how we can understand those aspects of the text that seem to be incoherent or even simply "bad writing." Pratt defines an autoethno-

graphic text as one "in which people undertake to describe themselves in ways that engage with representations others have made
of them" (35). Although Pratt is not specifically discussing the
fictional format of the novel, her point that "autoethnographic
texts are representations that the so-defined others construct *in
response to* or in dialogue with" ethnographic texts written to
present the European self to the native other usefully describes at
least one of the motivations for publishing *Cogewea* (35). Such
autoethnographic texts involve, as *Cogewea* does, dual collaborations, both concrete collaborations between individuals composing the text and "a selective collaboration with and appropriation of idioms of the metropolis or the conqueror. These are
merged or infiltrated to varying degrees with indigenous idioms
to create self-representations intended to intervene in metropoli-
tan modes of understanding" (35). By combining elements of the
western romance and the nineteenth-century sentimental novel
—both writing forms addressed to a white, and largely female,
reading audience—with more traditional storytelling art forms
rooted in traditional Okanogan oral culture, by relying on predictable dichotomous stereotypes in some scenes while under-
mining such stereotyping in others, and by incorporating what
reads to a contemporary audience as wildly disjunctive and dis-
ruptive shifts of discourse, *Cogewea* is a particular kind of writing produced at a particular historical moment. Moreover, *Cogewea* not only employs collaboration, it relies upon it in a host of
varied forms and, in turn, these collaborations become an indelible part of the "story" the novel tells.[8]

One of the key collaborations performed by *Cogewea* takes
place in the intertwining genres of the western romance and the
sentimental novel; both the novel's plot and the ways in which it
is structured work to represent Native Americans to a popular
reading audience who would recognize, even rely upon, particular stereotypes. *Cogewea*'s plot appears straightforward: its title character, Cogewea, is a young woman of mixed Native and
Anglo-American heritage. Her two sisters' opposing cultural

identifications embody the struggle Cogewea resists throughout the novel: to construct an ethnic identity that is represented as either Caucasian or Indian. The oldest sister, Julia, has adopted an Anglo-American lifestyle through her marriage to white rancher John Carter, and the youngest sister, Mary, has been raised with traditional Native beliefs by the Stemteemä, their grandmother. Unlike either of her fictional sisters, however, Cogewea is torn between Native American and Anglo-American cultures throughout the novel. Julia's husband, John Carter, employs the numerous ranch hands whose stereotyped representations provide much of the novel's comic relief and satisfy many of the conventions of the western romance that *Cogewea* sets forth and, perhaps inadvertently, parodies. A somewhat predictable romantic triangle is composed of Cogewea; Jim, a skilled ranch hand who, like Cogewea, is a "breed"; and Alfred Densmore, a white "tenderfoot" Easterner who, mistakenly believing that Cogewea is rich, plots to wed, rob, and abandon her. Cogewea ignores the Stemteemä's repeated warnings as well as signs from her spirit powers about Densmore's duplicity until she is finally betrayed by him. The novel ends when Cogewea realizes she returns Jim's love and learns that an error in her white father's will has resulted in a substantial inheritance for her and her sisters.

The western romance genre shapes—and constrains—the form the novel takes. Character development and plotting throughout the novel are self-consciously predictable. *Cogewea* is populated by stereotypical cowboy characters, whose comic antics and practical jokes on one another pay tribute to their dime-novel predecessors, situate the novel in a specific region and time, and help establish the sense of masculine community and affection upon which Cogewea's ultimate rescue from Densmore will depend. Frequent descriptions of the mountain vistas surrounding the Flathead region of Montana further establish the Frontier West setting of the novel. In addition to establishing a regional setting, however, these descriptions also suggest the wider-ranging implications of the irrevocable changes forced on Native peoples as a result of white contact, an emphatic politicization of the genre: "[Cogewea's] reveries were broken as the range riders burst into view over a distant swell. She saw them thrown into sharp silhouette against the sun, leaving its last crimson touch to plain and the beautiful Pend d'Orielle, as its blue waters swept southward around the Horseshoe. . . . She thought of the canoe which ruffled its bosom no more. The huge Clay Banks on its eastern shore loomed grey and somber in the shadowy gloaming, never again to reflect gleam of signal or camp-fire. The buffalo no longer drank of its cooling flood, nor thundered over the echoing plain" (17–18). This passage is sentimental but not merely so. Since the novel also owes its shape to the sentimental novel, a genre made popular during the nineteenth century by white women writers, sentiment here can be read as an effective evocation of political power. A call to emotion as the impetus to cultural change underlies the cultural work sentimental novels were intended to accomplish; *Cogewea* in this regard employs sentiment not as a form of fading nostalgia but instead as a specifically politicized call to action. Read from this perspective, the novel's use of sentiment paves the way for a subtle subverting of readers' expectations for Native characters. While Cogewea considers the effects on Native people of the ongoing white occupation of the American West at several points in the novel, the past she represents is always unrecoverable; there is no salving white guilt by creating an otherworldly Montana frontier, where the effects of colonization and assimilation have no impact. Neither Cogewea nor Jim is a "noble savage" who can satisfy desires for an "authentic" Indian to reassure white anxieties. The novel's action takes place in its contemporary early-twentieth-century time frame, and this focus on the present forces Jim and Cogewea to face thorny problems of identity that surpass stereotype or melodrama: "Regarded with suspicion by the Indian; shunned by the Caucasian; where was there any place for the despised breed!" (17). Neither white culture nor traditional Native tribal culture is able to accommodate the liminal identities Jim and Cogewea embody, and in that sense, the novel offers few of the comforting platitudes or reassuring plot resolutions that are generic components of both the western and the sentimental novel.

In *The Location of Culture*, Homi Bhabha describes the stairwell as a key image in understanding the concept of liminality: "The stairwell as liminal space, in-between the designations of identity, becomes the process of symbolic interaction, the connective tissue that constructs the difference between upper and lower, black and white. The hither and thither of the stairwell, the temporal movement and passage that it allows, prevents identities at either end of it from settling into primordial polarities. This interstitial passage between fixed identifications opens up the possibility of a cultural hybridity that entertains difference without an assumed or imposed hierarchy" (4). Mourning Dove and Mc-Whorter's collaboration occupies and embodies just such a liminal space, and the sense of disorientation and disturbance, the restlessness of the novel's form, its "failure" to cohere or unify, is the collaboration's lesson to us. *Cogewea* resists codified or stable identities, whether of the writers, of the novel's characters, or in this case, of the novel's collaborating genres.

In this regard, the collaboration between the western romance and the sentimental novel produces a version of Pratt's autoethnographic text: *Cogewea* utilizes both genres in order to reframe and reintroduce Native American characters and culture to an audience who can be expected to enter the text initially via familiar stereotypes. The novel's self-representations of the intermingled Native and white worlds refuse division into the safety of binary definitions, thereby intervening in contemporary constructions of polarized racial identities. In a particularly complex example, *Cogewea* inscribes a wide range of stereotypes that, while straining the novel's attempts at realistic representation, perform curious and sometimes contradictory cultural work. Indian characters in *Cogewea* are represented as superstitious and as possessing an innate ability to work with animals. These representations may spring from governmental and cultural beliefs regarding Indians: BIA (U.S. Bureau of Indian Affairs) schools regularly taught the Native American children, who were literally held captive, that their tribal beliefs were superstitious and prevented these children from speaking their native languages or observing their traditional ceremonies. In addition, Native Americans were considered by Europeans to be more "primitive" and thus more closely associated with animals. It is likely, therefore, that most white readers of the novel would immediately recognize the stereotypes *Cogewea* draws upon, even if some readers consciously rejected them. Yet, in an intriguing shift from these embedded cultural attitudes, the text makes clear that Cogewea herself is tricked because she fails to attach enough importance to vitally real spiritual signs and as a result is not sufficiently suspicious of Densmore, the western-style villain. In addition, with the character of Densmore, who wants to "rough it a while among Indians and cowboys," *Cogewea* mocks stereotypes of Native Americans and of the western frontier held by whites: "Fresh from a great eastern city, he had expected to see the painted and blanketed aborigine of history and romance; but instead, he had only encountered this miniature group of half-bloods and one ancient squaw" (43–44).

   Cogewea's stereotypical representation of white characters can also be read as a function of the novel's form, although it also may result from Mourning Dove's and McWhorter's joint concern to generate sympathy from the novel's intended white audience. White characters in the novel are either wholly good or entirely bad. John Carter, the oldest sister's husband and owner of the ranch where Cogewea lives, is represented as "good natured and amiable," kind to Cogewea despite her "escapades," and "more of a father than otherwise" to her: "She never failed to get back into his good graces with an additional link forged about his great, affectionate heart" (19). Densmore, on the other hand, is an utter villain, "thin lipped and with a cold, calculating grey eye" (43). This dichotomous split into good and evil preempts a great deal of anxiety for white readers because it establishes the possibility of identification with a number of "good" white characters.

Cogewea's reliance on stereotype, then, is one of the sophisticated ways in which the novel incorporates contemporary expectations regarding Native Americans in order to alter or challenge those expectations; to the degree it succeeds, *Cogewea* ultimately presents Native American characters and culture from an unexpectedly new vantage point. One way it does succeed is by persisting in presenting ethnic groups as dynamically changing, unstable, and multiply constituted entities. When Cogewea wins both the "ladies' race" and the "squaws' race" at the Fourth of July celebration described early in the novel, she is resisted angrily by both whites and full-blood Indians. A white woman who placed second, behind Cogewea, in the ladies' race stares "contemptuously" and loudly asks, "Why is this *squaw* permitted to ride? This is a *ladies* race!" (63). At the beginning of the squaws' race, one of the Kootenai riders responds to Cogewea by saying, "You have no right to be here! You are half-white! This race is for Indians and not for *breeds!*" (66). By employing the term *race* both to signify racial categories and to suggest a series of contests, as well as by having Cogewea win both events, the text documents a racist American practice of discrimination based on essentialized categories of race and insists that these categories inevitably collapse when contested.

Because of both the collaborations between literary genres and the collaboration between two writers, *Cogewea*'s apparent disjunctions read like shifts in voicing, shifts that are invariably attributed to one or the other collaborator. For example, Mourning Dove spoke Salishan and English, and she struggled to produce grammatically correct Standard English—the language of published literature—for the balance of her life. Therefore, in critical evaluations of *Cogewea*, formalized rhetoric, typically rhetoric that takes the form of righteous and often angry diatribes against white institutions, is invariably attributed to McWhorter and the less elaborate rhetorical constructions are attributed to Mourning Dove. In her introduction to the novel, Dexter Fisher points to what she identifies as one of McWhorter's particularly polemical rages against the Bureau of Indian Affairs: "A nasty smear on the Government escutcheon . . . a stagnant cesspool swarming with political hatched vermin! stenchful with the fumes of avarice and greed; selfishly indifferent to the Macedonian cry of its victims writing under the leash wielded by the hand of Mammon! Pitch is a fastidious cosmetic, compared with the Bureau slime!" (xvi). Fisher compares this frenzied rhetoric to what she identifies as Mourning Dove's "own unadorned style" (xvii), usually located in the oral storytelling style of the Stemteemä, while Donovan writes, "What endures in the novel is of Mourning Dove's creation, while McWhorter's contributions ironically appear frozen in a quaint time warp" (119). The critical coding of an easily discernible distinction between Mourning Dove and McWhorter, between an authentic (and so, apolitical) Indian story and a politically motivated (and so, inauthentic) white one, is a particular interpretive strategy that deserves closer investigation. By separating the text into such binary oppositions as "simple and direct" (Mourning Dove) and "complex" (McWhorter), between "real" (Mourning Dove) and "rhetorical" (McWhorter), critics do a disservice to both collaborators. There is no reason to believe that Mourning Dove was not an astute critic of white culture or that she was unable to compose the slang-riddled dialogue or some of the critiques of white culture attributed to McWhorter (xviii, 120). Likewise, there is no convincing evidence that McWhorter, who was a skilled student of Native American traditions, could not have written with substantially less rhetorical excess. My initial emphasis here is that, although the critical distinction between writing styles is at times apparent for scholars who have studied McWhorter's and Mourning Dove's letters, it is nonetheless impossible to separate completely each collaborator's contribution within *Cogewea*. More to the point, however, is that such impossibility is the nature of literature. *Cogewea* is like every other literary text in this regard; what sets is apart is, rather, the variety of ways in which it reveals rather than suppresses its collaborative mode of production.

It is important to remember that Mourning Dove had completed a first draft of *Cogewea* before meeting McWhorter in 1914. Although we no longer have access to this draft, we know that it was a novel-length fictional western romance, a localized variation on a traditional European literary genre. Moreover, as we consider the implications of Mourning Dove's and McWhorter's published collaboration, it is important to resist constructing her absent first draft as a destroyed example of "authentic" Native American literature in order to avoid simplifying an enormously complex relationship into that of victimizer and victim. To do so is to reemploy a dichotomous construction of racial authority that continues the work of colonization. Relations between race and gender (a Native American woman and a white male editor) are at the heart of this collaborative effort. Citing a 1924 letter from McWhorter to Joseph Latimer in which McWhorter claims that he "feel[s] that the publication of this work, coming as it does from the pen of an Indian, would be a potent factor in bring about a reformation and cleaning up of the Indian Department," Alanna Kathleen Brown has written, "The novel now had two writers with separate purposes. Mourning Dove's story remained focused on the spiritual struggles of her generation and the blatant racism of the times. McWhorter's sections added extensive ethnographic commentary to the novel to preserve a knowledge of Native American ways he believed were quickly vanishing. He also used the work to attack the Christian hypocrisy of his peers and the corruption of federal agents. The disruption to the narrative was severe" ("Legacy Profile" 54). Even without the original draft to compare with the published version of *Cogewea*, Brown's assertion of narrative disruption is undeniable. Dexter Fisher remarks that the novel "sags at times under the weight of vituperation" (xiv), and Paula Gunn Allen has referred to *Cogewea* as "a maimed—I should say martyred—

book" (83). More recently, Donovan argues that McWhorter's additions to the novel, "which were probably crucial to the novel's publication, now seem to be annoying distractions from the real story," relegated "to the category of propaganda" (119, 120). In varying degrees, however, each of these assessments emphasizes what appear to be the negative effects of the narrative disruptions and implicitly regrets that the novel is not either a more unified collaboration or, alternatively, more clearly delineated into two distinct authorial voices, one disingenuous and one "real." Even Bernardin, whose essay is one of the most theoretically cogent and challenging discussions of Mourning Dove and McWhorter's collaboration, asserts the primacy of Mourning Dove's "authorial control" over McWhorter's "in the text's privileging of Okanogan values" (501).

The issue of voice is, of course, of paramount importance, particularly for feminist scholars interested in establishing Mourning Dove as a critical authorial presence in the text. In fact, because the narrative disjunctions are so immediately apparent and, for most readers, irresolvable into a desired unified voice, Mourning Dove's authorship of *Cogewea* was challenged after the novel was published.[9] Yet the well-intentioned desire to account for and privilege Mourning Dove's contribution to the collaboration frequently results in assertions of identity politics in the form of claims to identify Mourning Dove's real voice.[10] The desire to establish and locate Mourning Dove's voice is understandable and functional; particularly when dealing with Native American texts, amid a history of translating, rephrasing, and reframing oral narrative in order to meet expectations of white readers, the concept of voice promises a reassuring authenticity. Yet the desire for an essential voice, particularly for an essential Native American woman's voice, contradicts the lessons of the text. As *Cogewea* makes plain at many junctures, any claims to an essential, unified identity, while poignant, are flawed misrepresentations of the more complex, liminal identities that characters in the novel negotiate. What's more, as the title page makes clear, whether we focus on Mourning Dove or on McWhorter, Hum-ishu-ma or Sho-pow-tan, there is no individual author behind any voice we might isolate. Both Mourning Dove and McWhorter were complex cultural subjects who occupied various overlapping positions and spoke from those various positions. In other words, while I applaud the feminist recovery efforts that have generally succeeded in claiming to identify and acknowledge Mourning Dove's voice after so many years of perceived silencing or suppression by McWhorter's, the "voice" we think we hear is already presented in far more complex, ambivalent, and polyvocal ways within the text and within the collaboration that is the occasion for such a presentation. Moreover, what becomes coded as "authentically Native American" also becomes coded by association as authentically spiritual. This critical move has the potential to obscure *Cogewea*'s more radical insights by reintroducing the dichotomous racial categories *Cogewea* undoes elsewhere. To attempt to cleave one voice from the other can result in reifying beliefs in the "simplicity" of Native American literature, when in *Cogewea*, the binary oppositions of simple/difficult, and the associations of primitive/sophisticated and authentic/counterfeit that they evoke for white readers, collapse.[11]

An example of these kinds of collapsing boundaries can be found in *Cogewea*'s mingled representations of Christianity and Native American spirituality, which present endless difficulties for critics and readers seeking an "authentic" Native spirituality or a clear distinction between traditional Indian and Christian beliefs. The autobiographical manuscript Mourning Dove left at her death suggests she held mutually faithful beliefs in traditional Catholicism and Native spirituality during her life: "To some extent we have tried to live in both worlds. An Indian knew he could be faithful to his native creed and still pray every day to the God of the whites. When in actual need from the troubles of the world, however, he did not hesitate to turn to the sweat lodge, never understanding how this could conflict with the white God, since the missionaries always said that God had many ways of helping people in distress" (141). As with the representations of a bicultural ethnic identity, *Cogewea* again refuses to choose either side of a binary opposition in regard to religion. *Cogewea*, like the lives of both Mourning Dove and McWhorter, relentlessly and courageously crosses boundaries. For example, an image of Eden appears in *Cogewea*:

> The splendid Flathead valley lay below. . . . A vision of the dim misty past rose up before [Cogewea]. A stately buffalo roved in the distance, while the timid antelope stood sentinel on the neighboring heights. An Indian village on the move, wound its way like a great mottled serpent over the crest of the highest ridge. . . . "My beautiful Eden! I love you! My valley and my mountains! It is too bad that you be redeemed from the wild, once the home of my vanishing race and where the buffalo roamed at will. Where hunting was a joy to the tribesmen, who communed with the Great Spirit. I would that I had lived in those days,—that the blood of the white man had not condemned me an outcast among my own people." (109)

This Eden differs from its biblical echo. Despite Cogewea's longing for a past prior to white contact, the paradise she describes is, in fact, physically before her in the present. The "great mottled serpent" is not the snake in the garden; it is a community she knows and implicitly values. Eden here is destroyed because of the entry of white colonization and assimilation, not because of the presence of Native Americans or of their expulsion, readings that might be suggested by Christian interpretations of the serpent's symbolic function. Rather than either rejecting or embracing Christianity here, Mourning Dove revises its imagery and then uses it to foreground for her people a message of tolerance.

Later, however, at another juncture, the issues become more thoroughly politicized when Cogewea says, "The white man's God has not saved my people from the extermination which came hand in hand with this 'spiritual light bursting on a darkened New World'. Woe! and degradation has been our heritage of the invaders' civilization; the invader who taught that our God was a myth. His teachings and example have failed to fit us for his heaven, while they have unfitted us for our own Happy Hunting Grounds. I am wondering if there will be any place for us in the hereafter. As a half-blood, I suppose that I will be left entirely out in the cold" (134). Again, however, the text insists less on the need to choose between two forms of belief than it expresses both regret and realization that Cogewea's mixed heritage prevents the comfort of a unitary identity. Within the novel, Cogewea is consistently placed in situations that demonstrate her difference from essentialized understandings of both Anglo- and Native American identities. Just as the title page of *Cogewea* suggests that the text is the product of a complex collaboration, so Cogewea negotiates between these cultures and their ideologies.

In one of the more hopeful early readings of the novel's conclusion, Brown writes that Cogewea's eventual marriage to Jim is the creation of "the 'new people'" who are "born out of the Indian and White clashes of the present," and who "united those worlds, the Spirits of the Earth, the knowledge of those who have gone before, and those who have come [after]" ("Mourning Dove's Voice" 12). In my reading, however, this union is less a celebration of the end to oppression through a union of Indian and white than it is a defense against continuing racism and even genocide, as Cogewea points out when she says to Jim: "We despised breeds are in a zone of our own and when we break from the corral erected about us, we meet up with trouble. I only wish that the fence could not be scaled by the soulless creatures who have ever preyed upon us" (283). There is no indication that Cogewea and Jim believed that the protective "fence" around them would hold, and the threats come from both cultures. As Bernardin notes, "While marriage in mainstream westerns and romances often signals a renewed social order, marriage in *Cogewea* gestures to the unhealed rifts between native Americans and Euro-America. . . . Following the long tradition of the western romance, *Cogewea* offers no projected reconciliation of Euro-Americans and Native

Americans—a move that belies Mourning Dove's hope to act as a hinge between cultural perspectives" (503). Rather than reading the text with an ultimate critical goal of establishing coherence or locating an essential voice—whether Mourning Dove's or Mc-Whorter's—I read it as one that is exciting and important because its splinters and fractures are so evident. *Cogewea* resists simplistic and stereotyped understandings of an essentialized Native American harmony, one perhaps desired by a white audience in search of a redemptive spirituality or a wise Indian elder. Rather than being a failure because it does not achieve a unified wholeness, *Cogewea*'s accomplishment is that it refuses such narrow expectations. The novel questions the very possibility of such wholeness: *Cogewea* presents us with the complexities of the bicultural identities that both collaborators claimed. Mourning Dove did not position herself "outside" of her culture—which was, by the time she wrote, already a mixture of Native and white beliefs.

While important, the content of *Cogewea* at the plot level is not the only story the novel tells. Elizabeth Ammons writes that "Humishuma's story tells a truth about race, class, colonialism, and female authorship in the United States that it has been in the interest of mainstream writers, critics, and literary historians to ignore and deny" (138). Mourning Dove was among the generation of young northwestern Indian people to be directly affected by United States assimilationist policies. She was a member of the Colville Confederated Tribes of Eastern Washington State and became active in tribal politics late in her life. She married twice and spent her adult life as a small farmer, migrant laborer, and caregiver to others' children; the work was relentless and extremely draining. Although Mourning Dove wrote and published during the span of years we have come to call the modernist period, she did not have the economic privilege, the formal educational preparation, or the leisure to directly participate intellectually in that movement. Mourning Dove's contribution to the collaboration springs from a different life. She remembered the final western buffalo roundup and the animals' removal to Canada, and in *Cogewea* she and McWhorter reconstruct that roundup and the poignant and violent sense of loss it represented: "It was pitiful to see the animals fight so desperately for freedom. . . . They seemed to realize that they were leaving their native haunts for all time. To the Indian, they were the last link connecting him with the past, and when one of the animals burst through the car, falling to the tracks and breaking its neck, I saw some of the older people shedding silent tears. . . . [The buffalo] were considered too dangerous for the white settlers, but we never found them dangerous when we were here alone" (148). The description of the buffalo capture, while hinting that a parallel between the treatment of the buffalo and that of Native Americans exists, is not the overtly complex, allusive, or densely self-conscious literary presentation privileged within modernist circles. Quite the opposite, this passage strives for immediacy and directness. The rich interplay of autobiography, history, and fiction as it is presented by these two collaborators provides us with a complex story that is crucial to acknowledge, particularly as our understanding of literature of the American West continues to develop. *Cogewea* is steeped in specific historical conflicts that shape both the form of the novel and the strategies both collaborators used to present themselves as writers and as storytellers. At the levels of both plot and production, *Cogewea* is a collaborative history of oppression, and its conclusion points to the ongoing threats to bicultural identity by both full-blood Indians and Caucasians.

A prominent form of literary collaboration in the early twentieth century is debated early in *Cogewea*, when Cogewea considers "becoming an authoress" in order to preserve her history: "[Mary], like Julia, had imbibed more of the primitive Indian nature, absorbed from the centuries-old legends as told them by the Stemteemä. Recognizing the new order of things, Cogewea realized that these threads in the woof of her people's philosophy, must be irretrievably lost unless speedily placed on record" (33). While in one sense, *Cogewea* is this record, the novel also makes it clear that the written record is not infallible and that it is not only whites who contribute to misrepresentation in print. The creation of written records of Native American literature was not pursued in most Native American cultures until the late nineteenth century, when ethnographers such as Franz Boas and his students collected and recorded "folklores" and oral stories from numerous Native American tribes. Until that time, Native American literature was primarily an oral culture and was also, in a sense, collaborative. Rather than the typical Western understanding of collaboration as consisting of two or more individuals composing a text together, Native American collaboration refers to a collective or tribal understanding that the meaning of a story is highly contextual, performative, and dependent on audience interaction. Stories are communally owned; they are passed on from teller to hearer and from generation to generation. The notion of the author as the singular creator of a text was simply not viable; literature grew out of the tribal relationship.[12] In the text, Jim recalls meeting a writer who was recording information directly from Indians: "I was there when the boys was a stuffin' one poor woman. . . . Well, you know how the boys are. They sure locoed that there gal to a finish, and while she was a dashin' the information down in her little tablet, we was a thinkin' up more lies to tell her" (93, 94). Ethnography, itself a central form of Native-white collaboration in early Native American texts, is susceptible to false information, of which the usually white ethnographer, in an eagerness to seize upon the "authentic" and in ignorance of the culture, may be unaware. Moreover, and perhaps because ethnocentrism and ignorance can so thoroughly shape ethnography, "lies" here are a form of resistance. In his discussion of anthropologist Elizabeth Colson's *Autobiographies of Three Pomo Women*, Greg Sarris elaborates on the collaborative roles inherent in ethnography: "I have watched Pomo informants, as they have been called, make an art of editing what they tell 'them scientists.' One Pomo woman calls it 'giving-them-a-piece-of-work.' She says: 'I give them pieces of this and that. I tell them a few things. Even things we shouldn't talk about [to non-Indians]. They never get the whole picture, not with just pieces of this and that. Besides, they make up what they want anyway. They tell their own stories about whatever I tell them.' . . . Speakers will often compare notes about their stories for anthropologists, and these discussions are full of raucous laughter" (105).[13] Ethnography—and the translation of oral literature into written stories—is not merely (or clearly) true or false; it is a method of interpretation, and so issues of competing interest inevitably arise.

For Mourning Dove, the act of writing immediately put her in some conflict with cultural traditions in which "authority" and the signature of the author do not function in the same ways they do in the European tradition. Arnold Krupat states:

> American Indian discourse, until very recently, has been notoriously lacking in its possession of named authors, and this has assuredly contributed to Euramerican neglect of it. As Foucault . . . notes, "Discourse that possesses an author's name is not to be immediately consumed and forgotten; neither is it accorded the momentary attention given to ordinary, fleeting words. Rather its status and its manner of reception are regulated by the culture in which it circulates." But can one attach an author's name to American Indian discourse? and if so, Whose? For its "status and its manner of reception" have always been tied to its presumptive anonymity, its lack of named authors. (120)

Krupat's point is one that Native Americanists must constantly keep in mind: oral literature is traditionally a collaborative literature in the sense that an author's signature is unrecorded. Instead, stories are told, and their telling is authorized by another storyteller, often in the past, who is invoked in the telling. In *Cogewea*, the Stemteemä demonstrates this conception of authoring and authority when she refers to her father as "giving" her the story that she then passes on to Cogewea and, somewhat ironically, to Densmore: "This story I am telling you is true. It was given me by my father who favored me among his many children. . . . He told me the tales that were sacred to his tribe; honored me with them, trusted me. Treasured by my forefathers, I value them. I know that they would want them kept only to their own people if they were here. But they are gone and for me the sunset of the last evening is approaching and I must not carry with me this history" (122). The context of the story and its telling are paramount, and both call into question the distinction between a single authoritative history and the separate realm of fiction that is so valued in European literary traditions. While Densmore is also given the story, he is completely incapable of recognizing the importance and validity of a system of literature and history that does not rely upon written records, an ironic commentary on literary valuation within a novel that so fully collaborates between specific literary genres and between written and oral traditions of literature. Giving Densmore the story is also an important political act within the novel. Although he neither understands nor values the story he is given, the Stemteemä's act of giving it explicitly brings a white man into the collaborative process of Native American literature.

The concept of the unified author is simultaneously challenged by this collaborative method of literary creation. As Donovan points out, "Tribal communities do not necessarily perceive the composer of the songs or stories as a unified subject in the Foucaudian notion of the author as owner of that which s/he creates" (118). The stories the Stemteemä tells are collaborative histories that consist of remembered events and accumulated wisdom. It is through verbal transmission, rather than the written record, that histories are traditionally and dependably "recorded." Collaboration across time and in performative events creates histories and passes them on. At the same time, lest we get swept away by a wave of oral storytelling, which is to say the desire to privilege the most apparent "Indian" aspect of the text, this scene in the novel functions ironically to remind us that, how-

ever valuable traditional tribal collaborations were, they are represented here in writing, in a novel, by collaborators who both
very much want to be recognized as authors of written literature.

Cogewea requires that we grapple with questions surrounding
nineteenth- and twentieth-century collaboration in Native American texts and with the gendered and racial implications of the results we find within the competing ideological frameworks of the
novel. Competing interests arise throughout Cogewea. The traces
they leave in the text account for much of the readerly neglect of
the novel. They also emphasize why we must foreground the collaborative nature of Cogewea's production. For Mourning Dove
to have written at all is a triumph, and the genres of the western
romance and the sentimental novel she used when writing Cogewea were perhaps dictated less by choice than by necessity.
Writing in established literary genres provided Mourning Dove
access to the identity and stability of "authority," and McWhorter's additions were aimed at reinforcing that authority. At the
same time, bringing two diverse genres into collaboration with
each other, in a sense paralleling the collaboration between Mc-
Whorter and Mourning Dove, highlights their constructed nature
when the process of collaboration itself resists the prescriptive
"happy ending" of the western romance or the sentimental novel.
In Cogewea, the security of a safe marriage is rejected for the am-
biguity and uncertainty of Cogewea's marriage to Jim, a union of
two mixed-blood Indians who consciously experience themselves
as not fully belonging anywhere. Only a "technical flaw" in white
inheritance law provides Cogewea with money from her white father's will, and both Jim and Cogewea are fully enmeshed in a
contemporary and potentially hostile present.

We can see elements of that present in a letter from Mc-
Whorter to Mourning Dove written in November 1915 in which
he implores Mourning Dove to collect and record Native American oral stories, casting her as a Christian savior. After urging her
attention to his commanding voice, "Listen, Mourning Dove of

the Okonogans; while the Old Wolf of the Yakimas speaks," Mc-
Whorter presents Mourning Dove with an explicit choice—two
paths, one easy and one difficult:

> Why should this young woman hesitate—dreaming while her camp
> fire burns out? I see in her vast possibilities. I see a future of renown;
> a name that will live through the ages, if only she will decide to take
> the right-hand trail. . . . Helping hands are held out to her, and the
> trail will not be so rough as it appears. Your race will be of actual
> benefit to her in this work. It is a duty she owes to her poor people,
> whos [sic] only history has been written by the destroyers of their
> race. Let the Mourning Dove of the Okonogans take cheer and step
> out from the gloom of ghostly fears, into the light of opportunity, ex-
> ulting in her own strength and show to the world her nobility of pur-
> pose to perpetuate the story of her people in their primitive simplic-
> ity. Nothing is in the way of your success. [11–13, 392][14]

McWhorter glorifies the role of the artist and storyteller as one
leading to a spiritual salvation. The role of artist-author Mc-
Whorter promotes is a distinctly European one, wherein the transcending personality is one whose sensitivity and suffering fit the
artist for the sacrifice. By addressing Mourning Dove in both the
second and the third person, McWhorter's syntax, along with
the visionary cast of his urgent exhortation, suggests the way in
which Mourning Dove is simultaneously objectified and utilized.
The urgency with which McWhorter charges Mourning Dove to
record stories collected from tribal peoples reflects his belief in
the fixed dependability of the written record and the inevitable
disappearance of Native Americans. As a documenter of her people's stories, she will preserve those stories in the face of what
McWhorter believes to be the inevitable extinction of a (primitive) race of people. However, McWhorter also understands that
histories are social constructs and knows that because they are
usually written by white historians, "the destroyers," existing
versions of history will legitimatize a different reality than will
Mourning Dove's stories. The "duty" McWhorter believes
Mourning Dove owes her people is to provide an alternate his-

tory, one that validates the oral literature and the different world-view of Native Americans. Yet, despite McWhorter's reliance on the transcendent figure of the artist, he cannot overcome his own culture's embedded racial constructs. In fact, it is the race of the historian, rather than the method of recording, that determines accuracy for McWhorter, and he identifies it as Mourning Dove's primary qualification, the "actual benefit to her in her work." What McWhorter does not see is his own racial positioning in this unique collaboration, and his 1915 reference to a "young woman . . . dreaming while her camp fire burns out" seems a particularly romantic conflation of European fantasies of authorship and stereotypic expectations of Native American self-indulgence and laziness.

McWhorter's blindnesses, while retrospectively regrettable, are not unusual. In fact, they are the historically dominant approach to Native-White interactions and, as such, are what we must strive to contextualize and historicize. If Edward Said's claim that "ideas, cultures, and histories cannot seriously be understood or studied without their force, or more precisely their configurations of power, also being studied" is true, then McWhorter's individual contextualization as a member of a hegemonic society, one that constructed images of Native Americans partly in order to validate their destruction, is important to examine (*Orientalism* 5). To the degree that he collaborates with Mourning Dove, not as an individual but as a mythic, salvific image, McWhorter's words reveal the underpinnings of his literary authority and, consequently, one aspect of his contribution to the collaboration. He is the individual; she, the image. He is the knowledgeable literary insider; she, the outsider. And while we could argue that, as a white man, he is equally an outsider in Native American culture, he would not be seen as such in the white literary world of his time, particularly given his previous study of and commitment to Native American causes, which the careful inclusion of his appellation "Old Wolf" signifies. Although McWhorter acknowledges his need for Mourning Dove's particular, individual insights, *Cogewea*'s title page makes clear that the meaning, the value, and the final authority to express those insights to a reading audience are constituted "through" him.

By employing theoretical terms and by resisting the urge to make claims for Mourning Dove's "voice" in either opposition to or agreement with McWhorter's "voice," I am not suggesting that it is unimportant either that Mourning Dove's original text was revised by McWhorter without her full knowledge of the extent of his changes or that the differing rhetorical strategies in the text we currently have are impossible to ascribe definitely to either writer. On the contrary, to dismiss the implications of that act and our subsequent uncertainty is to employ theoretical insights to enact yet another self-interested violence on the text. But from its title page to its conclusion, *Cogewea* insists on the collaborative and performative nature of literature, whether oral or written, and makes the particular Western desire to locate a single author who (himself) writes an individual text by dint of artistic brilliance seem obtusely wrongheaded, a yearning born of anxiety and doubt. In a very literal way, neither Mourning Dove nor McWhorter could have produced *Cogewea* without the other, a fact that both of them knew and appreciated. As Donovan describes, "The relationship between Mourning Dove and Mc-Whorter . . . even today resists categorization. If he considered her his daughter, she made it equally clear that he was like a father to her. While she frequently chafed at his editorial demands, she was capable of insisting on her own way or of reaching a compromise. If he sometimes appeared to be exploiting her, she recognized his usefulness" (102). And at the same time, this particular collaboration is not "the same as" the collaboration, across seasons and generations, that produces Native American oral literature, nor is it the same as the consciously selected, mutually publicized collaboration Dorris and Erdrich shared. Once again, we see that collaboration is a contested term and is neither inherently benign nor politically neutral. A collaborative event is always simultaneously a cultural event, and we cannot understand the first without investigating the second. With *Cogewea*, we can see a particular cultural struggle, one that the text performs with each reading.

The collaborative effort between Mourning Dove and Mc-Whorter reveals a more complex story—and one ultimately more spiritually challenging and historically informative—than reading for harmony would generate. In the most extraordinary ways, *Cogewea* represents, embodies, and performs a compelling series of collaborations crossing gender, race, religious, and interpersonal boundaries. The novel *Cogewea* is multivocal, incorporating numerous stories and depicting characters telling stories to one another, an aspect of Native American history that the novel reenacts with each rereading. When we read for a simpler story, one that does not recognize the text as a collaboration, the result is likely frustration over what will appear to be a dismally fractured text. Yet, when we do see *Cogewea* as a collaborative text at many levels, that narrative disruption is, among other things, *Cogewea*'s valuable contribution to the ongoing conversations surrounding Native American and western American literatures. *Cogewea* provides us with an opportunity to theorize the nuanced and various forms collaboration can take at one historical moment without sacrificing the ethical complexities of either Mourning Dove's or McWhorter's contributions to the text. To our lasting benefit as readers of this unusual collaboration, it is because *Cogewea* "fails" to deliver on readers' desires for either authorial or narrative unity that Mourning Dove and McWhorter achieve their greatest literary and social commentary.

4

Mary Austin, I-Mary, and Mary-by-Herself
Collaboration in Earth Horizon

We might pool our separate knowledges in a work of fiction around the destiny of one of those rivers which have meant so much to the development of the west. . . . Indeed, I'm not thinking of a conventional collaboration. No two people whose styles are as highly individualized as yours and mine could possibly write together, but there is no reason why we shouldn't create together our of our funded knowledge. . . . Dear friend, don't turn this aside because of a traditional objection to collaborating with a woman. I know I'm feminine, damnably feminine, and not ashamed of it, but I'm not ladyish. You can count on my behaving like a gentleman.
MARY AUSTIN TO SINCLAIR LEWIS

Making authorship visible in unexpected ways, literary collaboration thus put in relief the rules its own practice resisted, illuminating the very structures that necessarily excluded it from the category of authorship. In so doing, collaboration provided a platform to return to certain fundamental questions: What is an author? Who gets counted under this rubric? What forms of authorship are sanctioned and what forms marginalized at a given historical moment? . . . . What forms of authorship have particularly attracted women?
BETTE LONDON, *WRITING DOUBLE*

IN HER 1931 LETTER to noted American writer Sinclair Lewis, Mary Austin proposes a collaborative project in which, she assures Lewis, they need not actually "write together." Instead, Austin suggests pooling their knowledge in order to "create together." Less concerned with who does the actual writing than with the possibilities of mutual creativity, Austin's conception of collaboration highlights collaboration's potential for adaptability. But lest she be accused of painting a utopian vision of collaboration as instant creative harmony between the sexes, Austin also brings forward the obstacle hidden in plain sight: gendered expectations regarding women's writing. In a style typically both evasive and evocative, simultaneously claiming several gender positions and none, Austin reassures Lewis that collaboration with a woman should pose no problem: while she is feminine, she is no lady, and—as a final overture directed at soothing male anxiety regarding women writers and their presumably ladyish literary creations—she'll behave like a gentleman. For Austin, then, the most satisfactory collaborator is one who views collaboration as a flexible process that can literally skirt around the conventional constraints imposed by gender and one in which who holds the pen is secondary to the knowledge each collaborator brings to the experience.

A year later, in her 1932 autobiography, *Earth Horizon*, Mary Austin again focuses on gender when she relates a "prophetic" event in the life of her maternal grandmother, Hannah Graham. This time, however, although the collaboration Austin attempts to establish is metaphorical, the behavior that prompts it is equally resistant to gendered limits on female behavior. Austin tells us that Hannah's husband, a tailor, made his wife a custom-fitted dress from fine broadcloth, "an act so unprecedented that it narrowly escaped being scandalous" (19). Because she offended the conservative tastes of the community, Hannah was promptly disciplined by the Methodist Church and publicly called forward while a sermon on vanity was preached: "One must suppose that the church was well filled on that occasion, and that it was at the properly dramatic moment—I am sure that Hannah would have seen to that—the young matron walked down the aisle with her limping and totally unperturbed Scotchman beside her, *wearing that particular dress*! It was so exactly the thing Mary would have done!" (19–20). Using the genre of autobiography as her particular daring dress, her mode of resistance, Austin calls on a history of creative and innovative collaboration in order to assert the importance of female authorship. As *Earth Horizon* begins, she writes about her grandmother's "scandalous story," insisting upon her affinity with her grandmother in order to claim Hannah as a collaborative source in Austin's own refusal to capitulate to cultural expectations that violate her vision of female creativity. The life Austin represents throughout her autobiography—Austin would have us believe—is a spiritually superior one and thus is "prophetic" both in its visionary aspects and in its fulfillment of a maternal lineage of individual resistance to cultural constraints. As *Earth Horizon* continues, however, Austin will bring together these versions of spiritual prophecy by creating an emblematic collaboration with parts of her own psyche she calls Mary, I-Mary, and Mary-by-herself; by expanding her sense of collaboration to include her role as inheritor of a female tradition of mediumship that is reformulated and expressed in her professional commitment to Native American spirituality, literature, and culture; and by emphasizing the importance of the American West as the setting where these versions of collaboration unfold.

Like her maternal grandmother, then, Austin dons a "particular dress," her autobiography, that is designed to startle. As her persuasive plea to Lewis makes clear, when conceiving of alternatives, Austin routinely refuses the conventional on behalf of the more provocative. Carefully created and tailored to an unexpected but nonetheless carefully fitted form, Austin's life story strikes a sometimes awkward balance between overemphasizing its own careful construction and insisting on its visionary otherness. Like the anecdote it contains of Austin's grandmother, *Earth Horizon* is a story meant to endure; by documenting a professional, emotional, and linguistic collaboration with her own psyche in it, Austin challenges the basic tenet of autobiography: individual authorship. She investigates female subjectivity and its relation to creativity by positing an influential female heritage to form a collaborative history of resistance; she establishes a collaborative, multivocal subjectivity in place of the traditional singular subject of autobiographical writing; and she points to Native American literature, in its traditional oral and collaborative forms, as a prior text underlying her success as a writer.[1] Yet, like most prophecies, Austin's life story tells us less about what is to come than it does about what already exists but is obscured to the point of literal invisibility by dominating ideological assumptions and expectations, particularly those regarding female creativity and authorship. What *Earth Horizon* reveals—in the sense that it displays its evidence more readily than most texts, and especially more than most autobiographies—is that even a traditionally defined individual author is a collaborator involved in multiple collaborative relationships.

In *Earth Horizon*, the influential female heritage Austin inherits takes two collaborative forms: first, a specific inheritance from her maternal ancestors, and second, the ways in which Austin inherits a legacy of female mediumship, a practice of female collaboration that incorporates a spiritual counterpart in the process of creating a literary product. In her introduction, Austin states one of her clearest goals for her autobiography: to credit "the stamp of ancestral influences." She claims she was fortunate "to have been brought up intimately in touch with ancestral history, and so aware as few people are, of the factual realities of transmitted experiences"; she insists that her sense of "ancestral rootage" has been both her "greatest pleasure" and "the major importance" for writing the autobiography (viii). In the first section of *Earth Horizon*, a tribute to Austin's great-grandmother entitled "The

Saga of Polly McAdams," Austin transforms oral stories into an alternate written history. There she claims Polly as a temperamental and emotional mentor: "Except for Polly, you might suppose that Mary was hatched from a cuckoo's egg" (14). By crediting her own female ancestors for their "influences," Austin creates a prior text from their lives, a text she claims collaborates in the creation of her identity: "Whatever in Mary makes her worth so much writing about has its roots in the saga of Polly and Hannah and Susanna Savilla, in the nurture of which she grew up" (14). Austin's search for origins denies the illusion of the "self-made" identity in traditional forms of autobiographical writing, while her insistence on the centrality of female ancestry as a collaborative component of identity privileges an earlier cultural understanding of collaboration as intertextuality.[2]

Yet despite Austin's efforts to construct a usable, coherent text from her female ancestry, she faces an obstacle in her mother, Susanna Savilla Hunter, whose responses to crucial events in Austin's life undercut the image of collaborative female resistance. Instead of support, the figure of Susanna Hunter more frequently represents opposition and voices the collective force of cultural condemnation of female ambition. Throughout *Earth Horizon*, Austin traces her recurring sense of abandonment to her relationship with her mother. She describes Susanna's reaction when Austin's first story is published in the *Overland*: "Susie read it aloud to her, but she could never be got to express an interest in it. 'I think you could have made more of it,' Mary finally dragged out of her. Where was now the triumph and encouragement that should go to one's first professional adventure!" (240). After Austin's daughter, Ruth, is born with severe mental disabilities, Austin receives a letter from her mother: "I don't know what you've done, daughter, to have such a judgment upon you" (257). Her mother's blame creates in Austin a "grief too long borne in secret for surface recovery" (257). By quoting her mother's words, Austin creates a competing text documenting women's distance— and difference—from one another, a text that erupts only to be silenced in secret grief where "no one ever does speak to me about it" (257). But if the grief itself is unwordable, the text makes clear with whom the reader is expected to collaborate: Susanna's judgments and recriminations elicit subtle but sure admonitions from the dominant narrative voice, the "I" of the autobiography.

Austin addresses this narrative and emotional disjunction by positioning her mother as a strong activist in the public arena. Involved in the Woman's Christian Temperance Union, Susanna took her daughter with her to meetings. The Prohibition movement and her mother's commitment to it stand out for Austin as a bridge between mother and daughter, between abandonment and love: "I remember the first woman who was allowed to speak in our church on the right of women to refuse to bear children to habitual drunkards, and my mother putting her arm across my knees and taking my hand in one of the few natural gestures of a community of woman interest she ever made toward me" (142). Although Austin is unable to invest her mother with the same subversive feminist tactics she sees in her grandmother, she is careful to strike a balance between Susanna as a model she can claim fully and as one she must repudiate utterly. Instead, Susanna becomes the narrative embodiment of a boundary blurring, upon which the subversive aspects of the autobiography rely. Neither wholly this nor completely that, Susanna exemplifies the cultural obstacles to female creativity that Austin both internalizes and struggles to reject.

Austin clarifies these competing aspects of collaborative female inheritance when she discusses her mother's death. Although she is not with her mother when Susanna dies, Austin is preparing to travel to her. At the hour of Susanna's death, Austin has a vision of her: young, happy, telling her daughter that "there was no need for Mary to take the train now, since everything was well with her" (273). Later, in a telegram from her brother, Austin learns that Susanna's last words were "take care of Mary." Her vision of her mother culminates in an unassailable union never experienced in life, which, coupled with the uncharacteristic tenderness of her mother's final words, offers Austin some consolation for a lifetime of distance. The experience itself is cast in a prophetic and otherworldly tone, which works rhetorically to posit Austin as a medium of her mother's previously unspoken concern, emphasizing the autobiography's claim for Austin's superior spiritual status.

However, the language Austin uses to express her grief at her mother's death reasserts the simultaneous union and division that marked their relationship: "There is an element of incalculable ravening in the loss of your mother; deep under the shock of broken habit and the ache of present grief, there is the psychic wound, the severed root of being; such loss as makes itself felt as the companion of immortality. For how should the branch suffer, torn from the dead tree? It is only when the tree is green that the cut bough bleeds" (273). Although Austin goes back to her grandmother and great-grandmother to assert a prior text that she can claim collaborates in creating her identity, it is the conflicted text Austin makes of her mother's life and death, the image of a "severed root of being" in a matriarchal family tree, that most consistently informs her vision of female subjectivity as multiple—collaborating together but replete with fissures, linked but not identical.

With this representation of female collaboration as decidedly problematic, a site of struggle as much as of support, Austin anticipates the branching developments of feminist theoretical approaches to collaboration during the 1980s and 1990s. Virginia Woolf famously claimed in *A Room of One's Own* (1929) that "we think back through our mothers if we are women"(79), and both American and French feminist critics, such as (most famously) Sandra Gilbert and Susan Gubar as well as Catherine Clément and Hélène Cixous, have long identified collaboration as an important method of understanding women's metaphorical and practical writing strategies. As Bette London has argued, "Positing a form of women's writing that privileges the interactive features of orality . . . collaboration could even be seen to open up the possibility for a model of literary production explicitly feminist in orientation. . . . From this perspective, collaborative writing by women, as it articulates itself in the turn-of-the-century British literary arena, could be seen as the precursor of a self-consciously feminist critical practice that emerged in the academy in the 1970s" (76).[3] While earlier feminist discussions of collaboration tended to describe it as a harmonious process, one emphasizing friendship, equality, and mutual respect, "more recent work tends to emphasize—and often self-consciously stage —its difficulty" (London 88). Austin's construct of a collaborative maternal lineage cannot simultaneously accommodate her mother *and* a vision of utopian solidarity and like-mindedness; always, her mother's presence in the text is a reminder of division, difficulty, and struggle. Despite the counterversions of collaboration offered here—collaboration as an identification with an equally defiant and subversive ancestor, as with Polly, and collaboration as an uneasy affiliation with a recalcitrant and resistant ancestor, as with Susanna—both are equally components of the female inheritance Austin claims as collaborators.

Austin takes this image of division, difficulty, and struggle, which is first associated with her uneasy collaboration with her mother, and ultimately turns it into one of the most fundamental challenges she offers to the reign of the individual author. Austin develops her complex understanding of female subjectivity in her self-construction throughout *Earth Horizon*. Her subjectivity is cleaved, not simply in half but rather into various personae. With remarkable fluidity, some of these personae are subtly differentiated, marked by inconsistent changes in voicing, grammar, or syntax, while others are announced in the text. The most obvious persona is "Mary Austin" the traditionally understood individual author, whose achievements justify the autobiography and who is reconstructed by the text. Closely related is "Mary Austin" the writer-narrator, striving for omniscience but, as she often interrupts her narrative to tell us, frequently baffled at the complexity she encounters in relating her life story. In addition, there are the yoked personae of Mary, Mary-by-herself, and I-Mary, a representation of multiple subjectivity central to the collaborative aspects of the autobiography because Austin associates each persona, directly and indirectly, with her early development as a writer.

As she writes, Austin alternates between the first and the third person, frequently referring to herself as "Mary" or using the subjective or objective case to refer to herself as "she" or "her." Although an awkward narrative approach, her alternation repeatedly challenges the assumed stance of unitary selfhood privileged by traditional forms of male autobiographical writing by announcing these differences within herself rather than suppressing them. Despite its claims to unmediated truth telling, the "I" of autobiography is specifically gendered. Sidonie Smith writes: "Single letter, single sound, the 'I' appears unitary, bold, indivisible. In its very calligraphy and enunciation (in English at least) it defies destabilization, dissemination, diffusion. But that 'I' is gendered and it is male" (79). In *Earth Horizon*, Austin grapples with the obstacles encountered by female writers writing autobiographically in a literary genre conventionally dedicated to telling the life stories of great men, where a woman must claim the narrative authority of the autobiographical "I" in a genre that excludes her as other, while at the same time subverting the constraints of the unitary subjectivity that justifies her writing. In *Earth Horizon*, Austin does both by refashioning the traditional subject of the autobiography, the bold "I," to present herself as multiple selves who never coalesce into a unitary subject or a singular author. The linked personae Austin calls Mary, Mary-by-herself, and I-Mary, in combination with the other divisions of selfhood represented in the text, complicate even this critique. Austin inevitably introduces competing desires and conflicts among the varying deployments of personae. Each of these personae, in their fluid interconnection, forms a part of the collaboration that is *Earth Horizon*, and through them Austin contextualizes the autobiographical "I," revising and revealing it as a collaborative construction when she attributes agency for her writing to a variety of personalities, events, and influences.

On one level, Austin's use of a collaborative mode of narration is pragmatic, a recognition of the multiple selves, multiple voices, and multiple influences she felt defined her writing. On another level, it is an extremely effective writing strategy, anticipating recent work in the collaborative nature of textual production. As we have seen, multiple authorship, whether defined as process or as result, has been difficult to theorize adequately in the humanities in part because the concept of individual authorship has been made to seem inevitable. Collaborative textual production challenges that inevitability. With it depart claims to autonomy, the individual as the site of originality, and the privileged status of the author in the production of a text, all concepts that help consolidate the idea of the self as unitary, organic, and self-knowing, and literature—in this case, autobiography—as a transcendent medium through which experience can be directly represented. Recall again from chapter 1 Martha Woodmansee's point that "from the Middle Ages right down through the Renaissance new writing derived its value and authority with its affiliation with the texts that preceded it, its derivation rather than its deviation from prior texts" (281). For Austin, the idea of derivation from prior texts is a key to her collaborative endeavor in *Earth Horizon*. The prior texts she chooses to identify and claim, however, are not masterpieces of male autobiography; rather, they are the oral stories of women's history, as we have seen, and Native American storytelling, traditions that repeatedly deny the single authority of a named author, traditions that, in other words, refuse the coherent gendered identity of the authorizing "I."

In the introduction to their edited collection *Decolonizing the Subject: The Politics of Gender in Women's Autobiography*, Sidonie Smith and Julia Watson write that "what has been designed as Western autobiography is only one form of 'life-writing.' There are other modes of life story telling, both oral and written, to be recognized, other genealogies of life story telling to be chronicled, other explorations of traditions, current and past, to be factored into the making and unmaking of autobiographical subjects in a global environment" (xviii). If this is so, then Austin asks us to consider another form, one that stresses its collaborative construction. However, even in this, Austin does not fully forgo the authority of the autobiographical "I." Indeed, she cannot, because that "I" signifies an authority Austin wishes to claim, one that gives her entry into the realm of autobiographical representation and helps to limit criticism for transgressing the bounds of gendered expectations of female creativity. Austin herself apparently has the traditional male-gendered template for autobiographical writing in mind when she writes in the introduction, "When first it was proposed to me that I write my autobiography, I anticipated great pleasure in the undertaking, for I thought it meant the re-living of my important occasions, the setting of them in their significant order, and so bringing the events of my life into a pattern consistent with my acutest understanding of them" (vii). Austin understands that ordering events, creating the normative linear narrative, is a part of the pleasure of autobiographical writing, and yet she often assumes the pose of striving to meet, rather than to challenge, the formal expectations of autobiography. We are justified for refusing to take Austin at her word, or at least at her first word, because her forthcoming hint, "I anticipated . . . ," immediately alerts us that this traditional strategy failed. When she continues by writing "but I found that there was more to an autobiography" than her expectations first suggested, including "the choice of incidents," she launches her critique of the tenets of autobiography and the notion of the organic and unified self it seeks to reveal (viii). Austin's critique is linked to the collaborative aspects of *Earth Horizon* at the point when the different representations of "Mary" appear and the stable "I" of the introduction dissolves.

The process of subverting the tenets of formal autobiography continues throughout the introduction, which is signed simply "M. A.," a designation signaling the reader that it corresponds to

Mary Austin, the singular, even familiar, author of the upcoming autobiography. Yet this correspondence between identities traditionally presumed stable is quickly rendered more fluid when Austin seeks to call forth the more prophetic aspects of the autobiography. When she asserts that "it has always been a profound realization of my life that there was a pattern under it" (vii), Austin lays claim to a spiritual essence, a prior text from Native American culture, the "Rain Song of the Sia," which provides the conceptual "Earth Horizon" of her title: "the incalculable blue ring of sky meeting earth, which is the source of experience" (33). This prior text precedes and guides Austin's life story, further undercutting the notion that formal autobiography rests upon and re-creates: that of the self-made subject free from the impingement of culture. Austin insists upon the pattern rather than the more traditional autobiographical frame. By deflecting attention from herself onto the spiritual symbol of another culture, Austin resists the claims to singular genius that autobiography implies.

Austin's implied claim to apprehend, interpret, and include that spiritual symbol has its roots in another form of female collaboration with a long history of neglect or dismissal—that of the female medium. In both the United States and abroad, the late nineteenth and early twentieth centuries saw the growth of women positioning themselves as spiritual mediums and engaging in automatic writing, the process of receiving material from deceased people or other spiritual entities and "automatically" transcribing, sometimes with great difficulty, that material. As London has noted, "Mediums were rarely, if ever, considered as authors, despite the fact that mediumship made many women prolific writers. By the 1910s and 1920s, these women were increasingly of the same sort (in class, education, and professional aspirations) as those who became conventional authors. To recognize mediumship as a form of authorship, then, was to recognize that women often became authors in ways not institutionally legitimated" (8). With Austin's customary ambivalence toward institutionally legitimated forms of authorship—she eschews footnotes in her attempt to delineate an American rhythm in her study of the same name, but she nonetheless utilizes a form of scientific discourse in the text, for example—she is careful to insist that she does more than receive and transcribe. In titling her autobiography after the Native American spiritual concept of Earth Horizon, she is both paying homage to another culture's valuable contribution to her understanding of the meaning of life and filtering that understanding through the construction of that life, including in her "choice of incidents" a wide variety that emphasizes the underlying Native American spirituality that guides her. What's more, her cross-cultural appropriation, while debatably a colonizing maneuver that I will discuss in more detail later, emphasizes the differences between cultures rather than insisting on universality.

The "pattern" Austin identifies in her introduction is itself a multiple construct, affected by her cultural positioning as a heterosexual, white, midwestern female artist struggling for financial and emotional security at a particular historical moment when to be female and to be an artist were considered opposing roles.[4] These elements of the pattern are sometimes in conflict with each other, and Austin must balance her occasional desire for an essential, unchanging identity with her awareness of identity as shifting and contingent. The difficulty of maintaining that balance is evident in the apparent contradictions of the text, the ways in which Austin's representations of her "selves," her attitudes, and her actions sometimes conflict with one another.

One of these points of conflict appears almost immediately in the first-person address throughout the introduction, which seems to claim a coherent subjectivity. However, while the "I" of the introduction is aligned with the signatory initials "M. A.," much of the introduction's purpose is to emphasize and explain the difficulties of maintaining that coherent self in the process of writing autobiographically. Austin elaborates on the difficulty of knowing which events are important and in so doing links the status of authorship with the presence of the pattern: "It is not enough to say that, since one has arrived at the point at which an autobiography is demanded, the pattern has not been wholly defeated" (viii). This passage, along with the entire introduction, alerts her readers to a tension that exists throughout *Earth Horizon*: Austin's affinity for abstract rhetoric, the passive voice, and multiple negative constructions undermine authority while linear assertion gives way to qualifications, digressions, and abstraction. A second tension is evident in Austin's attempt to claim a unified self in the face of a heightened awareness of the fractures in that unity, fractures that are compounded by her acknowledgment of multiple sources of agency. It is an astutely doubled strategy, because by asserting the inspiration of the preexisting pattern, Austin lays claim to a higher authority, yet the intimacy of the first-person address works to coalesce the persona of Mary Austin, author and subject of the ensuing life story.

As Austin interweaves those collaborative forces into her autobiographical narrative, she creates a textual form that is itself a challenge to established forms of autobiographical writing. Once the autobiography proper begins, Austin chooses an unconventional narrative mode to relate her autobiography, assuming a more removed narrative stance by referring to herself in the third person. Rather than apologizing for the shifts between first- and third-person address, she insists on their validity as true to her experience. She is aware she risks critical denouncement: "I must write these things the way they happened to Mary, swiftly flashing, in a flame spurt. . . . Often [the idea, the event] would be new in the thought of her time. And nothing Mary does has so irritated the critics against her as her habit of writing these things in all the shining sharpness of her first perception of them" (216–17). Challenging the expected division between fact and fiction, or between past and present, could make Austin a publishing risk, but she nonetheless vents her annoyance with the strictures of autobiographical expectations: "All this Mary business is a nuisance; having to stop and tell why she did things and what she thought about them" (204). Well into the second half of *Earth Horizon*, Austin interrupts her third-person narrative with a lengthy first-person description of the difficulty and responsibility in writing an autobiography:

> Here I come upon the unfeasible task, the true presentation of a life-story uninformed by the contributory solutions snatched in passing from lives unable to profit by their own instruction. . . . I suppose every life that attains any degree of expressiveness is largely lessoned by these things. . . . I recognize no right of mine to minute particularly in the lives that did not actually press constructively on mine, and at the same time admit my indebtedness to the truth those lives revealed. I am aware that any autobiography written with due regard to such acknowledgments must seem to present the chief figure in it as moving through the ample space of admitted importance. (245–46)

Unhesitatingly revealing that she knows the constraints placed on autobiography do not coincide with the actualities of a life, Austin consistently shifts her notion of autobiography to include the effects of others in both her writing process and her identity. Austin's characteristic abstractness in this address further undermines her authority as a "chief figure" by requiring the participation and substantial interpretative abilities of her readers.

The literary persona of Mary Austin is at once troubling and necessary. Austin works to create this persona, but at the same time she also feels separate from it and separated from others by it. Her discomfort is evident when she returns to her college years later as a published writer: "I was shocked even to find figures warmly remembered out of that so happy intimacy, putting me apart across the years as Mrs. Austin" (175). The distance in this sentence between the "I" who was shocked and the public figure, "Mrs. Austin," can be measured in more than years or accomplishments: the palpable difference between the two identities precludes a return of "happy intimacy." The "I," signifier of identity and indivisibility, cannot traverse the distance to include "Mrs. Austin." The self is divided by the gaze of others, resulting in a loss that Austin does not attempt to suppress or recover. When Austin shifts between first and third person elsewhere in the text, the echo of division is recalled, but so is Austin's insistence on the illusionary intimacy of the autobiographical "I."

The most baffling and intriguing aspect of Austin's autobiography is her representation of Mary, Mary-by-herself, and I-Mary. Austin describes Mary-by-herself as a shy, uncertain persona who most fully feels the absence of her mother's love, while I-Mary is the more confident, capable persona Austin associates with books and, significantly, with her eventual authorship. Mary and Mary-by-herself become conflated identities after what Austin describes as the arrival of I-Mary when Austin was four years old, learning to read a primer with her older brother, Jim. Contrary to autobiography's assumption that "I" "defies destabilization, dissemination, diffusion" (Smith 79), when trying to understand the letter "I," Austin mistakes it for "eye" and her mother must correct her: "I, myself . . . I-Mary" (46). The ensuing experience transforms Austin: "Something turned over inside her; the picture happened. . . . And inside her, I-Mary, looking on. I-Mary, I-Mary, *I-Mary!*" (46). This scene of literal "self" awareness comes to Austin as a surprise, suggesting that women's subjectivity is not a foregone conclusion, an inevitable event. This inaugural moment of subjectivity functions as a key to Austin's association of I-Mary with the ability to write and with her conception of collaboration: Austin bestows selfhood onto I-Mary; only I-Mary can withstand criticism and remain unaffected by it. I-Mary does not replace the other persona, Mary-by-herself; she assists her.

Austin consistently writes of I-Mary as a distinctly separate entity, although she is clearly aware that I-Mary is indistinguishable from Mary or Mary-by-herself to others: "She came so suddenly and always so inevitably that I doubt if anybody ever knew about her, or could have been made to understand" (46). Austin insists on I-Mary's reality: "Certainly she would not have described the I-Mary experience as a feeling. It was a reality, as real

as when in dreams you pick up your feet and go floating in the desired direction. . . . I-Mary was as real as that" (74). She steadily
upholds this sense of an alternate reality as a valuable component
of her creative ability and spiritual insight: "When you were
I-Mary, you could see Mary-by-herself as part of the picture, and
make her do things that, when you were she, could not be done at
all; such as walking a log high over the creek, which gave Mary-
by-herself cold prickles even to think about" (74). Austin's association of I-Mary with writing explains her importance: "Always
until she was quite grown up, I-Mary was associated with the
pages of books. The mere sight of the printed page would often
summon her, and since her coming was comfortably felt . . . it was
sought in the contemplation of print" (46). Because it was in the
process of learning to read that Austin had her first experience of
"self" awareness, the link between I-Mary and printed text was
tightly forged. I-Mary would then, quite understandably, become
a collaborative partner later in Austin's life when she began the
difficult and demanding process of writing. I-Mary offered not
only comfort but also a singularly trustworthy experience of ability and confidence unmatched elsewhere.

The dangers of a life as a woman writer are emphasized later
in Austin's autobiography, when the metaphor of I-Mary travers-
ing the log reappears linked with authorship: "There was that
stream of knowingness which ever since adolescence I had felt going on in me, supplying deficiencies, affording criterions of judgment, creating certainties for which no warrant was to be found
in my ordinary performance, setting up in me the conviction,
which as experience I have named I-Mary, that all I know has always been known by me and used as known. At any rate, it was
as I-Mary walking a log over the creek, that Mary-by-herself
couldn't have managed, that I wrote two slender little sketches"
(230–31). The "two slender sketches" signify a beginning that
I-Mary literally enables because she brings to Austin the experience of a competent self and binds that experience to the realm of
books and writing.

Austin's understanding of I-Mary fluctuates throughout her autobiography. What is claimed as a separate entity, coming to her at age four, and whose appearance can be coaxed, becomes the name for an experience of self-knowledge that Austin takes as evidence of the pattern she claims underlies her life. Although Austin's conception of I-Mary shifts, she remains in a collaborative relationship with Austin, upholding her as a writer, giving her confidence and self-assurance. As a separate entity, I-Mary is a cocreator of Austin's "slender little sketches." I-Mary also implicitly collaborates in *Earth Horizon* when she is transformed into Austin's experience of "the pressure of knowledge, all the knowledge in the world" (154).

Just as Austin must find a way to include female ancestry as a prior text that collaborates in the construction of her identity, Austin also searches for a way to claim her religious inheritance; in this case, however, it is a text she radically revises by incorporating Native American beliefs. Austin felt ill suited to the Methodist beliefs of her family and community, feeling that "Heaven sounded more boring than church" (53), and she eventually links a long period of spiritual unhappiness and alienation to her participation in organized religion. As a young child, Austin had an experience she describes as "earth and sky and tree and wind-blown grass and the child in the midst of them came alive together with a pulsing light of consciousness. . . . I remember the child looking everywhere for the source of this happy wonder, and at last she questioned—'God?'—because it was the only awesome word she knew" (371, n. 13). Here Austin seems to fulfill the traditional obligations of autobiography by linking herself to an experience of universality, and the search to recover this experience is central to Austin's eventual conception of herself as a writer. But Austin's apparently traditional approach also functions as an acknowledgment of her difference from those around her, steadfast Methodists with whom she is at odds even as a child. Austin's description of God is not a claim to wholeness but instead is evidence of her incompleteness, the partiality of subjectivity, a point she emphasizes when the feeling leaves her for much of her childhood. It is also one of many narrative episodes in which Austin's struggle to find usable prior texts illuminates the role of collaboration in her development as a writer; she regularly describes her achievements, both personal and professional, as the culmination of external sentient forces acting in relationship with her, forces she reorganizes and revises for inclusion in her autobiography.

Even after it is revised to incorporate God experientially and I-Mary's function as granting transcendent knowledge, Austin's Methodist religious training cannot sustain crisis. During her adolescence, following the deaths of both her beloved sister and her father, I-Mary disappears, along with the experience of unity and unique individual vision Austin associates with her: "No longer were things experienced vizualized [*sic*] as things seen. . . . God was not found under the wide elms and cloudy maples with which the way to school was lined. There was no sort of emergency in which I-Mary came, nor answered to if called" (94). Apart from suggesting the difficulties of adolescence, Austin offers no concise explanation for I-Mary's disappearance, but we can find a hint when she writes, "Against the trauma of grief children are doubly helpless" (91). Austin's helplessness ceases only after her college graduation, when she moves to California with her family. This move west, although a dubious one financially, since the Hunters were ill prepared for the rigors of dry farming and subsistence living, is established in the autobiography as a key prelude to Austin's spiritual breakthrough and her eventual writing success. In California, she directs her mind to learning about the desert landscape, its indigenous peoples, and the animals there and is "released from the long spiritual drought that was coincident with her commitment to organized religion" (198). This "release" enabled Austin to incorporate collaborative aspects of Native American oral literature into her spiritual perceptions and writing, a point I will return to shortly.

Feminist theories of autobiography show us the risks Austin takes with her representations of multiple selfhood traced across prior texts. Austin's metaphor of the log high over the creek, which she uses twice in nearly identical phrasing, emphasizes the risks women take when they write and the fear they face of being unable to maintain a necessary delicate balance between success and failure, praise and blame. The stakes of writing for women here are high, and terrifying. Austin's initial surprise at the concept of subjectivity, the "I" of "I-Mary," and her subsequent experience of her as separate, arriving to protect her, comfort her, or achieve for her, reveal another dilemma of female authorship: not granted subjectivity, women must create it and wrestle for it. While it is possible to read Austin's experience as a form of multiple personality brought on by the trauma of her mother's physical and emotional distance and later integrated into a single persona, the autobiography does not bear this reading out. Although I-Mary is mentioned less frequently as the narrative focuses on Austin's adulthood, continuing shifts between first- and third-person narration reveal that Austin never achieves a single, unified subjectivity, just as her autobiographical narrative never becomes smoothly or consistently linear.[5]

Late both in her life and in her autobiography, Austin emphasizes her ability to re-create herself. Austin was noted, perhaps even notorious, for acts of self-creation and calculated self-promotion during her lifetime, but as she matured, some of her most notable feats of self-creation concerned her commitment to Native American issues and artistic expression. Without formal training in literature, ethnography, or anthropology, Austin wrote numerous short stories with Native Americans as her theme, "re-expressions" of what she called "Amerindian verse." She sometimes took on the behaviors, associations, and beliefs of Native Americans in her personal life, often at the cost of pointed ridicule that reveals a thinly veiled contempt for both Austin and for Native Americans.[6] We might wonder why a woman who experienced the status of outsider so bitterly throughout her life would consistently re-create herself as a target for criticism? The answer may be related to Austin's experience of subjectivity through the appearance of I-Mary, her association of I-Mary with writing, and her experience of Native American beliefs as usable, prior texts for her formulation of collaborative identity. In *Earth Horizon*, Austin writes of an encounter with the Paiutes: "She entered into their lives, the life of the campody, the strange secret life of the tribe, the struggle of Whiteness with Darkness, the struggle of the individual soul with the Friend-of-the-Soul-of-Man. She learned what it meant; how to prevail; how to measure her strength against it. Learning that, she learned to write" (289).

Austin's dichotomous and elusive view of Native American spirituality constructs the Native American as an exotic other whose wisdom both surpasses those of Austin's Anglo-American culture and justifies her appropriation of it. Here again, Austin emphasizes the partial over the unitary, but unlike her self-construction, her representation of Native Americans is decidedly stereotypical; cast into the realm of writing, Austin's encounter with the Paiutes emphasizes their mystery and primitiveness, their strangeness because primitive. Although for Austin, a charge of primitive would be a positive thing, the autobiography acts to recapitulate the cultural stereotypes of the Noble Indian— without power to stop his own destruction; with wisdom to offer those whites (such as Austin) wise enough to recognize it.

Despite Austin's polarization of Native American spirituality into light and dark, individual and universal, her attribution is clear nonetheless: she learned her craft from the Paiute Indians she encountered in the Southwest. The personal struggle, the collaborative relationship formed out of that struggle, and the experience of eventual literary success echo Austin's earliest experiences of texts: reading, and then writing, with I-Mary to guide her. For Austin, autobiography is a form in which she can credit the forces of her life, and the distinct personae of her self, for their collaborative relationship in her writing. Austin acknowledges this relationship when she writes that this form of prayer "is described here because it proved, though in the beginning I had no notion that this would be the case, the answer to the problem of creative activity" (277). Although here Austin attributes her ability to write to the Paiutes, the experiences do not so much suggest that Austin found a substitute for I-Mary and the pleasures of selfhood that she conveyed as that she found another manifestation of that experience, one that integrated her unconventional spiritual beliefs with her experience of subjectivity residing in texts.

Near the end of her life, Austin published *The American Rhythm: Studies and Reexpressions of Amerindian Songs* (1930), perhaps her most extensive claim to expertise in American Indian literary forms. Criticized for being inadequately researched and documented, and presented in Austin's own rather mystical vocabulary, *The American Rhythm* nonetheless utilized the collaborative strategies she valued elsewhere in her writing, and it did help to solidify her reputation as an expert on Native American literature. In *Earth Horizon*, Austin even claims to have a "far-off and slightly mythical Indian ancestor of whose reality I am more convinced by what happened to me among Indians than by any objective evidence" (267), an assertion that one critic appropriately questions as "problematic if Austin made such a claim to enhance her status as an Indian expert" (Langlois, "Marketing the American Indian" 165). Any biological Native American ancestry is doubtful, and it is more likely Austin was simultaneously appealing to a sense of spiritual compatibility, appropriating Native American literature and culture in response to her own need to establish herself publicly as an expert on Native American concerns, and searching for a way in which to record her cross-cultural experience in a genre not meant to accommodate divergences from its established boundaries.

We can recognize Austin's degree of cultural privilege—the status she already had as an American writer, her connections to the publishing world, the intellectual and creative communities that functioned to support her—when we compare Austin's claim for an Native American ancestor with Mourning Dove's concern (discussed in chapter 3) that too much attention to her possible white ancestry would deflect from her identity as a Native American writer. Both Austin and Mourning Dove recognize the challenge to literary authority and authorship implicit in collaboration: both writers recognize that claims to dual or multiple ancestry upset cultural ideas of unified selfhood and therefore unitary authorship. For Austin, such a Native American ancestor would enhance her perceived authenticity; even a passing query, such as she makes in *Earth Horizon*, functions to focus her authority to speak for and, to some degree, as a Native American. For Mourning Dove, however, the thrust of *Cogewea*, from the frontispiece to the multiple naming that takes place on the title page, is to emphasize her authority to speak as an authentic Native American, an authority both granted by her status as a mixed blood and put in doubt because of it. To point to white ancestry, Mourning Dove feared rightly, would undermine her authority since, at the time, a truly *American* literature was seen as arising from Anglo-American experience.

Austin's gesture to Native American ancestry is debatably a colonizing maneuver; in addition, she claims expertise without an intimate understanding of the tribes she studies or their languages, and her "reexpressions" tell us considerably more of Austin and her growing confidence than they do of historical Native American literature. While intention, to the degree that we can recover it, does not justify appropriation, it can render that behavior understandable. While Austin describes her use of Native American themes as an active collaborative relationship, it is unknown to what degree, if any, the Native Americans she knew agreed to that collaboration or even saw it in those terms.[7] On the other hand, and as we saw in the Mourning Dove–McWhorter collaboration, contemporary scholars of Native American literature have shown repeatedly that "authority" and the signature of the author do not function in the same ways in Native American literary forms that they do in a European tradition. Arnold Krupat writes that "American Indian literature, until very recently, has been notoriously lacking in its possession of named authors"

(120). The absence of an author's signature as well as the oral, performative basis of Native American literature make it traditionally a collaborative literature. Although Austin finds a compatible understanding of the collaborative nature of literature and rediscovers her childhood feeling of unity through her encounters with Native American cultures, she can never fully enter a tribal identity. Nor, I would argue, does she claim to, at least in *Earth Horizon*. Austin is careful to position herself in her autobiography as the enthusiastic and grateful student, a positioning that emphasizes a collaborative relationship but that also keeps her marginal, a white woman outside. Even the term Austin employed to describe her Native American influenced poetry, "reexpressions," has layers of interpretations. On the one hand, the term has connotations of superiority, presumably conferred by Austin's race and formal education. On the other hand, "reexpressions" points to Austin's active participation in re-producing a prior Native American literary form. She does not, in other words, present her poetry as original, either as the first or as the final word on the matter. Her reexpressions reveal her position as collaborator. Late in her life, Austin keeps to the lessons of that life by not abandoning the insight provided by her marginal position and by trusting in a collaborative process despite its cost in criticism and rebuke.

Earth Horizon is a provocative life story, detailing the conflicted desires of a child to be loved, a woman to be accepted, and a writer to be esteemed. Austin negotiates between the unitary subjectivity that is a generic component of autobiographical writing and her own deeply felt understanding of herself as multiple personalities whose ancestry and involvements with others all collaborate in her writing and in the creation of her identity as a writer. By refashioning the subject of her autobiography to incorporate multiple personae, the role of female ancestors in collaborative identity, and the importance of cross-cultural relationships in her writing, Austin revises the very form of autobiographical writing and insists on the need, particularly for women writers, to acknowledge the role of multiplicity and difference in their writing. Yet even more poignantly, *Earth Horizon* reminds its readers that to follow where her vision of creativity leads, a woman must create herself, going against a web of social conventions, often without support and in the face of ridicule and humiliation. The bold "I" of the autobiographic adventure remains bold in *Earth Horizon,* but it is no longer indivisible after Austin uncovers the hidden costs and struggles required to maintain it.

5

Collaboration and Contradiction in the Western Memoir

Ivan Doig, Mary Clearman Blew, and William Kittredge

And the voices from the past began to form a summer chorus.
IVAN DOIG, *THIS HOUSE OF SKY*

And so the story becomes a kind of communal novel, with twenty or more voices contributing their fragments of the known events, another hundred voices in the chorus, and one of the voices mine, retelling and revising, until the shifting truth spreads its own wings and casts the long shadow of fiction.
MARY CLEARMAN BLEW, *BALSAMROOT*

Over something like three decades my family played out the entire melodrama of the nineteenth-century European novel.
WILLIAM KITTREDGE, *HOLE IN THE SKY*

THE EPIGRAPHS that begin this chapter remind us of what much contemporary literary theory insists upon: the body is textual, but so is the voice, so that as we consider what we mean by "stories" and how we might interpret them, we also have to consider that part of what any story means may be found in the interrelationships between the story that is told, who tells it, who hears it, and the cultural and historical contexts in which all are multiply embedded. Greg Sarris makes this point when he writes that "storytelling is a fundamental aspect of culture, and stories are used in a number of ways and for a multitude of purposes. Stories can work as cultural indexes for appropriate or inappropriate behavior. They can work to oppress or to liberate, to confuse or to enlighten. So much depends on who is telling the story and who is listening and the specific circumstances of the exchange" (4).[1] If we understand stories as neither inherently liberating nor implicitly damaging, then to tell stories at all is to find oneself already engaged—or perhaps enmeshed—in a collaborative process of exchange in which meaning is dependent upon the complex and specific elements of that exchange.

The oral basis of storytelling—which notably is not governed by copyright law—forms the foundation of the written western memoirs I discuss here, Ivan Doig's *This House of Sky: Landscapes of a Western Mind* (1978) and *Heart Earth* (1993), Mary Clearman Blew's *All But the Waltz* (1991) and *Balsamroot* (1994), and William Kittredge's *Hole in the Sky* (1992).[2] Although Ivan Doig, Mary Clearman Blew, and William Kittredge approach orality and the concept of voice in storytelling with varying degrees of skepticism, all incorporate what they represent as others' voices into their memoirs. These voices and the stories they tell are not introduced into these memoirs as accessories to a "primary" text or accompaniments to the (single, individual) author's story; inescapably transformed through the creative processes of writing, others' voices are included as integral literary and conceptual aspects of these collaborative memoirs despite the single byline each carries. Perhaps more centrally, as the stories that comprise these memoirs are told and read, they construct western identity in fundamental and often conflicting ways. In each of these texts, an emphasis on voice becomes a way of representing the conflicted, sometimes mutually exclusive versions of authentic westernness and their relation to the multiply positioned collaborative writer. As an example of collaborative oral-become-written storytelling, the literary genre of memoir informs us about western identities in localized western landscapes at specific historical moments, and as this literary process works itself out in each of the western memoirs I discuss here, the process of constructing identity becomes a visibly collaborative endeavor, a work in progress continually revised by the stories we tell about it, frequently forcing the writers either to confront or to displace contradictions between the western identities celebrated as authentic by their texts and their own differences from those identities.

Doig, Blew, and Kittredge, all award-winning western writers, were born within a decade of one another, in the late 1930s or early 1940s, and, except for *This House of Sky*, which first appeared in 1978, all published their memoirs in the early 1990s. By representing the spaces of their Montana and Oregon childhoods, these western memoirists focus on a regionally similar time and place in western history as it is refracted through a variety of perspectives and personalities. Using these various voices in their memoir, each writer utilizes collaboration, with its inherent rejection of a unified text, very literally to construct the memoir: collecting and passing on stories remembered or recovered from the past, including stories gleaned or even directly excerpted from diaries or letters. As we have seen with Mary Austin, autobiographical writing is always engaged with re-creating specific textual representations of identity. Unlike formal autobiography, however, the autobiographical genre of memoir makes no claim to seamless representation or factual recall. From the outset, memoir is fragmentary; ostensibly, it situates itself as one person's literary representation of the tentative and often unreliable fruits of memory. Each of the memoirs I examine here explicitly calls on others' memories to create, question, or confirm events from the past. Consciously positioning memoirs as fragmentary does not mean, however, that the desire for coherent identity so integral to other autobiographical writing is absent; on the contrary, a yearning for coherence often drives these memoirs, creating unexpected disruptions and curious textual reversals. At some point, each of the memoirs asserts familiar essentialistic, even mythic, versions of western identity. Because I see the impact of collaboration within these memoirs, versions of an essential western identity are not fully convincing, either as a literary strategy or as a claim for universal truth. Instead, authority is dispersed in the texts through stories and storytelling; the texts (although not necessarily the writers) perform so as to refuse any unitary idea of westernness even when particular individual stories may advocate for a single authentic or universal western identity. Most interesting is the problem of identity these textual reversals suggest: the memoirists themselves are in frequent conflict with the models of identity they put forth.

In a part of the country where individualism is touted as a sacred story, Blew, Doig, and Kittredge see western identity as deeply intertwined with specific western landscapes and with the stories we tell about the landscapes in which we live. In both of his memoirs, Doig incorporates stories collected from people from his childhood, and in *Heart Earth*, he relies on selections from his mother's letters to his uncle in order to shape the text. By highlighting their words, Doig insists on multiple authorial presences throughout each memoir. In addition to the collaborations within each memoir, these two memoirs also collaborate with each other, particularly when *Heart Earth* returns to the question of identity when it attempts to represent the absent mother from *This House of Sky*. But in the process of reconstructing a childhood past, Doig privileges a nostalgic and essentialistic version of the rural folk that the memoirist's persona simultaneously celebrates and rejects. The resulting class tensions—between the writer as intellectual and the folk as uneducated, between the writer as thriving outside of the fictional Montana landscape and the folk as elementally linked to it—tell an alternative story of western identity and denial. In *All But the Waltz*, Blew likewise collaborates with letters passed down to her; hers were penned to an unknown audience by her surveyor great-grandfather and given to her by her grandmother. In *Balsamroot*, Blew turns to her Aunt Imogene's collection of five-year diaries to understand her connection to her aunt's life. In this way, *Balsamroot* returns to a key family story preserved in *All But the Waltz*, revising Imogene's story from the earlier memoir. In the explicit collaborations with her great-grandfather and beloved aunt, Blew challenges the viability of essentialized identities for western women and men, but in the final pages of *Balsamroot*, Blew reactivates a mythic western identity to claim as her own. Kittredge approaches collaboration more holistically in *Hole in the Sky*, passionately arguing for the importance of stories that help us recognize and value our interconnectedness with the rest of the world. Kittredge's construction of western identity rests on a presumably clear opposition between authentic stories and false stories, where authentic stories tell of interconnectedness and community and recognize a preexisting sacredness or wholeness, and false stories stress isolation, control, and individual acquisition. Ironically, however, Kittredge privileges the first kind of story and tells the second, leading the memoir to perform a more complex and ambivalent version of storytelling than Kittredge explicitly urges.

In his first memoir of his Montana childhood, *This House of Sky*, Doig's initial intention is to pay tribute to his father, Charlie Doig, and to "a way of life that seemed to be passing with him" (viii). Although Doig's father and Doig's grandmother Bessie Ringer are presented as the story's focus, the structure of the memoir instead establishes Doig's characterization of himself as the narrative center. Indeed, *This House of Sky* acts as a loving thank-you to his father and grandmother, but Doig's younger version of himself is the reason for the memoirist's gratitude and is therefore represented as the focus of their lives and the subject of the memoir. By recounting the construction of the young Doig's subjectivity though an investigation of the adults surrounding him, the text gives us the "landscapes" of not just one "western mind" but two: the semi-idealized Old West of the past as it is symbolized by Charlie and Bessie, and the New West as it is symbolized by Doig. But here, too, because it is so explicitly collaborative, refusing to cohere into a rhetorical or historical unity, the memoir itself is of at least two minds. Others' perspectives introduce contradictions and gaps that encourage alternate readings that undermine Doig's carefully crafted nostalgic framework.

This House of Sky offers the reader a textual Montana that is nonetheless recognizable today, boasting scarce population in comparison to the expansive grandeur of the land, endless hard physical labor, low wages, and plenty of bars. Doig uses precise place names and sweeping physical descriptions to anchor his text in an apparently realistic yet stylistically romantic mode. To secure this nostalgic re-creation of the past, Doig carefully resists the negative and avoids lingering on events or emotions with the obvious potential to wound, shock, or anger; instead, a sense of inevitability and fondness permeates this textual landscape. For example, Doig privileges the nostalgic when constructing his textual persona: he was not a boy wounded by a fractured family, but a man strengthened by those fractures and the opportunity to witness the love and work that went into bridging them. He may have been "miffed" at his grandmother's apparent nonchalance when he must wear a knee bandage to correct a knee fracture, but he ultimately praises her for being "the best possible company" for his temporary handicap: "that which shrugged it off and silently told me I had better do the same" (142). He may have been curious over his father's baffling lack of consideration when, during trips to town for groceries, Charlie leaves his mother-in-law angrily waiting in the car as he drinks and socializes in various bars, but Doig emphasizes that both his father and his grandmother were "an alliance, corded together only by the bloodline which knotted in me, and perhaps the best that could have been expected of them was the wary civility of allies" (157). Textual and familial unity is the focus, and young Doig is the necessary center making it possible.

Although *This House of Sky* inevitably recounts episodes that are open to readers' various interpretations and judgments, it attempts to displace the challenges presented by those alternative points of view. For example, his father, wracked by the death of his wife, Berneta, is a minimally responsible parent: young Ivan is witness to bouts of his father's temper and depression, and the remote, isolated location of his father's ranching jobs means that

Ivan frequently is boarded out with strangers in town. Even under the best circumstances, the sheer workload forced on Charlie Doig leaves him little time for attentive parenting. Instead, the memoir lingers on its presentations of affectionate, humorous, gentle recollections of Charlie Doig, Bessie Ringer, Ivan, and their friends. Indeed, repressing the negative aspects of Doig's childhood—not necessarily specific events but anything other than an understanding, cheerful response on the memoirist's part to them —helps to construct the nostalgic sense of a rough and tough time past: "The pattern to all this," Doig asserts, "was jagged but constant. . . . Everyone treated me fondly if a bit absentmindedly" (158). For many readers, part of the textual pleasure of this memoir is in the way it makes available a cultural fantasy of "the good ole' days" when even few resources, relentless poverty, physical overwork, and dramatically constricted choices leave no physical traces or emotional scars.

Through its collaborative construction and emphasis, however, this fantasy incorporates a presence most cultural illusions of the past West emphatically avoid: women. In a West that overvalues the lone, inarticulate man dispensing his own brand of outlaw justice, women's stories, which generally do not celebrate violence, isolation, or silence, have been frequently neglected or erased. Doig's initial desire to retrace his childhood and pay tribute to his father is not unusual; canonical literature, at least, is rife with stories of a boy's emergence into adulthood and of his relationship with his father. Nor would the absence of fully drawn female characters from this almost prototypical male coming-of-age story be unlikely: cultural scripts of marginalized and male-identified women—women as dead, devouring, or dedicated mothers, as long-suffering wives, muselike mistresses, or half-hidden servants—play out endlessly in our literature, telling stories of male desire that have too often been presented as the whole story. What is unusual about this memoir is the way it reshapes that desire into a story that explicitly emphasizes the fractures and suppressions of a western identity forged from women's absences. For example, Doig rectifies his initial erasure of his grandmother. In his 1992 preface, Doig describes how he remembers forgetting his grandmother Bessie Ringer and then altering the story he wanted, the portrait of the artist and his father he thought he was writing, in order to write the story that would include her: "As I tried to sort through life one more time, it became clear to me that what I'd been thinking of as a book about my father needed to be a book about her as well" (x). In its representation of women, the memoir confronts the pain that in other places it avoids. Doig's mother's death creates a palpable and sustained absence in the text, which he will attempt to address even more directly in *Heart Earth*.

Thus, in the structure of the memoir, two women—mother and grandmother—frame the story, and Doig's grandmother's life is threaded into that of young Ivan and his widower father. Yet, even with his deliberate inclusion of women, Doig's memoir is produced from the gaps and fissures, truths and falsehoods, of his and others' memories. As a writer, Doig knows that he has "prod[ded] away at all versions" of the story in order to "summon a kind of truth" rather than full meaning (14). Returning to Montana in order to remember and to record other's memories for *This House of Sky*, he selects and sometimes stumbles upon people whose stories eventually blend with and enhance his own, preserving an oral history. Doig repeatedly announces the memoir's collaborative structure, thus paying tribute to a range of those voices by giving them their own authority in the text; italics indicate when someone else's memory is inscribed, when someone else's story has joined the chorus: "Voices kept helpfully arriving. . . . My grandmother in particular would often meet one of my questions with 'Well, I don't just know about that, you better go ask so-and-so.' . . . Three or four times a year, another voice of so-and-so into the tape recorder" (viii). His father's friend Clifford's voice is distinct: "*Well, hell, y'know, me an' Charlie was like brothers. Closer, maybe. I seen your dad was havin' a hard time gettin' over your mother's passin' away. I don't think he ever did get over it, in a way"* (15). The self-generated, fully self-known individual celebrated by both formal male autobiography and the formulaic Western is recast in this memoir as fragmented and composed of questions and uncertainties that the memoirist is unable to answer. The collaborative structure of the text insures that there are no simple or exclusive identities here. Even Doig's desire to recognize and celebrate his father and his grandmother for the commitment they made to raise him is based in his recognition that they did so amid the tensions of uncertain identities and uneasy affiliations.

That celebration is, of course, Doig's stated goal, and the text overtly meets it. Yet achieving it ultimately places Doig, as writer and memoirist, in a contradictory and difficult position relative to what his memoir ostensibly celebrates. Although the text represents Charlie and Bessie, son-in-law and mother-in-law, father and grandmother, as overcoming tremendous temperamental obstacles as they join together to raise Ivan, they are also represented stereotypically. Bessie's character is fused with sentimentalized portraits of rural western women when she is cast as the enduring, nearly ageless caretaker: "It comes as a continual surprise to me to realize that even here, where she first came into my life, my grandmother already was nearly sixty years old. Everything I can remember of this time has the tint of her ageless energy" (141). Disappointed by her irresponsible husband, Bessie doggedly shifts her attentions to her children and eventually to her deceased daughter's family, her grandchild Ivan, and his father, Charlie. She commits deeply to Ivan and eventually to Charlie, but in emphasizing her loyalty and devotion, the text is curiously silent about her relationships with her other children. Except for a brief visit to her son Paul in Australia, whom she had not seen in twenty-five years, and the mention of another son who calls her regularly before her death, Bessie's life revolves around her daughter's family with single-minded devotion. Charlie too is represented stereotypically. He is the quintessential western loner, a tough but fair boss with an enviable work ethic. Charlie admits he needs help only in that most obscure of areas for men, parenting, and then only when an impending medical crisis forces his hand. Like Bessie, he labors physically with a determination matched only by his devotion to his son, who he decides to raise as "a miniature of how he himself lived" (54).

The use of these stereotypes helps solidify the nostalgia of this backward glance and, since nostalgic reconstructions of the West and its inhabitants fit most seamlessly with cultural fantasies of the West that require we repress what Patricia Limerick has famously termed its "legacy of conquest," nostalgia itself becomes equated with authenticity. Although the family unit—a man, his son, and his mother-in-law—initially appears as an innovative challenge to the fundamental, role-driven heterosexual unit, it ultimately functions merely as a variation of it, reinforcing the most traditional conceptions of the insular, nuclear family. Although there is enormous cultural power amassed in stereotypes, they are also risky strategies to pursue, even when the literary goal seems to be a positive one. In an essay exploring African American writer Zora Neale Hurston's controversial representation of folk culture in her novel *Their Eyes Were Watching God*, Hazel Carby highlights the risks writers run when relying upon stereotyped cultural images: "Hurston . . . assumed that she could obtain access to, and authenticate, an individualized social consciousness through a utopian reconstruction of the historical moment of her childhood in an attempt to stabilize and displace the social contradictions and disruption of her contemporary moment. . . . In Hurston's work, the rural black folk become an aesthetic principle, a means by which to embody a rich oral culture. Hurston's representation of the folk is not only a discursive displacement of the historical and cultural transformation of migration, but also is a creation of a folk who are outside of history" (77). My intention here is not to appropriate the insights derived from studies of African American literature, for certainly that literature has its own unique and complex tradition. Still, there are useful parallels between Hurston and Doig, if only as writers engaged in difficult strategies of representing their childhoods to a reading audience with predetermined, stereotypical expectations regarding the rural folk of the respective cultures.

One of the clearest places to see the difficulties Doig finds himself in when representing his father and grandmother as rural, and thus authentic, Montana folk is in "Ivory," the text's most stylistically abrupt section. "Ivory" begins with Doig's departure to college in Chicago, spans his college years and early writing career and his courtship and marriage to Carol, and concludes with the realization that his father is dying. In an effort to spring himself "free of the past" by going east to school in Chicago, Doig leaves Montana in the belief that education will change him, liberating him from his past, if not erasing it (236). To some degree it does, freeing him from the grueling seasonal ranch labor done by his father and grandmother. However, an internal contradiction in taking a nostalgic approach to the past is immediately present: Doig's text aims to celebrate precisely those things he seeks to escape and, moreover, it is Doig's successful escape—he eventually earns a doctorate and leaves Montana for Washington—that enables the production of the memoir celebrating the life he rejected.

Focused on Doig's life away from Montana, the "Ivory" section is truncated and choppy, lacking the lyricism, detail, or eloquence that comprise Doig's consciously honed writing style in other sections of the memoir. The shift in rhetorical approach away from "writing it all as highly charged as poetry" (x) emphasizes the strained relationship the New West has with the old and highlights irresolvable elements of the western identity Doig simultaneously privileges and rejects. His grandmother's letters are literally folksy: "*Well dear time for another few lines to let you know that Dad and I are both fine. And hope you are to . . . . Is the weather good where you are. We are haveing Indian Summer but it gets cold nites*" (241). Bessie Ringer's casual punctuation and incorrect spelling stand out against the background of Doig's reiteration of his college years, revealing the distance he has traveled from home in terms of class and educational privilege. Although Doig attempts to displace a confrontation with this class difference, arguing that "even with a doctorate on my wall I was hopelessly a writer rather than a professor" (viii), the ungrammatical, idiosyncratic discourse that Doig emphasizes as his grandmother's "voice" irresolvably distinguishes itself from his own carefully eloquent voice. While Doig's inclusion of his grandmother's letters is one of the ways in which the text employs collaboration to create multiple views of the West, this particular collaboration uncovers deep ambivalence about the past it ostensibly aims to preserve.

Although the most obvious example of *This House of Sky*'s collaborative approach is in its inclusion of various voices, the memoir also acknowledges a more diverse West than we might expect: "In that time I puzzled up into three other faces which were strange to me—the black faces of Rose Gordon, Taylor Gordon, and Bob Gordon" (88). The Gordons pass quickly in and out of Doig's remembered landscape but not before Taylor Gordon's voice remembers the Harlem Renaissance, a literary movement largely ignored in studies of American literature prior to the 1970s. It is an important inclusion, bringing into view what is usually repressed, not just in settlement stories of the West but, until recently, in most discussions of American literary contributions. Doig briefly touches on the underlying racism the Gordons encountered when they met "the transplanted Scots, my father's family and the others who had never seen black faces before and in all likelihood didn't care for them when they did" (92). Doig's text reiterates his own immigrant history here, but it also reveals his own racial privilege when it records that he doesn't know, doesn't have to know, whether his neighbors and family welcomed the Gordons or feared them. Despite Doig's concerted efforts to create a text that is inclusive, one that refuses gendered or formal literary expectations of autobiographical writing, Doig's story is solidly that of white, recently arrived settlers. The history he represents is the history these settlers and their descendants prefer to remember. We see this most clearly in Doig's representations of Native Americans.

The memoir begins with his mother's death and concludes with his father's and grandmother's deaths, but death also haunts the interior of the memoir in far less visible ways. Although the memoir presents an African American presence with some insight, it lapses into stereotypical and disturbing literary characterizations of Native Americans. Doig describes the Montana landscape with a classic sleight-of-pen: "A new country had been declared here, bigger than some entire states in the East and vacant for the taking. More than vacant, evacuated" (19). Although Doig's telling of it briefly acknowledges the Native Americans' "ragged retreat," his vagueness elides the reality of white conquest, creating instead a tribe of "vanished" Indians leaving only "empty acres" (20). Doig frames his story with one of America's greatest myths about western identity: white progress. By repressing differences between that story and the perspective of those who "vanished," Doig creates an empty wilderness, awaiting settlement. In a subtle parallel to the text's other absence—his mother—we are invited as readers to mourn "emptiness," to see it as loss, and to fill it with presence, in this case with the presence of those white settlers driven forward by that most valued of traits, "an outcropping of the family vein of stubbornness," where the representative immigrating Doigs "clearly went about life as if it was some private concoction they had just thought up" (24). Doig's recollections of pasturing sheep on the Blackfeet Reservation is a salute to stock images of Native Americans: "squinty leather-colored people, men with black braids dropping tiredly from under their cowboy hats, women so fat they seemed to waddle even standing still . . . entire families drunk by midday, cars racketing away with bodies spilled half out the windows" (209). Native Americans are made the guilty victims of alcohol, and references to midday drunkenness invoke a stereotypical image of laziness. By constructing a guilty, lazy band of Indians, Doig suppresses the historical reality of white alcohol trading, of poverty and disease, of land stealing, and of Native American resistance, survival, and creativity, and readers are left with a classic example of making what is different into what is entirely alien. Indians become other in Doig's text, while privilege and a sense of entitlement accrue to young Ivan and his father: "Since the Blackfeet never appeared out on their own landscape, we took advantage of the emptiness to become steady poachers" (209). Although Doig acknowledges the harsh unfairness of his remembered judgments—and in his role as historian, these attitudes appear in the memoir as consonant with the judgments arrived at by generations of white Americans in the absence of an alternative history—Native Americans are nonetheless portrayed as merely minor obstacles to a placid vision of the past.

Whether it is used to construct an ahistorical band of drunken Indians or an ageless grandmother devoted to her grandson and his father, nostalgia is itself an attempt at forgetting; we remember things as we wish they were, which is to say that we remember incompletely in order to remember harmoniously. While *This House of Sky* utilizes a collaborative structure throughout the text, its deepest yearning is for a further collaboration, one with his absent mother. Berneta Ringer Doig's death is the unbridgeable gap, the fundamental absence that the text recognizes but cannot fully heal, release, or make nostalgic. In a text filled with other voices, hers is emphatically absent: "But the one thing that would pulse her alive for me does not come. I do not know the sound of her voice, am never to know it. Instead she is wound in the other voices tracked through the years" (7). Psychoanalysts from Freud forward emphasize this most fundamental of all impossible desires, the yearning to return fully to the wholeness the infant experiences with the mother, before language and separation usher in selfhood. For Doig, that desire, while never literally satisfied, leads him to a literary and metaphorical collaboration with her in his second memoir, *Heart Earth*, in which Doig writes, "It turns out that the chosen world where I strive to live full slam—earth of alphabet, the Twenty-Six country—had this earlier family inhabitant who wordworked, played seriously at phrase, cast a sly eye at the human herd; said onto paper her loves and her fears and her endurance in between; most of all, from somewhere drew up out of herself the half hunch, half habit—the have-to—of eternally keeping score on life, trying to coax out its patterns in regular report, making her words persevere for her" (156). Published seventeen years after *This House of Sky*, *Heart Earth* precedes it chronologically by six months. *Heart Earth* re-creates the half year prior to the opening of *This House of Sky* from a thin bundle of letters his mother posted to her brother Wally during World War II. Yet, while *Heart Earth* offers Doig some consolation—he has at least gained his mother's letters—it is a memoir penetrated by grieving. Even the story of Doig's re-ceipt of the letters is embedded in conflict and resolved by a death: a quarrel between Doig and his Uncle Wally over an unpaid fam-ily loan (ironically about who will pay for a funeral) leads to a strained silence during his uncle's life. After Wally's death, Doig receives the packet of letters from Wally's sons. The letters are a belated bequest from his uncle of one of the few remaining physi-cal traces of his mother.

In *Heart Earth*, we have the fullest expression of Doig's desire for his mother; the book's very existence is itself proof of a life-time absence assuaged by her ghostly presence in her letters. Yet, because Doig has collaborated with others on his memories of his mother, he is able to read more than she has written: "To this day, people will wince when they try to tell me of asthma's torture of my mother" (16). Where *This House of Sky* seeks to understand and memorialize the bonds between his father and grandmother as a way for Doig to understand himself, *Heart Earth* tries to re-cover from almost thin air some lasting and reliable memory of his mother and her contribution to his identity as a writer. Where *This House of Sky* is flush with remembered anecdotes drawn from interviews as well as individual memory, *Heart Earth* is slen-der, drawing most of its story from her letters. In both memoirs, language becomes the medium by which his mother is represented, symbolized, and made to "mean." However, language eludes as much as it satisfies, and what Doig has of his mother is what we have of her: a slender volume formed from the collaboration between a son and his deceased mother's words to someone else. Language cannot tell the whole story, and there is much of his mother's life that will forever elude him. The memoirist's challenge is to make language bridge the fissures of forgetting without promising false healing.

As in *This House of Sky*, Doig emphasizes that *Heart Earth* did not emerge as a product of his individual genius. The process of composition was collaborative: "Out of that unexpected narrative of hers comes this saga-within-a-family-saga, of an indelible young woman" (x). In *Heart Earth*, Doig most fully imagines his mother *as* language. If she "cannot be sculpted from sugar," Doig will use language (17). It is finally not a succession of classic male writers to whom Doig offers allegiance or from whom he draws his creative skill; it is his mother: "Some of me is indisputably my father and my grandmother, and some I picked up along the way. But another main side of myself, I recognize with wonder in the reflection of my mother's letters. . . . As I put words to pages, I voyage on her ink" (156). As a prequel to *This House of Sky*, *Heart Earth* is an attempt to satisfy Doig's desire for his mother's presence. To some degree, the strategy is successful: in Doig's small bundle of letters, he discovers her voice and the beginnings of his own love of language. Yet his mother's fundamental absence continues, and she eludes him: "What I know of her is heard in the slow poetry of fact" (12).

Theorist Julia Kristeva claims that "any text is constructed as a mosaic of quotations; any text is the absorption and transformation of another. The notion of *intertextuality* replaces that of intersubjectivity, and poetic language is read as at least *double*" (66). By reading Doig's memoirs with a doubled vision, as constructing nostalgic models of western identity and as a narrative performance of the contradictions involved in that construction, we can see the role and function of collaboration from an equally complex vantage point. Both memoirs construct the family from a fundamentally conservative perspective that reiterates the importance of the male child at the center of the narrative, and they attempt to return the reader to the consolation of a nostalgic past. But challenges to that narrative—the unpredictable and literally unforgettable Ruth, for instance, or the noticeable omission of nonwhite histories— coexist in the text as liminal events that tell an alternate story of western identity.

In a set of intriguing literary parallels to Ivan Doig's pair of memoirs, Mary Clearman Blew has also published two memoirs that use a variety of collaborative approaches to investigate possibilities of western identity. Blew's first memoir, *All But the Waltz*, wends its way through five generations of Blew's family, and her second memoir, *Balsamroot*, picks up a resonant, unresolved thread in the form of her Aunt Imogene's story from the first memoir and follows it both into the writer's adult life and away from the comfort of an unconflicted ending. Also like Doig, the collaborative strategies Blew uses throughout both memoirs question the nostalgic framework erected in the earlier memoir, although, for Blew, nostalgia is considerably more circumspect from the outset. Memory, too, is highlighted, but for Blew memory is as treacherous and punishing as it is vital to the meaning of the stories we tell about our lives. *All But the Waltz* begins by announcing its vexed relationship to memory when Blew's childhood memory of a sow and her piglets trapped by the rising waters of the Judith River in Montana is gruffly dismissed as illogical and impossible by her father. In the memoir, however, the memory remains important for what it represents: "Whether or not I dreamed her, the sow in the river is my story" (11). That story —evoking risk, abandonment, and the treachery of competing truths in a framework of uncertain meaning—is combined with others' stories to form the memoir's critique of rural nostalgia and rural life's limited and limiting opportunities for women.

Conflicting stories—their refusal to cohere or to align with particular memories in order to resolve into a single, final truth—

return throughout both of Blew's memoirs, and these stories have much to say about western identity and the cultures from which it emerges. Of the impossibly trapped, vividly remembered sow in the Judith, Blew writes: "What I remember is far less trustworthy than the story I tell about it. The possibility for connection lies in the story" (11). As the memoir progresses, Blew remembers, overhears, and seeks out various, sometimes partial and fragmented, stories of five generations of her family, beginning with her great-grandfather Abraham Hogeland and leading to her own generation. In a family in which the patrilineal inheritance of a ranching ethic sentenced most of the women to ceaseless physical labor and financial uncertainty, Blew's great-grandfather Abraham's letters initially and vividly demonstrate the multilevel collaborative reverberations that roll through *All But the Waltz*.

Abraham's letters are all that remain of "an oppressor, a traditionalist" whom Blew "came to disapprove of" and "to believe that he would have disapproved of me" (16). Turning to Abraham's letters in an effort to understand her own father, a man Blew believes succumbed to the western myth that masculinity shows itself through cruelty, isolation, and silence, Blew slowly deciphers the words of "this man who had shaped my life without ever bestowing a word or perhaps even a glance at me" (23). What she finds in the disintegrating wad of "pencil on the softening envelopes and backs of official correspondence and unused letterhead from the Office of the Fergus County Surveyor" is an uneasy combination of the expected and the unlikely (17). A surveyor who often wrote while he was working, Abraham, as we might predict, writes little of his family and friends; his attention is focused on the land he measures and maps. A man of his time and its temperament, Abraham "discovered that writing about the northern plains was another means of transforming them into space he could measure and control" (28). His descriptions are sentimental, his thinking linear, and "he seems not to have been aware how much he was concealing in the telling, or how much, in the process of his mapping, he was erasing of a landscape and a way of living" (34). Yet unexpectedly, Abraham, like Blew, is a writer, lavishing attention on carefully composed descriptions of the landscape that compels him, writing on whatever material is available, revising his words carefully and saving them even though Blew eventually comes to feel that she "was the only person ever to have read most of these notes" (23).

By including his letters in the memoir both as his story and as an integral part of hers, Blew engages in a complex literary collaboration with her great-grandfather. Through Blew's retelling of Abraham's stories about the places he maps and of others' stories about him, he emerges as both an artist and an oppressor, as someone captivated by the majesty of the land and determined to parcel it into psychologically coherent parcels, as a pioneer attempting to explore possible meanings of his place in the specific landscape so important to him and to limit those possibilities through surveying and through the process of writing. In short, he is trying to construct an identity for himself and to understand that identity. In these ways, he is not so different, either in goal or in method, from the memoirist who incorporates his words as a part of her family's saga. In a word portrait of Abraham, Blew captures the memoirist's goals as well: "His narrative has to do with how he sees himself, A. Hogeland of Bucks County, honors graduate of one of the most prestigious Presbyterian colleges in America, as he kneels in the alkali dust at the side of poor senseless, anonymous Frenchy and watches his bull team stampeding down the raw frontier grade. What a sight! What a story! . . . He is itching for the slip of paper and pencil stub" (27). Like Doig's memoirs, *All But the Waltz* implicitly takes its narrator as its subject; in Blew's representations of Abraham, her selection of his letters to include, her reconstruction of him in her imagination, we learn about Blew. By including Abraham's words, Blew writes him as a writer, joining them in the collaborative event of the memoir where together they produce "words, words, words, more words, the shapes for what we otherwise would never know, the stuff by which we reduce the terror of endlessness, as you, Abraham, understood so well" (38).

As important as the inherent collaboration between Abraham and Blew as writers is their connection through their responses to the landscape. Although she wonders where she could "find certain footing or even air to breathe in his world of right angles" and claims that "as I had suspected from the beginning, Abraham and I had nothing to say to one another and no way to say it if we did," Blew's dismissals ring flat in relation to the layered collaboration emerging between them (36). Reading his letters, Blew is captured by "Abraham's exact sense of time and place": "I was pretty sure I knew almost to the mile where Abraham had sat in his buggy on a winter night in late 1902 or early 1903. I knew about the snow-fields on both sides of the dark running water, and about the bluffs ('over hanging cliffs'), and the clear thirty-below-zero night. I knew where to find his road, and these things I knew not so much spatially, geographically, as internally, as I might slowly recognize a map of my own arteries. Abraham had seen the bluffs and running water of my childhood, of my father's childhood, and, in the act of writing about them, had told me he saw what I saw" (21). Both in his own writing and in the stories others tell of Abraham, his love for Montana's Judith Basin is prominent. Blew's love of the landscape is clear in her claim that she is "bone deep in landscape," a phrase she will later use to title a book of essays.[3]

Although Abraham's letters are stylistically sentimental, they are not nostalgic, and his story evokes no nostalgic response from Blew. Instead, the text's representation of Imogene in "Auntie" is the most nostalgically inflected portrait in the memoir. Whereas Abraham's letters open the memoir, establishing a literary collaboration between Blew and her ancestors and setting the tone for the interweaving stories that will follow, Aunt Imogene's story is literally at the center of the memoir, and in *Balsamroot*, it will eventually lead to a contemporary collaboration between Imogene and Blew that demonstrates how "one story can be narrated only by denying another" (*Balsamroot* 149). Imogene is Blew's favorite aunt, described as possessing "the laugh of eternal summer" (*Waltz* 120). The skeleton of her story concerns a nearly fatal mowing accident in 1942, when Imogene, on summer break between one-term positions in rural Montana schools, helps with the haying and accidentally slices her foot in the sickle bar of the mower. The cut is nearly fatal, and although Imogene survives, in large part due to her own cool head, she is on crutches for a year. Because Montana schools refuse to consider her while she is recovering, her best opportunity for teaching is in the Pacific Northwest, where the war has created prosperity in the shipyards and a teacher shortage in the classrooms. Imogene moves to Washington, where she will live for most of the rest of her life, returning to Montana for visits. She never marries, and her financial and personal independence, which seems both exotic and unseemly to many of those she left behind in Montana, make her an important figure of identification for Blew.

In her discussion of Imogene, Blew gives us a character who literally escapes Montana and the punishing life for women it too frequently imposes by coming "as far west as she could" (*Balsamroot* 2). This characterization links her to Blew, who will also "escape" her father's expectations to return to the ranch, as well as her first husband's and his family's expectations that she be fulfilled by her husband's career and her son's potential. In *Balsamroot*, Blew returns to Imogene and the implied happy ending that her escape to the farthest reaches of the West presumably secured for her. Imogene's story unfolds far differently here than in *All But the Waltz*. Through the lens of advancing age, encroaching dementia, and years of diary entries, rather than the idealized aunt who appears with gifts and bubbling laughter, the Imogene of *Balsamroot* appears weakened and confused, irresponsible, and often angry. She is connected to Blew through the collaborative story *Balsamroot* tells: "I possess more of my aunt's repository of memories than she does, nowadays, though I don't understand all the connections. The thread of narrative attaches itself, spun thin, endless, stretching across the parking lot and the street. . . . It will stretch as far as I will ever go. In a sense, I am possessed. My life is hers, after all" (*Balsamroot* 91). That life, as revealed by Imogene's diary and her stories, is more complex than the nostalgic, eternally happy one described in *All But the Waltz*.

After finding Imogene's diaries and reading some of the entries, Blew's daughter, Elizabeth, remarks, "She was so unhappy. I never knew she was unhappy" (*Balsamroot* 119). The connections between Blew and Imogene, between *All But the Waltz* and *Balsamroot*, are laid bare: "The words chased themselves around my brain. What could Elizabeth mean? Auntie unhappy? Until the cruel blows of the past seven months, she had always seemed to me the merriest, the stablest woman I knew. . . . Of course she had been happy; otherwise, what about my secret belief that, if only I tried harder to be like her, to pare my life down as she had to its essentials of teaching and gardening and love of children, I would be spared pain?" (*Balsamroot* 119). As Blew reads a tiresome string of entries that record a dreary and lonesome fall teaching in a distant school in Montana, before the mowing accident, she muses: "What kind of an ending would we write for Imogene if we could? Do we want to see her married and stuck on some godforsaken ridge or coulee ranch in Fergus County, spending her days scrubbing and baking and helping with the harvest and the cattle? Holding together a few depleted acres? Or not even that much—having to work for wages on somebody else's acres? For the sake of Lud's dark face and his grin and the tension in his arms? Imogene? Without resources, without choices? What kind of a story would that be?" (174–75). It would be, in short, one of very few acceptable stories for western women's lives. Moreover, it would be the story Blew rejects for herself after it culminates in a repeating dream in which her husband "took me in his arms, smiling fondly, and squeezed and squeezed until, still smiling fondly, he had cracked my ribs and choked the breath out of me" (*Balsamroot* 128). But in love, or at least hopeful about the possibility of love, Imogene would have written for herself precisely the story Blew rejects: "*Guess I'm an introvert. I live within myself—but of my most important thots & hopes & dreams I cannot even discuss with my mother. She still would like to see me finish college. If anything happens to Lud or our affair or plans I probably will but O for my own home—garden—cellar—chicken, pigs & milk cows—flowers—cattle*" (176). But Imogene is unable to author that story, and her diaries provide tantalizing hints at a larger story that will never be uncovered. Her family disapproves of Lud, who is later sent to jail for breaking the western code by stealing a saddle, and soon she will nearly lose her foot in the mowing accident. As the second memoir collaborates with the first, the character of Imogene deepens and grows more complex; her move to Washington becomes as much an exile as an escape.

With the exception of the story of Imogene, which the second memoir revises through its collaboration with the earlier memoir, Blew largely eschews the nostalgia she simultaneously sympathizes with: "I can understand the current tendency to idealize agrarianism and the rural community. I can understand nostalgia for the way life ought to have been. But what I remember is a way of life that it was getting harder and harder to pretend was sustaining" (*Balsamroot* 143). In *Balsamroot*, Blew takes an image that many readers are likely to interpret positively as symbolizing the careful craftsmanship of a bygone era and reframes the image when she asks:

> Ever wonder why the women crocheted all those lace doilies and starched and ironed them and pinned them like so many white cobwebs over every piece of furniture? Ever wonder why all the embroidered pillowcases? All the embroidered dishtowels? All the embroidered dresser scarves with the crocheted edges lining the rooms with the bare studs of wall and the rusty linoleums and the windows that looked out at pointless horizons? If they looked long enough into the windows, they could see their own faces reflected back at them, and the terrors that they had to keep secret.
>
> *I never knew she was unhappy,* said my mother. *I never knew.*
> (184)

Through their collaboration with other sources, the memoirs peer more deeply into the pretty picture of a nostalgic past West symbolized by an embroidered pillowcase, revealing its darker shadows. By recalling a past where "one story can be narrated only by denying another," the memoirs give us a set of stories without denying their possible mutual exclusiveness (*Balsamroot* 149). It is likely that Abraham would have disapproved of Blew's rejection of the ranch life, just as she suspects he would have, and he may well have expressed it with a brutal cruelty comparable to her father's. But Abraham's writing reveals his own likely awareness of "the distance between the West as romantic invention and the West as he knew it, for it is on his description of the real landscape that he lavishes the most care" (*Waltz* 28). Imogene's diary hints at sorrows and losses even in her choices.

In Doig's memoirs, the family, in the formidable figures of his father and grandmother, is represented as a protective barrier against personal devastation. In Blew's memoirs, family itself can be precisely the devastation. Repeatedly, both *All But the Waltz* and *Balsamroot* record the growing distances between the generations, the sacrifices made to ensure physical or emotional survival, and the rejections that ensue when an individual breaks from the traditional expectations. In Doig's memoir, no sacrifice for the child at its center is too great; in Blew's writing, the sacrifices required for bare survival too often mean that children are not at the center. Blew's mother, Doris, becomes the casualty when her mother must begin teaching to support the family on Doris's birthday, ending the reassuring tradition of four-layer birthday cakes and instilling a lifelong sense of insufficiency and resentment. Elizabeth, Blew's daughter, "was part of the price I paid for myself" upon Blew's divorce (*Balsamroot* 128). Blew points to the paucity of possible stories for women's identity as the cause of such sacrifice when, prompted by the birth of her first child and the pressure she encounters from her in-laws to quit college, she says: "She knows how the plot is supposed to turn out. Basically, she has two choices. One, she can invest all her hopes for her own future in this sleeping scrap. *Son, it was always my dream to climb to the stars. Now the tears of joy spring at the sight of you with your college diploma.* . . . Or two, she can abandon the baby and the husband and become really successful and really evil" (*Waltz* 177–78). The first alternative is the story line of *This House of Sky*, and certainly Doig makes it appear appealing, at least for the sacrificed-for child; the second alternative is unthinkable, "as out of reach from ordinary daylight Montana as Joan Crawford or the Duchess of Windsor or the moon" (178). Those stories, with their focus on women either supporting a masculine sense of entitlement or abandoning their family entirely in a spontaneous eruption of female evil, are part of the limited range of possible identities available to women that both memoirs work to undo. At the same time, however, both memoirs counter the paucity of livable stories for women with "the power of story, the lifeline of narrative that links us across the generations" (*Balsamroot* 90).

In a final collaboration with the memoir that precedes it, *Balsamroot* recasts the story of the river and links western identity with the landscape once again. In *All But the Waltz*, the Judith River of Blew's uncertain memory threatens destruction. In its affinity to memoir, the river is "ruthless," with "muddy roiling water" (5). Because *All But the Waltz* refuses to accommodate nostalgic myths of female identity in the West, identity itself is revealed as tenuous and changeable. But in *Balsamroot*, the image of the river takes on a different meaning when, in 1992, the Snake River is "drawn down to its original level . . . before the construction of the dams had deepened and widened its flow" (192). What reemerges is a powerful hidden river: "Now I saw that . . . buried under those tons of slowly moving water, a tough western river with real gravel bars and a real current had been flowing all along" (194). One way to read this ending is that the collaboration between Blew and her aunt is recast to include her daughter, Elizabeth, whose own failed marriage and reemergence into a life of her own choosing become important components of the tapestry of women's interconnected stories the memoir tells; the inherency of the river is a metaphor of identity that women can claim and deploy successfully. A more ominous reading is simultaneously present, however, in that the later memoir, which ruthlessly revisits the nostalgic conclusion of Imogene's story from the first memoir, cannot sustain its own purported vision of unfixed identities and instead resurrects an essentialist construction that realigns women with the perceived strength and endurance of the western landscape. It is precisely the text's collaborative framework that prevents either reading from being either fully satisfactory or easily dismissible; the text itself performs so as to refuse a single, unified notion of western female identity.

Like the other memoirs I've discussed here, William Kittredge's memoir, *Hole in the Sky*, recalls selected events that form a narrative family history of several generations. More emphatic and self-conscious than either Doig's or Blew's memoir, however, is the pervasiveness of the interconnecting, inherently collaborative nature of stories and storytelling that supply the memoir's guiding philosophy. The title "Hole in the Sky" comes from a Tsimshian totem pole in British Columbia, where a hole in the house pole served as a ceremonial doorway to the Tsimshian families' home and as a literal doorway to heaven: "The Tsimshians believed that stepping into your house was stepping into a place actually populated by your people, all of them, alive or not—the dead at least to the extent that they were remembered by anyone. It is a lovely notion, the space inside the house connecting to the landscape of communal imagination, the actual place bound together with story and recollection" (*Hole* 10). The memoir that follows, whether by way of stories told across generations or cultures, of individual memory, or of hopeful invention for the future, is a collaborative event resulting from the often unwilling and sometimes unnoticed efforts of the many people, "alive or not," who populate it.

Of the five memoirs discussed in this chapter, Kittredge's understanding of story, and therefore of collaboration, is closest to the Native American understandings of story as a living entity that we have seen in earlier chapters. "We tell stories," Kittredge argues, "to talk out the trouble in our lives. . . . It is one of our main ways of making our lives sensible. Trying to live without stories can make us crazy. They help us recognize what we believe to be most valuable in the world, and help us identify what we hold demonic" (67). Ever powerful ways of shaping our understanding of reality and our conceptions of identity, the stories we live with need not be factually true, as Kittredge suggests when he relates the story his mother tells him about a great-great-aunt who was a writer: "I think it is a story my mother got from her mother, one of the stories my mother told herself all her life, a story which sustained her. . . . I think that story was one of her solaces in life. I think she passed it along as a way of insisting on her own worth, and, in consequence, mine. And I thank her" (28). Knowing such stories about "your people," Kittredge says, "means knowing the names of places, and who named them, and what happened there. In this way the incessant world is closer to becoming a territory where you might be able to take some rest" (28). Knowing such stories also positions Kittredge as a storyteller who shares the stories that both create and maintain the world we know.

By establishing himself as a western storyteller, Kittredge occupies a dual position in contemporary culture and literature. Despite more nuanced contemporary understandings of the construction of standards of excellence in academic circles—and Kittredge is, among other identities, an academic—oral storytellers do not occupy the privileged position that traditional authors of literary works have. On the other hand, storytellers have a long history of folk recognition, and Native American cultures regard storytelling as a central function of existence and storytellers as essential to survival. What's more, Kittredge's memoir, composed as it is of stories, is nonetheless a piece of written literature and Kittredge is a recognized western writer. This dual position of the privileged but denigrated storyteller is consonant with how Kittredge casts the stories he tells. For Kittredge, there are stories that tell of our interconnections; those are the stories that have been lost or ignored and must be revalued. There are also stories that emphasize isolation, control, and individualism; those are the stories that have come to stand for the culturally fantasized West of popular literature and film and, not incidentally, those are the stories that have led the West as a whole into destruction. There are, in short, good stories and bad stories, stories that will save the West and stories that will endanger it. A central contradiction in the memoir is Kittredge's insistence on our need, as a culture, to return to telling stories of the first kind, while the memoir as a whole more often cannot avoid recalling and even emphasizing stories of the second kind:

> But by my time, among the people who had got hold of some land, people with something to lose, a man who told stories was regarded as suspect and sappy. Perhaps people imagined that stories about the strength of ambition and will involved in climbing out of poverty were too lurid for polite mention. They turned closemouthed and secretive. For whatever reason, the stories died, and nobody told us anything revealing from the history of our family, or our neighbors' families. It was right there, as I understand it, that our failures, in my family, began. Without stories, in some very real sense, we do not know who we are, or who we might become. (25–26)

The contradiction is evident: Kittredge's story is that he had no story. *Hole in the Sky* reconstructs a past that Kittredge represents as laden with stories that lead to cultural suicide, a past he dismisses as "being without" stories altogether. Yet of course there are stories: in telling the story of his past, he tells the stories that created it. The memoir as a whole breaks this binary opposition by implicitly telling complex stories that can be interpreted in contradictory ways, stories that are neither good nor bad.

In the best instances, stories stave off what Kittredge calls craziness, a "nearly catatonic fearfulness generated by the conviction that nothing you do connects to any other particular thing inside your daily life" (177). But, as Kittredge's memoir demonstrates through its own collaborative storytelling, they can also reinforce a kind of cultural insanity. Throughout *Hole in the Sky*, Kittredge's family history—building an agricultural empire in Warner Valley, Oregon, followed by its subsequent collapse—collaborates with individual memory and musing to uncover the stories Kittredge argues we have lived by in the West and the ones we need to replace them. Too often, those stories compete with one another, resulting not in possibility and plurality but rather in dead ends and isolation: "Accumulation was my grandfather's game. . . . In his story, if we took enough care and sacrificed enough—and here the story goes sideways—we would eventually get to live in town most of the year, as he did, in a big rock-walled house, and own linens and painted china and silver tableware. . . . It was a story he wanted to believe, and one he used to manipulate everyone" (39). His grandfather lived his story; he was responsible for acquiring the vast tracts of land whose "management" would eventually splinter the family.

For Kittredge, western identity is connected to landscape and the stories we tell about it: "In a family as unchurched as ours there was only one sacred story, and that was the one we told ourselves every day, the one about work and property and ownership, which is sad. We had lost track of stories like the one which tells us the world is to be cherished as if it exists inside our own skin. We were heedless people in a new country; we came and went in a couple of generations. But we plowed a lot of ground while we were there" (27). Ignoring the inherently collaborative nature of the world, Kittredge warns, will lead to our demise as individuals and as a western culture: "We are animals evolved to live in the interpenetrating energies of all the life there is, so far as we know, which coats the rock of earth like moss. We cannot live, I think, without connection both psychic and physical, and we begin to die of pointlessness when we are isolated" (234). By telling stories that examine the nature of storytelling and its impact on our lives, *Hole in the Sky* embodies collaboration as a method to call for a collaborative mode of existence: "We are part of what is sacred.

That is our main defense against craziness, our solace, the source of our best politics, and our only chance at paradise" (238). Like both Doig and Blew, Kittredge reaches for an essential truth, an authentic westernness located in the landscape. For him, the stories that have the potential to save us are also about the need to recognize a preexisting sacredness or wholeness. In ways akin to Blew, this reiteration of essentialism within a text that otherwise emphasizes the constructedness of reality and our responsibilities to what we create is both a useful, even necessary, deployment of a western identity and a simultaneous return to a worn-out mythos that posits the West as the salvific force for a disintegrating culture.

Thus far, I have examined these memoirs individually, arguing that each employs collaborative strategies and urges readers to recognize that collaboration, rather than isolated production, is an inescapable aspect of writing. Read alongside one another—as a cluster of western memoirs similar to one another in regard to the time period they examine, the landscapes they explore, and the dates of their publication—we can also see these memoirs overlapping with one another, collaborating in unexpected ways. For example, class and gender divisions that are sometimes obscured in each separate memoir stand out when we view them together. Kittredge's memoir paints a portrait of a family successfully achieving what generations of Blew's family desired: the pioneer's dream of property and prosperity. Kittredge's representations of much of his own behavior also echo many of the men in Blew's memoirs: men caught up in denial, despair, and isolation because they are unable to either succeed in the dream of control over the land or abandon the pioneer story for a more livable one. There are exceptions of course. In Blew's *Balsamroot*, Elizabeth's boyfriend Brian deliberately takes on the demands of caring for Imogene, taking much of the burden of her care off of Blew and her daughter because he wants to become a part of their family; Kittredge survives both himself and his family's stories about an ideal masculine control in order to form loving relationships with others. But Kittredge's memoir is situated across a class divide from Doig's and Blew's memoirs. Of the three writers, only Kittredge "had inherited the right to pick between more lives than one" (54).

For example, Doig's memoirs do not record the endless desire for more and better land or for ever lengthening reaches of control over the landscape that we see in Kittredge's memoir. Neither does *This House of Sky* document the withering deterioration that follows such desires. And, although the work is as unending in Charlie and Bessie's life as it is in the life of any of Blew's ancestors, their labor is noted and passed over; it is not prominent in any story, nor is it implicitly or explicitly protested. The "escape" that Ivan manages is applauded by his family; their grief is only that they see him less often. Similar escapes by Blew and Kittredge are interpreted within the family story as betrayal and failure. If Doig reconstructs a different past than either Kittredge or Blew, his story is also invisible in their memoirs. Perhaps because the Doigs do not aspire to landownership in the same way (or are financially prevented from such aspirations), they are not driven by the same story of conquest that spurs on Blew's great-grandfather and father in *All But the Waltz* and Kittredge's grandfather and father in *Hole in the Sky*. Yet, even if we could fold Doig's narrative into these memoirs, it would still be invisible. Blew's story would have us wonder about the "secret terrors" Bessie faced, and Kittredge's story is about the successors—the landowners and their sons—rather than those they employ. The latter does not see, much less tell, the stories of the cooks or foremen. In a kind of New West answer to Doig, Kittredge's text is not peopled by "the folk" of cultural fantasy; instead, members of his family are represented as far more materially privileged and far less intuitively wise. Kittredge tells of his "grandfather's idea that we should sit down with the men who worked for us and eat what they ate, off tin plates," calling the periodic events "a fraud" in which "nobody was actually sharing anything." Kittredge assesses the scene in terms of the privilege it was meant to deny: "In retrospect those meals look like self-serving political bullshit designed to reveal our family as common and decent. They look as if they might have been designed to breed loyalty among the workmen, and to feed the family ego. We were poor people who had risen; we were naming ourselves. It is an old story" (44). Whether Kittredge's family lived out their lives within the scope of a known framework of meaning in which acquisition and control equaled success or whether Kittredge himself can interpret their behavior only from the perspective of that framework is unanswerable; more to the point may be the fact that, in either case, it is an oppositional framework that begins to collapse when pressed.

Because these collaborative memoirs depend so heavily on others' stories, language and the ability to make oneself articulate to others become an integral part of the storytelling. Consumers of the western mythology have long looked to the silent hero at its center to stand in for the model of western masculinity; in various ways, each of the memoirs here investigates silence and the idea of voice. Because a self-conscious focus on collaboration structures both the form and the content of Ivan Doig's memoirs, *This House of Sky* and *Heart Earth* call attention to other voices whose points of view shape the nostalgic past promoted in each memoir. For Doig, articulateness is less a matter of the quantity of words or one's facility with language as it is the quality of expression and voice, which Doig presents as a unified whole even as the use of multiple voices challenges traditional models of autobiographical writing, dispersing authority for and authorship of the texts. Although Doig's writing is notable for its distinctive poetic, metaphor-laden qualities, the memoir itself is carefully attuned to the folksy sounds of those less formally educated. His father's sense of humor is recorded: "*As the fellow says, a fool and his money are soon parted, but ye can't even get introduced around here*" (19). His grandmother "talked a small private language which must have come from those two islanded times of childhood, her own growing up on the Wisconsin farm and her children's years at Moss Agate. Words jiggled and bellied and did strange turns then: *I'll have a sipe more of coffee, but if I eat another bite, I'll busticate. . . . Get the swatter and dead that fly for me, pretty please? . . . Hmpf, I been settin' so long my old behinder is stiff"* (130). Bessie converses with animals, and both Charlie and Bessie tell the stories that eventually compose *This House of Sky.* Elsewhere in the text, however, are pockets of silence. Bessie retreats into silence when angry; Charlie and his second wife, Ruth, endure lasting bouts of silence during their marriage; and "no trace of Ruth—reminiscence, written line, photograph, keepsake—has survived" save Doig's and a few others' vague memories of her after the marriage ends (69). In his response to Ruth, Charlie adopts the enduring silence of the western hero, freezing her memory into the disparaging nickname "Flip." However, the most unforgettable silence is "the new silence" that follows Doig's mother's final breath (3). For Doig, language and communication are the keys to survival and silence is represented as either pointless, as in Ruth's case, when even Charlie's enduring silence about her fails to erase her from his life, or as something that itself calls to language to fill the gap, as it does with Doig's efforts to fill the obvious silence left by his mother with her words.

Mary Clearman Blew has much to say about silence and the escalating costs required to maintain it. Many men in Blew's memoir are notable for their inarticulateness and their punishing use of silence. When Blew deserts the family script of returning the ranch, her father doesn't speak to her for years. He eventually pursues a solitary death shrouded in "inarticulate strength" (45). Her second husband is trapped in a spiraling denial of the pulmonary disease that is killing him, and it is the denial rather than the disease that leads to their separation and divorce. Finally, her daughter Elizabeth's new boyfriend Brian is notable because, in contrast to Elizabeth's ex-husband, "Brian talks" (*Balsam-*

root 55). From Blew's perspective, silence becomes a patriarchal weapon, something that ultimately damages the men that wield it as much as it harms the women it is frequently aimed at.

Kittredge's memoir is itself an attempt to heal the silences that permeated his family and eventually the land where they lived when "storytelling drifted to a stop" (26). *Hole in the Sky* presents storytelling and silence in somewhat conflicting ways, first suggesting that the stories about his family ceased and later revealing that the stories did not cease so much as they changed: the stories that emphasized connection to and interaction with one another and the landscape changed into stories that emphasized independence, isolation, and control over one another and the landscape: "Our actual model was industrial. We worked hard to be analytic and coldhearted. The places around us were not alive with history but they could be useful. It was another way for the world to be dead. It was a way of thinking which distanced us from everything we might have loved, like each other, and the place where we lived." The resulting memoir is an attempt to remember the history, "to fit it together in strings which reach from generation to generation, trying to loop myself into lines of significance" (27). The memoir enacts its collaborative basis by retelling as many of the stories as Kittredge can remember or reinvent.

For Doig, Blew, and Kittredge, collaboration is the complex state of autobiographical writing, and explicitly foregrounding the collaborative structure and content of their memoirs allows them to present differing, sometimes conflicting versions of western identity. However, the cultural power that still suffuses the mythic version of the Old West and its rural inhabitants, or the presumably elemental link between westerners and the landscapes they inhabit, still dominates much of our autobiographical writing in the West. These memoirs' collective vacillation between identity as constructed and identity as essential suggests that the West as a concept is still laden with assumptions that its writers have yet to adequately recognize or theorize.

One of the assumptions western writers (and readers) have not yet questioned is our ability to recognize plagiarism. In the preceding chapters, writers have reproduced works in collaboration with themselves, with other writers, and with stories explicitly passed down or imperfectly remembered. Nowhere, however, has an accusation of plagiarism erupted. Ironically, Wallace Stegner, perhaps the West's best-known and most revered writer, is accused of plagiarism regarding *Angle of Repose*, one of his most distinctly collaborative novels. Why is Stegner accused of plagiarism and not Doig, Blew, or Kittredge? I believe the answer has to do with some of our deepest assumptions about western identities and authorship.

6

"Her Future and My Past"

Collaborating with History
in Wallace Stegner's Angle of Repose

*These fragments of my past are presented merely as back-
grounds and the figures upon them are placed by instinct
in a selected light and seen from a certain point of view.
To that extent I suppose I am still the artist I tried to be.*
    MARY HALLOCK FOOTE, *A VICTORIAN GENTLEWOMAN IN THE FAR WEST*

*If I had written a biography of Mary Hallock Foote I would have
put her in the book by name and made acknowledgment to her
papers. But it is a novel, not a biography. It has nothing to do
with the actual life of Mary Hallock Foote except that I borrowed
a lot of her experiences. So I don't, I guess, feel very guilty about
that. It is a method I've used . . . to mix history and fiction.
And whenever fact will serve fiction—and I am writing fiction
—I am perfectly willing to use it that way.*
    WALLACE STEGNER

*[T]he clashes and the conflicts of Western history will always
leave the serious individual emotionally and intellectually
unsettled.*
    PATRICIA NELSON LIMERICK, *THE LEGACY OF CONQUEST*

I N THE second epigraph above, Wallace Stegner defends himself from what he called a "holier-than-thou attack" on his extensive use of western artist and writer Mary Hallock Foote's letters and reminiscences as the basis for his Pulitzer Prize–winning
1971 novel, *Angle of Repose*.[1] Stegner's self-defense hinges on one
of his favorite themes: the distinction between history and fiction.

Stegner no doubt had this distinction in mind when he offered up his thanks to Mary Hallock Foote's descendants in the opening pages of *Angle of Repose*, almost in premonition of the criticism his use of Foote's papers would eventually provoke: "My thanks to J. M. and her sister for the loan of their ancestors. Though I have used many details of their lives and characters, I have not hesitated to warp both personalities and events to fictional needs. This is a novel which utilizes selected facts from their real lives. It is in no sense a family history" (9). In this acknowledgment of his thinly disguised literary use of Foote and her relatives, three sentences that would later cause him much trouble, Stegner attempts to position himself as a fiction writer rather than as a historian; by his way of thinking, fiction and history are separate entities that can be profitably mixed by the fiction writer without losing their fundamental identities as either fiction or history. Creative mixing of history and fiction justifies what he terms the "borrowings" from Foote's papers that form the basis for the title of the novel and for numerous scenes, letters, and characterizations within it, including the main character of *Angle of Repose*, Susan Burling Ward, who is closely modeled on Mary Hallock Foote.

Elsewhere, however, Stegner argues convincingly against such a clear distinction between fiction and history. In his essay "On the Writing of History," Stegner states that it is his "impression that too many trained professionals consider narrative history, history rendered as story, to be something faintly disreputable, the proper playground of lady novelists" (*Sound* 202). Initially in the essay, Stegner makes several claims for the separation of history and fiction: fiction can have many voices and points of view; history can have only one voice, the historian's, and point of view is, for Stegner, a question the "historian never has to raise"; the American West, he also implies, gives the historian "a greater story and more colorful people than any he could possibly have invented" (*Sound* 210–12). However, these apparently inevitable distinctions between fiction and history begin to collapse when we consider, as Stegner does, the ways in which his own novels combine history and narrative in order to take advantage of novelistic and fictional approaches. Stegner sees a vital importance in combining narration with history and argues that "the novelist's skill with scene, character, and symbol may be used, not to cheapen history but to enhance it" (*Sound* 210). History for Stegner is not a series of facts but rather a legacy of stories that the historian must tell. If he does so properly, he will have "set far sounder standards of how to tell the stories that history provides, without either missing the drama or leaving out the footnotes" (*Sound* 222). In short, he will render narrative history reputable by removing it from the ladies' playground into the realm of serious, masculine history.

Stegner's comments in his essay "On the Writing of History" revise the definition of "good" history to include the more nebulous realm of story and storytelling. In the process, however, he reasserts this revised history as a serious male endeavor. Stegner's belief that men possess history reasserts itself when he revisits the epigraph of *Angle of Repose* in an attempt to clarify his intentions and his use of that particularly telling word *warp*:

> I wasn't warping any of the history which people know; I was warping the biography of the woman on whom I was drawing as a model, but I wasn't warping her life. If I had been writing her life, I wouldn't have done any such thing. But in writing fiction you have to keep a character flexible. . . . I don't know what I meant by "warping" history. I suppose I meant I use history as a plastic, malleable material out of which fiction is made. . . . It would only be a certain kind of history that I would feel justified in doing that to. I wouldn't warp anything in the life of George Washington, for instance, if I was writing a book about the Revolutionary War. Any time Washington appears there, he would have to appear as history would justify. (Stegner and Etulain 162–63)

What begins here as an attempt to clarify, explain, or perhaps settle the question of his motivations regarding the use of Mary Hallock Foote's letters and papers deepens into a murky and contradictory defense laden with unacknowledged gender assumptions.

Stegner's point here is not that history and fiction are fully distinct, since he figures history as a tool from which he creates fiction. Rather, the point seems to be that, for Stegner, some kinds of
history are more amenable to "warping" than others. In this instance, the most serviceable kind of history appears to be that of
a woman artist, largely unknown at the time of the novel's composition and, significantly, one whom Stegner would not consider
an important historical figure. Stegner's representation of history
and its relationship to fiction is troubling in that, while Foote was
recognized as an important regional writer and artist during her
lifetime, her work fell into relative obscurity after her death. Stegner's insistence that he "wasn't warping any of the history which
people know" implicitly reveals his reliance on the continuation
of Foote's obscurity.[2] By comparing her life to Washington's, Stegner insinuates that Foote's life was not the stuff of real history, the
sort made by male American generals and presidents, and thus
not the kind of known, and therefore valuable, history to which a
fictional writer must remain factually responsible.

In numerous interviews, when asked about the composition
process of *Angle of Repose*, Stegner makes virtually identical arguments: "I used her as a model, but whenever her papers didn't
suit me, I changed them, which is why it is a novel and not a biography. If I'd been writing her biography, I couldn't have changed
them" (Hepworth 36). Yet, returning to his conception of history
as implicitly a man's province, Stegner reveals why he chose a fictional format for his use of Foote's life. Stegner says that, after
reading her letters to Helena Gilder, "I knew there was a book
there, but I wasn't sure what it was. I had thought of writing her
biography, as apparently [Rodman Paul] was doing. I decided,
quite frankly, that she wasn't worth a biography. She wasn't an
important enough literary person, though she was pretty good.
And her art was hard to judge, because she drew so commonly,
particularly in later life, directly onto wood blocks, so there
are no originals. . . . So I decided against writing a biography. I
wanted her to cast a bigger shadow than that interesting but

rather modest success that she had had as a Victorian gentlewoman with gifts" (Hepworth 69). In this description, Stegner
takes yet another curiously contradictory stance toward the historical Foote. First, he dispenses with her historical significance;
she does not warrant a biography because her writing isn't good
enough and her drawing didn't endure. This is an odd statement
itself, given that Foote published twelve novels during her life, at
least a moderate testament to her literary stature, and her drawing was illustration work, by its very nature intended for reproduction rather than cherished originals. Stegner's evaluation of
Foote's art is, like all evaluations, political. By the evaluative standards of her time and ours, Foote's drawing would be considered
"low" art; she literally drew "commonly." But my complaint is
not so much with Stegner's gendered vision, which seems stead-
fastly unable to grant Foote any lasting importance except as a
prototype for his fictional character Susan and her life, as it is
with the contradiction buried here, one that undermines Stegner's
claims that he was not writing about the historical Mary Hallock
Foote. Stegner seems to want it both ways: the novel is not about
Foote, Stegner claims; yet, if this is so, who is it he wants to cast
a bigger shadow, and why? After all, if (as Stegner would have us
believe here), there are such clear delineations between biography,
history, and fiction, how would fictionally aggrandizing Susan
Burling Ward in any way bolster Mary Hallock Foote's shadow?
What was it about Foote, through her letters and memoirs, that
captivated him enough to collaborate with her writing—while
never acknowledging it as a collaboration—in order to produce
Angle of Repose?

Stegner's contradictory response to Foote has, I think, a great
deal to do with his unexamined investment in the ideal of the individual author, with himself a preeminent example, and with
the unavoidable challenges and problems of maintaining such a
belief while discussing his relationship to Foote and her work. In
interviews in which he discusses her work, Stegner generally represents Foote as a writer whose work he valued enough to study

and teach. But in discussing her work, he frequently finds himself mired in a kind of ethical quicksand, for certainly our contemporary idea of plagiarism describes well his use of Foote's material in *Angle of Repose*. As we've seen, Stegner attempts to deflect charges of plagiarism by asserting his intentions: he intended a novel, not a biography; he intended that his readers not interpret Susan Burling Ward's experiences as those of Mary Hallock Foote. Authorial intention, which implicitly relies on a faith in the encompassing authority of the author, is promoted as the key to the text in general and the plagiarism debate—as well as Stegner's reputation as a western author—in particular. None of this prevents the text from performing in very different and, I would argue, exciting ways from Stegner's stated intentions. In fact, because the novel so fully engages a collaborative focus, which in turn problematizes the key terms at play here—originality, plagiarism, authorial intention, individual authorship—Stegner often appears quite clumsy and defensive in his anxious efforts to articulate how his relationship to Foote's work is different than the term *plagiarism* would suggest. Unfortunately, by laying claim to the author's intention rather than the text's performance, the way out Stegner creates for himself is disappointingly familiar. At fault, finally, is Foote herself, for not being a better author, a better artist. She, not Stegner's response to her (which is, after all, designed to help her cast a larger shadow), is the problem. It is a move oddly reminiscent of *Angle of Repose*'s male protagonist's focus on Susan, and on women in general (Shelly, Ellen), as the problem the western man must solve. But what *Angle of Repose* makes clear is precisely what Stegner works hard to repress in his comments: there is no simple other who is the problem, nor is there an individual author who can narrate the solution.

As we have already seen, history for Stegner is literally "his story": his to do, his to tell. However, authorship, particularly western authorship, is also a male enterprise for Stegner. This is not to say that Stegner does not praise particular western women writers—he does, citing Louise Erdrich and Willa Cather as important western writers, among others. But the concept of authorship is masculine, as we see in his essay "Born a Square," in which Stegner traces the development, potential disillusionment, and eventual promise the representative western writer offers the rest of the nation: "[The western writer] is forced to see everyone except himself fulfilled. Southerners, expatriates, beats, Jews, Negroes, homosexuals, junkies can all achieve the status of Man as Victim. But our Westerner stands unwanted, ashamed, still a rank outsider, and he knows that, incorrigibly wholesome and life-acceptant as he is, he deserves no better, because an artist is by definition a victim, a martyr, a loser, a self-loather, a life-hater" (*Sound* 176). This representative western writer, Stegner makes clear, is misunderstood and unappreciated by a culture that mistakes his optimism and hope for naiveté. Emphasizing the essential masculinity of the representative western writer promises other protections as well. As Debora Halbert has argued, "The very development of intellectual property, which carefully established the paternity of the text, is indebted to appropriation. By ignoring the connections between ideas and highlighting originality, intellectual property favored those who could be authors —men. Plagiarism is what happens to men, not women" (114). In one of his more salient images, Stegner's thoroughgoing "square" is revealed as unmistakably male: "It is going to occur to our naïf that he doesn't feel as alienated as he knows he should, and yet to demur at this literary model is to be a square, and who wouldn't rather have his sex torn out with a red-hot pincers than be one of those?" (*Sound* 174). Like his representative hope-filled western author, Stegner too was "born a square" and has to negotiate his relationship with western models of masculinity against a backdrop of potential castration that charges of plagiarism threaten. In *Angle of Repose*, this negotiation can be traced in the text's investigations of femininity.

By representing femininity as a key conundrum the western male must address, *Angle of Repose* calls into question conventional codes of masculinity as Stegner's protagonist, Lyman, struggles with his own ineffectual and rigid interpretations. At the same time, however, the novel performs a double maneuver by representing femininity as fundamentally, even definitionally, a western story about *masculinity*. In other words, while the novel is seemingly "about" Susan Burling Ward (and by association, Mary Hallock Foote), the constructs of femininity within the novel ultimately function to uphold, explain, or console key male characters in their quests for a practicable masculinity. When seen from this perspective, the novel, so densely layered with desires and projections, in turn sheds light on the circumstances surrounding its production and reception. Despite Stegner's denials (and perhaps to some degree because of his persistent, dogged reiteration of them), Foote's words refuse to submit themselves to Stegner's conscious intentions to turn history into fiction. Mikhail Bakhtin makes this point when he argues that "language, for the individual consciousness, lies on the borderline between oneself and the other. The word in language is half someone else's. . . . Language is not a neutral medium that passes freely and easily into the private property of the speaker's intentions; it is populated—overpopulated—with the intentions of others" (293, 294). And yet, the astute reader of *Angle of Repose* should not be surprised by the intricate collaboration of history and fiction, since the novel is deeply invested in exactly that collaboration and goes about examining it through a series of parallel collaborations. These parallels extend from the characters within the novel, in which Lyman collaborates with his grandmother's papers in order to understand her life, to the composition process, in which Stegner drew from Foote's papers, to the reading process, in which readers must sift through contradictory interpretations to form their own collaborative interpretations with and against the text.

Just as Stegner desires to see history and fiction as two distinct entities that, in the best cases, collaborate together to produce an improved text, so do many critics have a desire to see the collaboration between Stegner and Foote as taking place between two distinct, individual authors. Indeed, Stegner's fascination with the mutable, unstable boundary between history and biography, coupled with his belief that some kinds of historical records are ripe territory for use as fiction, have prompted a sideline dispute among critics and readers of *Angle of Repose*, some of whom see his heavy reliance on Mary Hallock Foote's writing as an example of dubious literary ethics at best and as downright plagiarism at worst. On the other hand, others grant with Stegner that fictional writing authorizes its own creative license, and the resulting novel, whose "genesis is clearly the Mary Hallock Foote papers," is transformed into a fictional narrative removed by definition from the actual life of Mary Hallock Foote (Stegner and Etulain 83).[3] Despite their apparent differences, both interpretations reify the individual author in the sense that, whether plagiarist or artist, Stegner and Foote are seen as individual artists who have either succeeded or failed in the task of producing original literature. These opposing interpretations of what Stegner and many of his critics refer to as his "borrowings" point to the underlying tensions that this fictionalized western history dramatizes: the ways in which women's lives become both the subject of and subjected to reigning cultural understandings of western fiction and history, which are related to conventional representations of masculinity, and the role a belief in sole, original authorship plays in shaping those understandings.

Whenever a collaborative text is considered, predictable efforts to delineate "who" wrote "what" reveal the tension multiple authorship creates.[4] These tensions escalate when we consider *Angle of Repose* not only as a collaboration but also as one that utilizes a collaborative structure to investigate that theme. While Stegner and Foote were not collaborative partners in the traditional sense of jointly and deliberately working to compose a text together, Foote's papers are integral to nearly all aspects of *Angle of Repose*. Stegner openly acknowledges his debt to Foote, both in the disguised acknowledgments preceding *Angle of Repose* and directly in conversations and interviews conducted later, but

he limits his debt to Foote's work to providing him with the "genesis" of a later, much-changed story that, he claims, ceases to be
about her "life" in the same way a biography would. Most readers familiar with Foote's work would grant that Foote's writing is
the starting point of *Angle of Repose*; however, many would have
significant trouble seeing exactly where "genesis" (Foote) leaves
off and originality (Stegner) begins. Although the resulting novel
is substantially changed from Foote's biography, Stegner nonetheless remained indebted to her writing for his characterization
throughout the novel, even when he invents apparently "new"
characters not directly from Foote's life. For example, the character of Frank Sargent is a compilation of several actual persons in
Foote's life. As Mary Ellen Williams Walsh has extensively documented, *Angle of Repose* relies heavily on Foote: "Her writings
are the source of the title of the novel, the metaphor and the theme
associated with the title, the outline and most of the major events
and scenes of the Susan Burling Ward story" (186). Rodman Paul,
editor of Foote's reminiscences, also argues that "the basic settings [of the novel] and the cast of characters have been re-created
out of Mary Hallock Foote's own descriptions, with few changes
and only the thin disguise of a slight alteration of names" (403). In
numerous places throughout the novel, Stegner directly incorporated passages large and small from Foote's letters to her friend
Helena De Kay Gilder as letters from Susan to her friend Augusta Drake.

Despite the immensity of Stegner's reliance upon, as well as
direct incorporation of, Foote's writing, the novel's "originality"
interests many critics. Unlike many other collaborative manuscripts, it is often possible to locate specifically which parts of
Angle of Repose originated with Foote, which are the result of creative changes Stegner made from her writing, and which are Stegner's contributions. However, once that has been done, the question of originality remains unanswered: is the completed *Angle of
Repose* original, or has it crossed some important but undefined
boundary into the realm of plagiarism or, at the least, small-

spiritedness? If all writing is always collaborative—indebted to other sources—why is Stegner's indebtedness to Foote such a difficult issue to resolve? Laurie Stearns's discussion of plagiarism helps to clarify these issues:

> People despise plagiarism not because it results in inferior works —indeed, by drawing from others plagiarists may produce better works than they could by themselves—but because it is a form of cheating that allows the plagiarist an unearned benefit. . . . Plagiarism is, then, a failure of the creative process, not a flaw in its result. Although imitation is an inevitable component of creation, plagiarists pass beyond the boundaries of acceptable imitation by copying from the work of others without improving on the copied material or fully assimilating it into their own work; by failing to attribute the copied material to its actual author; and by intending to deceive others about its origin. (7)

The insistence shown by critics to assert *Angle of Repose*'s originality, and therefore to deny that any significant form of plagiarism took place, is a veiled attempt to acquit Stegner of charges that he failed in his creative process and to assert not only Stegner's authorship but also his masculine authority. If the imputation of plagiarism challenges the creative process, then what simultaneously motivates both critics' and Stegner's defense against this "holier-than-thou attack" are deeply buried beliefs that masculinity is associated with, even depends upon, the possibility of originality. Not surprisingly, Stegner's character Lyman becomes the lynchpin for this argument. William Abrahams's review notes that Lyman Ward, "his grandparents, and all the other figures of the tale are created by Wallace Stegner; we are speaking of a novel, not history" (33). Kerry Ahearn, cautioning us to read Lyman with skepticism, argues that he "is Stegner's response to critics with tunnel vision, and perhaps represents some authorial self-parody as well" (122). Other critics find Lyman equally interesting and, quite often, the centerpiece of the novel. Clearly, Lyman is a character to whom many respond. The implication here is that Lyman, at least, is Stegner's original creation. Yet Walsh disagrees, arguing that Stegner "also 're-created' Lyman from a character in Mary Hallock Foote's unpublished story, 'The Miniature'" (185). Stegner claimed he never read the story and based the character of Lyman on his former mentor, Norman Foester (Stegner and Etulain 84).

The similarities between Foote's story and Stegner's character Lyman appear more significant than mere coincidence: "The Miniature" is set in a California mining location, and "the hero is a cripple, confined to a wheelchair" who still possesses an active mind (Walsh 185). Yet Stegner's account of Lyman's origin is equally persuasive: "The physical misfortunes I borrowed from the plight of my old professor. . . . The marital problem I took from the experience of a friend of mine" (Stegner and Etulain 84). Stegner adds, "I hadn't even read the story. . . . As far as I am concerned the Mary Hallock Foote stuff had the same function as raw material, broken rocks out of which I could make any kind of wall I wanted to—as poor Norman Foester's ailments, which I borrowed for that wheelchair point of view" (87). Clearly, even in a novel composed with papers and materials still existing in collections and available for comparison, there are interpretive gaps, places where "originality" is contested and cannot be attributed without doubt. Below one collaboration lies another. The very difficulty we encounter when trying to resolve this question points to the active process of collaboration, in which the whole created exceeds the sum of its parts and in which the process of joint creation itself prompts growth in directions that cannot necessarily be traced back to an individual presumed their originator. Indeed, the insistence, whether on the part of Stegner or of his critics, of the originality of either collaborator (usually at the expense of the other collaborator) registers an anxiety—one that in turn confirms that collaboration is taking place.

Collaboration challenges traditional conceptions of originality; if acknowledging the collaborative nature of literary production reveals the fictional status of the text's individual author, then that author's pure originality is equally impossible to claim.

More interesting to me here than the absence of the author or the impossibility of originality is the persistence of claims to both. It is likely no coincidence that Stegner's comments on his novel attempt to claim his work as original. After all, it is precisely because he insists on the distinction between fiction and history, and his particular suitability as a fiction writer to mix the two, that he can avoid describing his work as a collaboration. Undeniably, Stegner's contributions are equally important: utilizing Foote's writing, Stegner rewrites a narrative of western settlement by incorporating his own themes, perspectives, and considerable talent as a writer. However, the implicit assumptions buried in his approach—his reiteration of the term *borrowing*, a term many critics faithfully reproduce—are not politically neutral. Indeed, the very term *borrowings* elides the underlying ideological systems of patriarchal power that allow Stegner to recover and recontextualize Foote's words in the first place. Moreover, as we have seen with Austin, even one writer writes collaboratively. Even without Foote's work, Stegner would have written a collaborative text; even before Stegner, Foote wrote collaboratively. What we do have here is a keenly fascinating opportunity to see some of the usually hidden aspects of collaboration functioning more visibly. Viewing the text as a complexly collaborative one offers us a more ideologically comprehensive vision from which to explore the concerns that writing fictionalized history presents, offering insight into the complex power relations at work in the creation of a western literature.

If Stegner never openly acknowledged his collaborative relationship with Foote, he nonetheless investigated a strikingly similar collaborative relationship within *Angle of Repose*. From within the novel, characters explore collaboration as an interpretative process that is ultimately susceptible to the gendered and politicized agendas of the collaborators. Early in *Angle of Repose*, Stegner's protagonist, Lyman Ward, states what he desires to accomplish in reinterpreting his grandmother's life through her letters and personal papers: "I would like to hear your life as *you* heard it, coming at you, instead of hearing it as I do, a sober sound of expectations reduced, desires blunted, hopes deferred or abandoned, chances lost, defeats accepted, griefs borne. . . . I would like to hear it as it sounded while it was passing. Having no future of my own, why shouldn't I look forward to yours?" (25). Despite his desire to hear a future without the constraint of present knowledge, Lyman cannot hear his grandmother Susan Burling Ward's life as it sounded to her. Separated from her by two generations, gender, life experience, education, and differing motivations governing his writing, Lyman can hear only what he thinks she heard or, more precisely, what he needs to think she heard. As adept as Lyman is at intermittent empathy, his motivations for reconstructing the story of his grandmother, artist, Easterner-become-Westerner, beloved friend, and perhaps unfaithful wife to her steadfast but financially unsuccessful engineer husband, Oliver, are clearly stated: "Fooling around in the papers my grandparents, especially my grandmother, left behind, I get glimpses of lives close to mine, related to mine in ways I recognize but don't completely comprehend. I'd like to live in their clothes a while, if only so I don't have to live in my own" (17). What motivates Lyman's writing is his desire to escape from the rigid present of life in a wheelchair, where he is unable to move his head because of advancing disease, from facing his ever diminishing capacity to care for himself, from his failed marriage and humiliating sense of betrayal, and finally, from the undistinguished close of a distinguished academic career. He wants to find comfort and familiarity in the past, "the only direction we can learn from" (17).

But in Stegner's hands, Lyman's journey to the past becomes as fraught with contradictions as the present he seeks to avoid when he begins working on the writing Susan left behind, transcribing it, and reading his notes, imaginings, and conclusions into a tape recorder. The process of transcription and interpretation becomes a collaborative endeavor on the basis of its partiality: Susan has left hundreds of letters to her dear friend in the East, Augusta Drake, along with reminiscences, essays, novels, and other unpublished material, but neither these individual pieces nor the whole they appear to create will cohere enough to provide Lyman with any ultimate "truth" about his grandmother's life. More pertinently for Lyman, they also fail to provide him with the truth about his own life. It is here that the novel offers us a lesson about collaboration: in order to understand his grandmother, Lyman must actively collaborate with her, even in her absence. Yet, when he does so, he reveals that, in addition to bringing his own attitudes to her words, it is finally himself he is trying to understand. Of his grandmother, Lyman will never have more than a provisional understanding—and that shot through with his own unacknowledged need for a particular interpretation, which is in turn based upon constricting definitions of female desire and capability.

With something less than a full awareness of the implications of the collaborative process he is involved in, Lyman has difficulty separating his own partially hidden desires from his assessment of Susan's. He relies on decades of her letters to Augusta in order to comprehend her life but is troubled and embarrassed by the passion they display. Susan writes in an anguished letter to Augusta that "I only want you to love me" and that she wants "to put my arms around my girl of all the girls in the world . . . and tell her I love her as wives love their husbands, as friends who have taken each other for life" (57). Lyman directly acknowledges Susan's "complexity," which he glimpses in her passion for Augusta: "Instead of smiling at her Victorian ignorance of her own motives, I feel like emphasizing her capacity for devotion. The first passion of her life lasted *all* her life" (34). Nonetheless, his discomfort with "the suggestion of lesbianism in this friendship" appears in his condescension toward Susan's hard-won acceptance of Augusta's marriage: "The tide of love, as these romantic girls put it, never came full again in the same way. . . . Maybe your emotions and your good-loser attitude were learned from novels, but they worked, and they lasted" (34, 58). Although, as Lyman

himself points out, there are fifty years of letters that attest to
their devotion to each other, he cannot refrain from contextualiz-
ing their early, rhetorically passionate relationship as belonging
to "romantic girls."

We might argue in this case, and in others, that Lyman is
merely the narrator of Stegner's sweeping novel, that we must see
things through his scope of vision. Certainly, this is true. But there
are two considerations we must take into account when examining Lyman's understanding: first, his reliability as a narrator, and
second, his positioning as a male westerner, a position different
than his grandmother's and one in which he has considerable investment. As other commentators on the novel have pointed out,
Lyman's trustworthiness as a narrator is debatable. While Audrey
Peterson argues that "Lyman Ward [is] a fictional narrator who is
himself so believable that the reader comes to accept whatever
conventions he dictates" (176), Kerry Ahearn comes to a far different conclusion when he writes, "Yet as confident as he seems,
it soon becomes apparent that the 'biography' represents not the
conclusions of an objective mind that has weighed all evidence,
but rather the speculations and pre-judgments of a man groping
his way along" (119). Melody Graulich goes even further to assert
that "Stegner's text allows for many readings of Susan's character; in fact, I think it demands alternative readings from us"
("The Guides to Conduct" 94). Lyman's biography of his grandparents has come into being as a result of collaboration not only
between Lyman and his grandmother's papers but also, as Graulich points out, between Lyman as a reader of his grandmother's
papers, the reader of Lyman's narrative, and that reader's assessments and alternative readings of Lyman's conclusions.

As a representative reader, one who is confronted by the impossibility of unmediated stable truth, that Lyman conjectures,
deduces, and at times creates scenes and motivations out of whole
cloth is clear, although it appears not to trouble him unduly. He
acknowledges that Susan is "harder to imagine" as a young girl
than the "old lady" he knew (26). He speculates that she was

drawn to the man who would eventually marry Augusta and only
afterward turns her sights to the unlikely Oliver Ward: "I am
guessing, but not wildly" (56). Repeatedly throughout the narrative, Lyman encounters moments when he must conjecture,
and as readers we conjecture with or against him: "Did she feel
trapped in her complex feelings, caught in marriage as she was
caught on the wrong side of the continent? I shouldn't be surprised" (100), or "She felt, I imagine, both trapped with him and
abjectly dependent on him" (102). As the novel progresses, Lyman grows ever more speculative; he feels forced to fill in the increasing blanks with his own sometimes grasping interpretations.
His assistant, Shelly, points out the collaborative role he has taken
in regard to his grandparents' sexual lives: "It isn't history—
you're making half of it up, and if you're going to make up some
of it, why not go the whole way?" (266). Unlike Stegner, who substantially changed the life of his source, Lyman claims he "stick[s]
with the actual . . . what *they* would have done" (266) and insists
he doesn't "extrapolate" because "the resulting sex scenes would
have been mine, not hers" (268). Yet the resulting narrative *is* partially his, just as the silence around their sexual life is his, as Shelly
points out when she says, "It's *your* inhibitions that are showing,
not hers" (268).

Later, of course, extrapolate is largely what Lyman does do,
particularly in relation to the buried desire presumably between
Oliver's friend and assistant, Frank Sargent, and Susan. "What
would Susan Ward and Frank Sargent have said to each other in
the two hours before Oliver and Ollie returned from town? Having brought them together, I find it difficult to put words in their
mouths" (449). Yet put words in their mouths he does, claiming
he was only "guess[ing] backward from the consequences" (507).
As he does when trying to understand why his own wife left him,
Lyman arrives at a point where the collaboration becomes most
difficult: "Up to now, reconstructing Grandmother's life has been
an easy game. Her letters and reminiscences have provided both
event and interpretation. But now I am at a place where she hasn't

done the work for me, and where it isn't any longer a game. I not only don't want this history to happen, I have to make it up, or part of it. All I know is the *what*, and not all of that; the *how* and the *why* are all speculation" (524). Yet, as we have seen, Susan's letters have never provided for Lyman "both event and interpretation," or at least the interpretation they do provide does not suffice for Lyman, whose collaborative portion has been significant and frequent. Although Lyman denies attributing to Susan's letters the interpretation he has made of her life, he has always been collaborating with her letters.

What is surprising here is both Lyman's refusal to see the weight of his own perspective in the narrative he creates and that narrative's effort to displace recognition of that perspective onto a somewhat narrow focus on Susan as the central figure in his story. Lyman's Susan is a complex figure: a passionate woman whose commitments to friends and family endure across her lifetime; a professional artist whose financial success is crucial to her family's survival and, particularly, to her son's education; and a transplanted Easterner who struggles with her sense of identity in the West. We know, in fact, a great deal about Susan. Yet Lyman's focus on her is as the quintessential mystery. She is the enigma, the code that must be cracked, the problem that must be solved and resolved. While drawing together holes and gaps in order to dramatize an adulterous romance—Lyman's focus, and the crisis to which the novel builds—even Lyman acknowledges that Susan and Frank many never have been together in anything like the tension-riddled scenes he creates for them. Yet it is on the basis of these constructed scenes that Lyman is able to pronounce his grandmother guilty of desire for another man and the death of her child. In an instant of insight he is unable to turn on himself, he finds her "responsible, willing to accept the blame for her actions even when her actions were, as I suppose all actions are, acts of collaboration" (534).

Lyman would do well, of course, to hear the wisdom in his own words; this disjunction between Lyman's and the reader's awareness regarding the role of collaboration in the construction of the narrative is another example of the text performing its collaborative structure. Several times during the novel, Lyman veers away from the story of his grandparent's lasting relationship to focus on his own failed marriage with Ellen, emphasizing how much this narrative explores displaced desire—from Susan's love for Augusta, which is shifted to Oliver, to Lyman's need to understand his grandparents' marriage as a way to examine his own. His stated goal in sorting through his grandmother's life, along with the refuge it offers him from his own, is "how two such unlike particles clung together, and under what strains, rolling downhill into their future until they reached the angle of repose where I knew them. That's where the interest is. That's where the meaning will be if I find any" (211). Yet the marriage Lyman writes about is as much, or more, his own than it is Susan and Oliver's. Lyman chastises his grandmother for her eastern affectations, her apparent snobbery, and her willed social isolation, and yet, though it is the silent Oliver to whom Lyman likes to compare himself, he is much like he perceives Susan to be: verbally gifted, smugly convinced of his own rightness, doggedly isolating himself from friends and family, and focusing on writing at the expense of intimate connections with those nearest him. Yet Lyman has to keep this awareness at a distance, to project onto his grandmother what he interprets as the sins of his wife. And, although he has information about why Ellen left him, he cannot follow where it leads: "If she had left me when I *was* still a man, with two legs to stand on and a head that could turn aside in shame or sorrow, I would have hunted among my own acts and in my own personality for her justifications, and would have found them. I did take her for granted, I did neglect her for history, I did bend her life to fit the curve of mine, we did have our share of quarrels. But she didn't leave me after a quarrel. She left me when I was helpless. . . . The hell with her" (443–44). It is less Ellen's abandonment of the marriage that angers Lyman than that her leaving coincided with—he believes was because of—his amputation and physical deterioration, thus adding perceived emasculation to injury. But here, too, Lyman gives his readers enough information that we realize he collaborated in the death of their marriage, for although Ellen leaves him, there is more than slight evidence that he likewise left her—to "household routines" and a quiet life that would seem cavernous in the light of Lyman's self-absorption and preoccupation with developing an academic reputation. Put another way, Ellen's leaving plunges Lyman's narrative into chaos. Lyman's narrative is out of control, and without that narrative authority, he can no longer experience himself as a man. Control of the narrative, through control of the women who populate and interpret it with him, is what Lyman wants. However, the collaborative process of narrative production, which is so steadily emphasized in the novel, keeps getting in the way of Lyman's desires for sole authorship and for the secure masculine identity that authorial control promises to bestow.

As much as Lyman would wish otherwise—to be merely and innocently rendering his grandmother's life from clear facts she left behind, to be the victim of a careless and quickly punished betrayal—he is an actor in his life and wields a power for which he is loathe to take responsibility. While he can sometimes sympathize with Susan's struggle to move from place to place, following her husband "into exile" (371), leaving her friends, her family, and the community that recognized and supported her as an artist, he nevertheless holds to his belief that her aspirations and needs were appropriately set aside in favor of Oliver's, that her alleged behavior was more costly to their relationship than his actual behavior was: "She never blamed her husband for abandoning her in her grief and guilt, she never questioned the harshness of his judgment. . . . She thought he had suffered as much as she, and she knew that for his suffering she was to blame" (540). Susan's acceptance of blame is hardly surprising, since it is constructed through Lyman's creation of her as already the problem. Likewise, the story of Ellen's adultery, her lover's death, and her subsequent vague attempts to reconnect with Lyman also show more than traces of his authorship.

In these ways, the novel enacts a game of hide-and-seek in its representations of masculinity and femininity. Lyman's self-deceptions motivate his interpretations of Susan, but those interpretations are regularly (and obviously) punctured by other female characters in the text: as we have seen, Shelly challenges Lyman's objectivity, and in his final nightmarish dream Ellen flatly counters the despair he projects onto his grandmother when she argues against Lyman's too-pat summary of his grandparent's unforgiving truce: "Talking to Grandmother's portrait she said, 'Death? Living death? Fifty years of it? No rest till they lay down? There must be something . . . short of that. She couldn't have been doing penance for fifty years'" (562). Lyman's final dream embodies his desire for helplessness—freedom from emotional and interpretative responsibility for the narratives he creates—and his concomitant fear of the masculine control he spends much of the novel seeking. Awakening from the dream, Lyman acknowledges, "I am not so silly as to believe that what I dream about other people represents some sort of veiled or occult truth about them, but neither am I so stupid as to reject the fact that it represents some occult truth about *me*" (567). Exactly what that truth may be is left unanswered at the novel's end, but Lyman implies that it has to do with a new definition of masculinity: "I lie wondering if I am man enough to be a bigger man than my grandfather" (569). The need for a secure and fixed masculinity, figured as an impossible desire for narrative and interpretative control and hinging, in turn, on dubious representations of feminine sexuality as essentially chaotic and dangerous, is regularly undone not only by Lyman's undeniable physical dependence but also by the text's gradual shift from a focus on femininity to masculinity.

The damage incurred when men pursue masculinity is a recurring theme for Stegner. In *The Big Rock Candy Mountain*, for instance, Bruce Mason learns from his father's painful and destructive attempts to secure a masculine identity when he claims that "perhaps it took several generations to make a man, perhaps it took several combinations and re-creations of his mother's gentleness and resilience, his father's enormous energy and appetite for the new, a subtle blending of masculine and feminine, selfish and selfless, stubborn and yielding, before a proper man could be transformed" (563). Despite the text's ritualistic adherence to masculine and feminine dichotomies in the characterization of Bruce's parents, Bo and Elsa, Bruce's wish is to see those dichotomies collapse into a new masculinity. And although it takes Lyman an inordinately long time to arrive at his own realization of the limits of his grandfather's idea of masculinity, the novel's final words clarify the underlying basis of the text: a masculinity that requires men to sacrifice themselves to the illusion of self-contained authority is too high a price to pay.

Although *Angle of Repose* attempts to shift focus from femininity and female authority to masculinity and male authority, the novel's reception has kept the tension between these terms at the forefront. Although the degree to which Stegner utilized Foote's writings has already been well documented and discussed, the complexities surrounding authorial intention and the willingness of one of the collaborative partners—in this case, Foote—to engage in the process are significant. While Foote's intentions cannot be fully ascertained, she was a published author, writing many short stories, twelve novels, and creating numerous illustrations. Clearly, she valued publication and, although she argues in her reminiscences that she wrote for the money necessary to help support her family, she also continued writing and publishing after that financial need disappeared (Graulich, "Legacy Profile" 46). Throughout her reminiscences, Foote refers to her artistic production, suggesting that she saw herself struggling to produce art: "There is such a thing as a perfect spongecake—I have done pretty well in that line myself—but I never made a perfect drawing. My best work was mere approximation to anything like Art. If to begin was excitement and fresh hope, to finish was disappointment that often verged on despair. But one could always try again" (86). The deflection of her ability seems an almost rote example of female humility, particularly given her success in publishing in such important contemporary magazines as *Scribners*, *St. Nicholas*, and *Century Magazine* or in illustrating the works of such well-known authors as Hawthorne, Longfellow, and Whittier. Nonetheless, it is unlikely that Foote imagined that her life would become the basis for a Pulitzer Prize–winning novel or that her private letters to Helena De Kay Gilder would make their way into it. But inability to imagine is not refusal; we simply have no way to ascertain whether or not she would have consented to Stegner's use of her life and writing. Legally at least, the issue thus becomes one of the descendants' agreement.

In the novel, the descendants' issues are simple: Lyman is Susan and Oliver's grandson. At the level of the novel's composition, Stegner's relationship to Foote's work is decidedly more complex. The route Foote's papers took to their eventual incorporation into *Angle of Repose* is generally agreed upon. Doctoral student George McMurray was studying the Foote-Gilder letters and arranged with Janet Micoleau, Foote's granddaughter, and Rosamond Gilder, Gilder's daughter, to house them in the Stanford University Library, retaining permission for direct quotation from the letters. Stegner read the letters after McMurray, his student, decided not to pursue a dissertation on them. Stegner contacted Micoleau, but not Gilder, to discuss the possibility of writing a novel based on the letters; Micoleau agreed. Stegner describes the agreement as "Janet's notion that no names should be used—that we shouldn't recognize the source of this as her grandmother"; he then later offered to let her see the drafted novel, but she declined (Stegner and Etulain 87). From Stegner's point of view, Micoleau's need for anonymity led to the disguised epigraph, "to J. M. . . . ," and effectively prevented him from attributing quoted material to Foote. For Micoleau, however, the material used was indeed so lightly disguised, or even directly appropriated, that once Foote became known as the model for the story, any attempt at disguise was moot. Further, Stegner's belief that his actions preserved the anonymity of his source relies on the dubious assumption that Foote's work was "the kind of history" that either was not or would not become notable. Lastly, when Stegner fictionalizes the historical narrative in order to draw attention to a possible lesbian attraction and divisive marital difficulties, and to add a potentially adulterous relationship and the death of a daughter through Susan's inattention and potential infidelity, the possibility of slander arises.

The descendants' concerns begin to reveal the complex knot Stegner wrote himself into: as much as Foote's descendants and critics such as Walsh take Stegner to task for writing a novel that relies too heavily on the actual materials produced—scenes, historical figures, and other incidents in her life—they are also unhappy that, after having done so, he veered too far from the actualities. There is no evidence, for example, of any near-adulterous affair, and Foote's real-life daughter, Agnes, died in her teens of complications following an appendectomy rather than drowning. Given our cultural adulation of the individual author and Stegner's acute investment in his position as a representative western author, Stegner was mired in a no-win situation: to faithfully render Mary Hallock Foote's life through the character of Susan Burling Ward would have left him open to potentially devastating critiques of the book's originality, accusations that could have drastically limited both his reputation as a western writer and the impact his book might have had, while to fictionalize the events of her life—"warping" the "truth"—exposes him to charges of slander or deliberate misrepresentation of character. If Stegner is an artist taking license, then he should have taken more liberties and changed the text more fully; if he is a plagiarist, then he should have plagiarized more faithfully. Neither possibility fully satisfies everyone, it seems.

Yet there is something deeper at stake in this oppositional wrangle, because Stegner's changes to the "truth" rely on the dubious, and changeable, interpretation of available evidence. For instance, Stegner directly suggests at least the veneer of a lesbian attraction in the letters between Susan and Augusta, although he has Lyman favor a reading of "devotion." Nonetheless, the specter of culturally unconfined female desire is present in *Angle of Repose*, a point that Walsh argues is not in Foote's original letters: "Stegner also changes the wording of a crucial sentence. Foote wrote: 'I love her as wives do (not) love their husbands as *friends* who have taken each other for life. . . .' Stegner omits the phrase 'do (not)' and the emphasis on the word 'friends': 'I love her as wives love their husbands, as friends who have taken each other for life' " (191). Shifting tactics here and taking Stegner to task for *changing* elements of Foote's life, Walsh also points out that Stegner adds the anguished scene where Susan weeps after missing Augusta's boat to Susan's "Fishkill Landing" letter (191). If this weren't enough to rescue Foote from what Walsh reads as Stegner's inappropriate insinuations of lesbianism, she provides a footnote of further refutation, citing Caroll Smith-Rosenberg's argument that "the language in Foote's letter is quite typical of that used between women friends in the Nineteenth-Century" (209, n. 11).[5] Yet the energy displayed by both Stegner and Walsh to point out and then deflect a twentieth-century sexualized reading of a nineteenth-century phenomena of female friendship is startling and belies the impossibility on the part of both writers to stabilize the boundaries between past and present and between history and fiction. As Graulich has noted, "Despite his frequent comments that he's 'drawing the curtain' and not probing into the private moments of his grandparents, Lyman spends a lot of time on sex. He is fascinated by his grandmother's sexuality, though he claims he refuse[s] to enter very far into that 'inpenetrably female' area" ("The Guides to Conduct" 97–98). Stegner, I want to suggest, is equally fascinated with sexuality in his collaboration with Foote's letters. Neither Stegner nor Lyman takes seriously the possibility that a woman could choose another woman as a life partner, despite the example of "Boston marriages" of the time. Yet Stegner at least acknowledges the possibility of a "passion" that exceeded the circumscribed possibilities of the time. Even if Stegner, through his character Lyman's focus on devotion and eventual condescension, rejects such a reading, it exists in the text as a subversive possibility, the echo of a once-possible choice that renders Susan's marriage to the devoted but unsuccessful and often-absent Oliver ever more complex. Walsh is at pains to eradicate the possibility of lesbianism in the text, but even her excellent evidence pales next to the sheer accumulation of fifty years of letters.[6] In short, Walsh's reading is no less an interpretation than Lyman's, but if Lyman is ill at ease with his grandmother's potential for a lesbian attachment, Walsh is more so, actively working to reel Susan, and Foote through her, back into contained heterosexuality.

Another important example, the one that has caused the most problems with both critics and descendants, again concerns the changes rather than the appropriations that Stegner incorporated into *Angle of Repose*: Susan's attraction to, and possible affair with, Frank Sargent, which leads to the death of her daughter, Agnes, and causes the lasting distance in her marriage with Oliver. Walsh claims Stegner "chose to make Susan Burling Ward an adulteress, to make her responsible for the death of a child, to show her estranged from her son for ten years, and to create a terrible rift between her and her husband because of her adultery and her responsibility for the child's death. None of these negative events occurred in Mary Hallock Foote's life" (205–06). Arthur Foote's drinking, which does appear in the novel, seems to be the central cause for the Foote's temporary estrangement. These changes from Foote's biography are substantial and significant, and they result in the conflation of fiction and history Stegner claims he sought to avoid: "According to Mrs. Marian Conway, 'People who had barely known Mary Hallock Foote [in Grass Valley] would stop me on the street and say, in essence, "I never knew your grandmother did *that!*" Even though some of them listened politely to denials of all these evil doings, it was only a matter of time until a man in our local bookstore said to my brother-

in-law, "Don't worry—there's one in every family"'" (Walsh
208). Graulich accounts for these discrepancies when she argues
that all interpretations are inherently—and inescapably—political: "Stegner focuses on sexual estrangement, only one of many
possible themes emerging from Mary Hallock Foote's letters and
art, because he wants to explore the influence of the inescapable theme on an interpreter of western history" ("The Guides to
Conduct" 99). Graulich goes on to explain that Lyman "sees [Su-
san's] gentility as limiting and entrapping. . . . Although he wants
her to rebel, wants the West to liberate her, wants her to become
what he defines as 'western,' he is outraged when she does rebel. . . . As soon as Susan steps out of the role proscribed for her,
social chaos ensues—and paradise is lost" (100). Likewise, with
their description of Susan's behavior as "evil doings," the descendants' responses work to prove Graulich's point. Their desire to
separate their ancestor, while understandable, reflects these clear
proscriptions regarding femininity.

While the Foote descendants see in Stegner's novel a character
assignation, I see a collaboration that reveals much deeper tensions surrounding the gendered process of this collaboration and
the culturally imposed roles that set off male and female, historian and fiction writer, into opposing poles. The process, rather
than the end point, of this collaboration also gives insights into
the western myths of masculinity and femininity and their relation to artistic production. Foote herself bemoaned her aesthetic
ability, perhaps because she had so little time to focus exclusively
on it: "There *is* no *art* for a woman who marries. She may use her
gift if she has one, as a drudge uses her needle, or her broom, but
she must be content to see the soul of it wither and the light of it
go out."[7] Stegner, on the other hand, penned himself as the representative western writer, and he was publicly recognized as
an artist and celebrated as such with literary prizes and other rewards. Despite the fact that it is Foote's "art" that Stegner utilizes, the story he sees—like the story Lyman sees—is one defined
by limited convention: "[*Angle of Repose*] grew during the time

of reading [Foote's papers], perhaps because that story reinforced my own notion of what a story is. . . . It was the boomer husband and the nesting wife" (Stegner and Etulain 83). While Foote did leave many professional opportunities in the East to create a home with her husband, she was never what I would call a "nesting wife." She and her husband lived apart large periods of their married life, and Foote worked as a productive and financially successful writer and artist during their marriage.[8] Despite Foote's career successes, the descendants' responses and experiences suggest that this entrenched dichotomization of femininity and masculinity still determines many readers' interpretations, and Walsh's attempt to constrain the sexual interpretations of the Foote-Gilder/Ward-Drake letters also reveals the threat women's passion for one another has for contemporary readers.

The division of interpretations along sexual lines should not surprise. In fact, the text frequently represents the act of collaboration sexually. Collaboration is enabled by the female body, which is represented by the textual artifacts (letters, memoirs, stories) women left behind, only to be taken up, decoded, rearranged, and reinterpreted by the distinguished male historians. Women's sexual response—who or what they desire and how—is the narrative that historians and writers are trying to control, and it is the particular, sexualized "use" of Foote that her descendents object to. Yet, to at least Lyman's escalating frustration, control is exactly what he doesn't have, what he's never had. It is important to note that Susan does not necessarily have an affair with Frank Sargent. Even Lyman says, "I gravely doubt they 'had sex.' . . . I cannot imagine such a complete breakdown in my grandmother, who believed a woman's highest role was to be wife and mother, who conceived the female body to be a holy vessel, and its union with a man's—the single, chosen man's—woman's highest joy and fulfillment" (508). Lyman's doubts are telling, because it is exactly the belief that Susan wouldn't have transgressed the bounds of her marriage that the collaboration responds to and ultimately unsettles drastically. Lyman continues, "I cannot image it, I say. I do not believe it. Yet I have seen the similar break-down of one whose breakdown I couldn't possibly have imagined, whose temptations I was not even aware of" (508). This, of course, is the crisis Susan's presumed desire for Frank amplifies: that women might not believe what Lyman so articulately words on behalf of patriarchy or, worse yet, believing, may still escape from the restrictions placed on their sexuality. Moreover, because Frank is Oliver's best friend, Susan's potential adultery threatens not just her marriage but also destroys the bond between the two men and leads to Frank's suicide; this is the chaos to which Graulich refers. Susan's sexuality, and Lyman's inability to contain it rhetorically, erupts as chaos throughout the book, first in the suggestion of a passionate attachment to another woman and later as the cause of the rift in her own marriage, in the friendship between Oliver and Frank, and in the deaths of Frank and Agnes. So internalized is this dichotomous view of women as either monogamous "nesters" or sexually wanton destroyers, so dangerous is the potential of their escape from the sexual boundaries created for them, that Stegner's contribution to the collaboration is to bring the crisis to the fore, letting us examine more consciously a narrative that usually exists unconsciously.

For the descendants, the underlying anxiety unconfined female desire represents is compelling, so much so that in accordance with the agreement to the myth of the western woman as "nester" that readers of the novel display, they too want to recapture Mary Hallock Foote from the uncertain landscape of historical fiction and sexual indeterminacy and firmly replace her into the role of nesting and unambiguously faithful wife. Had Stegner turned his fictionalizing powers to provide his character Susan with domestic or artistic attributes unavailable to her model, Foote, giving her lasting artistic celebrity or a marriage devoid of even the tensions Oliver's drinking created, there would be little debate surrounding Stegner's use of Foote's papers. But that is not the threat that women represent in our culture's stories of western settlement or artistic production.

As Lyman notes, "All acts are acts of collaboration." This maxim extends to Lyman himself, to Stegner, and to the descendants and critics responding to *Angle of Repose*: we all collaborate in the readings of Susan, and thus of Foote and of Stegner, that the novel prompts. My concern is less about the historical Mary Hallock Foote and her behavior, or even about the fictional Susan Burling Ward and her behavior, than it is about the forces that shape our interpretations and, learning a lesson from Lyman, about the difficulty we have taking responsibility for them. If, as I have been arguing, collaboration is the nature of language rather than an exception to it, *Angle of Repose* demonstrates the complex web of interrelated collaborations in which we always function as readers, as writers, as critics. Realizing that we exist in this collaborative web has the potential to lead to new western narratives in which women and women's sexuality are not always the "problem" that requires solving, ones in which our cultural understandings of authorship, and particularly of western authorship, includes a recognition of all writers' inevitable and exciting collaborative interactions.

Afterword

Collaboration and Western Authorship

WHEN INVITED TO WRITE a piece on collaboration for *PMLA*, Holly Laird describes wondering, "disconcertedly, whether the topic was huge or quite small" and goes on to clarify that "*collaboration* ranges in meaning from any work in which one or more person has a hand (which makes it a huge academic topic) to full overt or covert coauthorship (which makes it considerably smaller)" ("A Hand Spills" 345). Despite the potential for criticism on the grounds that I have failed to adequately discriminate, my working definition of collaboration throughout this study has been the "huge" one, and although I've limited my study somewhat by focusing on examples of collaboration and collaborative relationships in western American literature, even that expands my landscape of inquiry since western American literature is currently such an open and changing field. Nonetheless, for me, the advantages to this approach have been many and have far outweighed the disadvantages. The approach I have taken has allowed me to explore a range of types of collaborations, which in turn makes the point that collaboration is complex and deserves attention in focused ways adapted to the individual circumstances of each particular event. At the same time, I've tried to show that complexity need not prevent analysis, that indeterminacy, while suspending "the" meaning, does not rid us of the possibility—indeed, the necessity—of making meaning and identifying agency.

In closing, let me return for a moment to the image with which I began this study: me, writing away in a moment of deeply felt, deeply satisfying authorship. As I described the scene in the introduction, I noted that I no longer recall what I was writing. That forgetting seems significant to me, but not because I think that it is in any way important to remember which specific essay or article occupied me at the time. It is important because it highlights one of the key points I try to address within this text: that authorship is a culturally defined (and therefore changeable) role that can, under certain conditions and at certain times, be taken up by particular flesh-and-blood writers. But because authorship is so bound to context, so entirely a product of history, it is not available to everyone who writes, and to some who write, it is never available. Viewing literature as collaborative allows us to study the shifting guises of authorship without denying its importance as a culturally constructed and privileged identity and, equally, without denying the literal presence and importance of writers who may or may not achieve the status of author.

The scene is also important in another way: whatever specific piece I was writing, it was criticism. So much of the current work on collaboration, including this study, focuses on literature, but the "critic" as much as the "author" writes collaboratively. However, the very structures we have in place to write and publish literary criticism simultaneously reveal and cover over that awareness. This study, for example, is published under my name as the visible, individual author-critic. The University of Nebraska Press holds the copyright, however, and in exchange for the substantial work of publishing and marketing the book, legally owns the words and ideas it contains. Within the text, I have tried to indicate my reliance on others' ideas and words by the traditional method of direct citation where possible (a method that also suppresses an awareness of collaboration since it typically refers to individual authors as my source but does not recognize the collaborative elements of those writers' writing) and by a more general insistence on the collaborative nature of writing elsewhere. On the whole, however, this book conforms fairly consistently to the image of the single-author study, and until there are more innovative writing strategies, publishing opportunities, and marketing approaches, it is likely that the collaborative aspects of this and other similar studies will be hard to discern.

Even being able to recognize these obstacles to acknowledging the collaborative aspects of literature demonstrates that we are already engaged in somewhat contradictory attempts to (again) dismantle the very conceptual center of our discipline: authorship. As someone who studies western American literature and works in the academic environment most likely to benefit by maintaining traditional views of authorship, the English department, it seems appropriate to wonder why, and why now? Certainly, there is much to be gained by keeping collaboration invisible or at least tangential, a theoretical query for those—like myself— pleasured and fascinated by the abstract. The structure of hiring, promotion, and university advancement, for instance, or of publishing, or of teaching literature and writing in the classroom can remain remarkably unaltered if collaboration is a merely abstract consideration. But the fact is that each of those areas is already changing as a result of economic shifts, of advances in technologies, and of the challenges offered by multicultural perspectives. Recognizing the presence of collaboration can be a way of understanding these changes and of contributing to them in thoughtful ways. It can let us recognize unusual or unexpected forms of authorship, and it can allow us to acknowledge more fully those many others who are essential to literary production. For our students, a less rarified authorship may also make the process of writing more accessible.

For me, however, the most compelling reason to keep collaboration in mind is its undeniable explanatory power; it helps make sense of the process of reading and writing in a way that the idea of the individual author does not. It literally helps fill in the gaps. Lastly, I hope that this study serves to remind us that western American literature is vitally and intrinsically involved in the questions about authority and authorship that are now being debated in terms of collaboration. Authorship is an important concern in western American literature because it is an important concern for writers and for readers. Coming to see western American literature both as collaborative and as telling a story about its collaborations brings it into conversation with the rest of American literature, not as the laughably backward country cousin nor as the spiritual superior with the market on literary scenery, but as one connecting branch of the diverse literature of the nation.

NOTES

INTRODUCTION

1. Other scholars might refer to the text as "multivoiced" or "composite" to capture the ways in which the text embodies various counterperspectives and ideological assumptions as they arise from a creative process involving (at least) two distinct authors. However, using the terms *multivoiced* and *composite* to describe texts (as opposed to using them to describe writers, for instance) tends to keep questions of authorial individuality and uniqueness at bay, essentially preserving the illusion that there are (at least) two distinct authors, while the term *collaborative* emphasizes the ongoing interaction between two or more authorial subjects—an interaction, I hope to show, that itself undermines the coherence and unity of those very authorial subjects.

2. Throughout this study, I make use of what I consider to be an important distinction between the author and the writer. My focus in these pages is to challenge the construct of the author, with all of the cultural muck of originality, authority, and "truth" that clings to him. *Writer* is a term I use to argue, sometimes implicitly, for a real, biological, historical individual who creates, however deeply embedded in contexts and collaborations that individual may be.

3. For other overviews and discussions of the developing (and currently chic) topic of collaboration, see the "Theories and Methodologies" sections of the March 2001 and May 2001 issues of *PMLA*. In particular, see the essays by Holly Laird (March 2001) and Heather Hirschfeld (May 2001).

4. One of the most recent literary battles took place between Suntrust Bank, on behalf of the Margaret Mitchell Estate, and Houghton Mifflin regarding *The Wind Done Gone*, Alice Randall's "parody" of Mitchell's *Gone With the Wind*. *The Wind Done Gone* collaborates with *Gone With the Wind* in a number of ways. Its (modified) title, characters, events, and setting all invoke and subsequently resituate and revise elements of the classic from a mixed-race perspective. Although Suntrust Bank initially won an injunction against the book's publication, a higher

court vacated the injunction and the book was published in June 2001. Although much remains to be decided regarding *The Wind Done Gone*'s literary merit as either a parody or a critique, it is an important example of the difficult terrain we travel when trying to sort out fair use from plagiarism—a distinction I see as less about any factual discriminations we may make between the two novels and more about the threat to cherished beliefs in individual creativity and, in this case, economic benefit that such collaborations foreground.

5. See Inge, 624. Other studies suggest that, even without an authorial signature, the identity of "the author" was frequently known, or at least knowable, by his rhetorical style (Hirschfeld 619). Of course, Masten reminds us that even to discuss authorship and "the author" in the seventeenth century is to consider a very different construct than our current one, a point that emphasizes rather than eliminates the complexities we face.

6. I do not mean to suggest that some work has not been done to address this issue, with new work coming out regularly. Nevertheless, there is not a widely accepted canon of western American literature to which we can refer, even if it is in order to refute and revise such a canon.

7. Though not quite so rigorous as Maine's notorious xenophobia, Montana, where I live, has its own code of insider-outsider (nativenonnative) identity. Antipathy to new residents, particularly those from California, who are perceived to bring with them the very attributes of big-city life they moved to Montana to escape, such as traffic congestion, road rage, escalating crime rates, high housing costs, and so on, can sometimes be palpable. Urban legend has it that one of the first things new residents from California do is get Montana driver's licenses and license plates, thereby avoiding identification as "outsiders." Yet becoming an insider is an elusive process. A friend who moved to Montana from Chicago more than a decade ago recently stated that only very recently has she begun to "feel like a native." All of this is especially ironic given that, as states go, Montana is still very young, having only achieved statehood in 1889, and that "native" in this context refers to those born in Montana but not necessarily to individuals enrolled in the eleven Native American tribes located in the state.

8. Two of the more recent and provocative studies help show the variety of approaches being taken. Blake Allmendinger locates five categories of literature: the formula Western, "canonical" western literature, literature of discovery, regional literature, and ethnic literatures. Yet Allmendinger too acknowledges the difficulties inherent in those categories, particularly in the category of ethnic literatures. His own study *Ten Most Wanted: The New Western Literature* seeks to "recon-

stitu[te] the existing field by exploring new works" in a field he considered "intellectually conservative and . . . unimaginative" (12). While introducing writing as "new" seems, on the one hand, somewhat premature given the absence of agreement on what constitutes the "old" canon of western literature, Allmendinger's premise is similar to my own in its attempt to prevent an entrenchment into categories by focusing instead on what is already rendered invisible. Approaching western American literature with a concern for the way literature impacts history, Krista Comer reconsiders some of the assumptions regarding western literature in her essay "Literature, Gender Studies, and the New Western History." There, she argues that " 'mythic' discourse does not always signal political regressiveness, nor does 'realist' discourse inevitably liberate" (127–28) and urges a view of literature and history also attuned to what is generally rendered invisible: gender.

9. Literatures that have been largely excluded from the canon of American Literature—the vast range of Native American literatures, Hispanic American literatures, and African American literatures, for example—may be similarly focused on identity but from a different vantage point. Rather than staking out and defending a unified national identity derived from European philosophies of individual selfhood, noncanonical literatures frequently investigate racial, multiethnic, and tribal identities. By their very existence, they emphasize the variety and diversity of models of identity in America.

10. See Baym, "Melodramas of Beset Manhood: How Theories of American Fiction Exclude Women Authors."

11. Although the credibility of the literary or formula Western is debated and many critics remain dubious about its artistic merit, some western literature and popular culture specialists are finally giving it the serious consideration it deserves. One of the most recent book-length discussions is by Jane Tompkins, *West of Everything: The Inner Life of Westerns*. See also John G. Cawelti, *The Six-Gun Mystique*; Lee Clark Mitchell, *Westerns: Making the Man in Fiction and Film*; and Will Wright, *Six Guns and Society: A Structural Study of the Western*.

I. WRITING TOGETHER/WRITING APART

1. See Hirschfeld for an overview of the various approaches to collaboration dealing with this literary period.

2. See the appendix, "Multiple Authorship from Homer to Ann Beattie," in Stillinger's *Multiple Authorship and the Myth of Solitary Genius*, for a more extensive and provocative listing of British and American examples of unacknowledged multiple authorship (203–13).

3. Koestenbaum argues for the importance of homosocial bonds in

male collaborative writing and figures collaboration as "intercourse," creating a relationship among men; Masten is also interested in the ways in which collaborative writing can be seen as metaphorical sexual activity while also investigating the ways in which literary texts from the early modern period in Britain challenge our ideas of authorship and desire. Laird argues for the importance of a "theory of desire" in our understanding of collaborative coauthorship (*Women Coauthors* 13). Leonardi and Pope argue that the romanticized sites of reading and writing usually include a single reader or writer and are therefore "fairly autoerotic." Collaboration, which represents a doubling of those individual pleasures of the text, therefore transgresses that model and can be called queer (633).

4. The University of Nebraska Press, for example, has a policy against identifying by name the editors who contributed to the final versions of texts they publish. However, since endnotes typically do the academic work of acknowledging sources, and since my argument throughout this book is not just about making these sources visible but about also recognizing them as inevitable, this book is also the work of Ladette Randolph, humanities editor, who read an early draft of the manuscript and has shepherded it, and me, through the publication process.

5. Although jointly authored articles, which are frequently described as collaborative writing within the discipline, are commonplace in scientific research, debates over primary or secondary listings as author continue, revealing the predominance of traditional understandings of authorship. The hierarchical nature of author listing in the sciences is closer in philosophy to the humanities' insistence on singular authorship than to the idea of collaboration I am investigating here. In whatever ways names are arranged in a scientific article, it is tacitly understood that each individual contribution somehow remains indelibly so and can be identified and merit granted accordingly, a "parsing" approach to collaboration that has at its foundation an unquestioned belief in the individual author. Particularly when the same strategy of primary and secondary listing is utilized in the humanities, I can imagine tenure committees bemoaning: "But *who* wrote *what*?"

6. For fuller discussions of the changing meaning of authorship than I explore here, see Woodmansee and Jaszi, *The Construction of Authorship: Textual Appropriation in Law and Literature*; and Lunsford and Ede, *Singular Texts/Plural Authors: Perspectives on Collaborative Writing*.

7. Hans Robert Jauss, "The Alterity and Modernity of Medieval Literature," 192, quoted in Lunsford and Ede, *Singular Texts/Plural Authors*, 78.

8. The collaborative nature of drama is still in high profile, as anyone sitting through the list of credits in virtually any film can testify. Stillinger notes that "as a rule . . . the authorship of films is so complicated and diffuse as to be, for all practical purposes, unassignable" (174).

9. Mark Twain to Helen Keller, regarding Keller's purported plagiarism of a childhood story, which was written by Keller for a friend but then published without her consent. Cited in Swain, 68.

10. As Lunsford and Ede describe their own writing process, it includes joint writing, where both writers are in physical proximity to one another as they write, as well as solitary writing. Yet the writers adamantly insist that their final text, *Singular Texts/Plural Authors: Perspectives on Collaborative Writing*, is a fully collaborative one.

11. In addition to Masten, Kostenbaum, Laird, and Leonardi and Pope, see Joyce Elbrecht and Lydia Fakundiny, "Scenes from a Collaboration: Or Becoming Jael B. Juba"; and Linda Hutcheon and Michael Hutcheon, "'All Concord's Born of Contraries': Marital Methodologies," for alternative readings of the erotics of writing together.

12. Debora Halbert discusses the ways in which the metaphor of paternity functioned to help define intellectual property as a masculine creation: "Copyright invites the author to own his work. The work is not only the child of the author, but his property. Authorship was a method for establishing paternity over a text, the male creation. . . . The paternity metaphor illustrates what later metaphors conceal—literary creation is masculine creation" (113).

13. There is some evidence that regionalism, particularly when it hails from the West, is fast gaining not only acceptance but a certain sought-after marketability. During a recent literary reading in Bozeman, Montana, in 2000, Mary Clearman Blew related how her recently published book of short stories, *Sister Coyote*, was subtitled "Montana Stories" by her publishers, presumably in order to appeal to a reading audience in search of a specifically western regionalism, even though one of the stories is set in northern Idaho. I cannot help but be reminded here of the classic story Norman Maclean told of trying to place his fictionalized memoir, "A River Runs Through It," with prominent publishing houses and having it returned to him with the then-dismissive comment that "these stories have trees in them" (Maclean ix).

2. PARTNERS IN COLLABORATION

1. *Love Medicine*, which carries Erdrich's name, has this dedication: ". . . I could not have written [this book] without Michael Dorris, who gave his own ideas, experiences, and devoted attention to the writing"; *The Beet Queen*, also with Erdrich's byline, says: "To Michael: complice

in every word, essential as air"; *Tracks*, with Erdrich's name, says: "Michael, The story comes up different / every time and has no ending / but always begins with you"; *Tales of Burning Love*, published under Erdrich's name, has the dedication: "To Michael ♥ Q, ♥ J"; and finally, *The Bingo Palace*, with Erdrich's byline, is also dedicated to her husband: "To Michael UR Lucky 4 Me." Fiction published under Dorris's name has corresponding dedications to Erdrich: *Cloud Chamber*, which was published posthumously, is dedicated: "For Louise, who found the song / And gave me voice"; *A Yellow Raft in Blue Water*: "For Louise / Companion through every page / Through every day / Compeer." *The Crown of Columbus* bears both writers' names in alphabetical order and is dedicated to their children by invoking the name of the child born to the central characters, Violet: "For our bouquet of Violets." The exceptions to this pattern are Erdrich's 1998 novel, *The Antelope Wife*, which was published after Dorris's suicide, and her most recent novel, *The Last Report on the Miracles at Little No Horse*, published in 2001. Although *The Antelope Wife* omits the full, even effusive, dedication to Dorris so typical of earlier books published with Erdrich's byline, it continues the writers' tradition of acknowledging each other on the dedication page by substituting this statement: "This book was written before the death of my husband. He is remembered with love by all of his family." *The Last Report on the Miracles at Little No Horse* has no dedication.

2. Erdrich and Dorris began living in separate homes in 1996; *Cloud Chamber*, published under Dorris's name, was published in 1997.

3. Their very first published collaborations, about which Dorris has said, "They're not terribly deep . . . but they're uplifting" (Trueheart 115), were published in *Redbook*, *Woman*, and abroad under the name Milou North, a combination of *Mi*chael + *Lou*ise + the area where they lived. Discussing the decision for the name choice, Erdrich addresses the real need to challenge certain audience expectations surrounding literature while meeting others: "You really think that's probably a female, but you don't know. It's one person. I think when readers read a story they want to read one by one person" (Wong 37).

4. When asked if literature develops a sense of pan-Indianness, Erdrich pointed out that *Love Medicine* was positively received by Indians from many different tribes: "Michael had lots of mail from readers of *Love Medicine*, Indians from different tribes who have read it and said, 'This is what happened here and it's so much like what happened to me, or to someone I know.' It's a kind of universalizing experience. The book does touch some universals, which is what we're talking about, Pan-Indianism. We wanted the reservation in *Love Medicine* to kind of ring true to people from lots of different tribes" (Coltelli 25).

5. Although the web of familial relationships is typically opaque in all of Erdrich and Dorris's fiction, that web includes *The Crown of Columbus*, in which Vivian Twostar descends from the Manions of *Cloud Chamber* and *A Yellow Raft on Blue Water* through her grandmother Angeline Begay Manion.

6. See John Elson, who claims that "the talent pooling has spawned a novel with as much spontaneity as if it had been plotted by computer" (76). Robert Allen Warrior also faults the collaboration when he insists that, because Dorris is "not capable of the language of Erdrich's sublime and ironic passion," "fans of Erdrich will find her voice disappointingly faint here" (393). Even more sympathetic reviewers find it impossible to avoid acknowledging the novel's problems. See Helen Hoy, who notes that "its plot [is] a patent absurdity" and seriously questions whether the "focus on Columbus and, eventually, on christianity . . . risk re-inscribing a eurocentric worldview?" (54); Peter Beidler states, "I have no desire to defend this plot. It sells books and makes successful movies" (47). In a significant departure from most critiques of the novel as a collaboration, Beidler points to the collaboration as the key in the novel's success: "*The Crown of Columbus* is a very good novel . . . not in spite of the collaboration, but because of it. We cannot know, of course, what the novel would have been had either Erdrich or Dorris written it solo. But if the dual voices in the book are evidence of collaboration, then I say, hooray for collaboration" (48). Beidler's comment, while positive, nonetheless implies that the characters Twostar and Williams somehow parallel the writers Dorris and Erdrich, another example of a critical need to separate the collaboration into its respective individual authors even while the reviewer celebrates that collaboration.

3. A QUESTION OF PERSPECTIVES

1. For another perspective on the importance of Mourning Dove's name, see Elizabeth Ammons's *Conflicting Stories*. Ammons, following Rayna Green's example in *That's What She Said: Contemporary Poetry and Fiction by Native American Women*, uses Mourning Dove's Indian name, Hum-ishu-ma, in her discussion. Green's and Ammons's choice seems to me both sensitive and appropriate. In her introduction to *Cogewea*, Dexter Fisher quotes from a February 1926 letter from Mourning Dove to McWhorter in which Mourning Dove says, "You asked me about Humishuma. As far as I can translate it, it really has no meaning at all besides the name of the bird Mourning Dove. And it does not mean Mourning Dove at all, and as far as I can judge it, the whiteman must have invented the name for it as Mourning Dove because the translation to Indian is not word for word at all" (xxvii). In other words, the name "Mourning Dove" may be another instance of the erasure of Indian cul-

ture by white assimilationist moves. On the other hand, Mourning Dove
used a number of English names during her life, particularly in her correspondence, and "Mourning Dove" was the name she appended to all of
her published material. While I do not wish to elide "Hum-ish-uma," I
do choose to foreground Mourning Dove's identity as a writer by referring to her by the name she consistently identified with authorship.

2. Mourning Dove always indicated she was born in 1888, and tribal
records place the year of her birth at 1882, 1886, and 1887. Jay Miller's
biographical research suggests that, contrary to the public identity
Mourning Dove asserted for herself as mixed-blood, she was in fact a
full-blood. See Mourning Dove, *Mourning Dove: A Salishan Autobiography*, ed. Jay Miller; and Miller, "Mourning Dove: The Author as Cultural Mediator." Other scholars disagree with Miller's conclusions.
Alanna Kathleen Brown claims that Mourning Dove was either one-
quarter or one-half Caucasian. See Brown, "Mourning Dove's Canadian Recovery Years, 1917–1919."

3. See, for example, the first epigraph of this chapter. The majority of
Mourning Dove's letters are in the McWhorter Collection, Washington
State University, Pullman, Washington. Kathleen M. Donovan has
rightly pointed out that critics use this passage "as proof that McWhorter had appropriated Mourning Dove's text as his own" and argues that
"this interpretation requires reading a degree of anger and resentment
into her words where none was intended." Donovan offers another reading: "She is complimenting him. . . . She is sharing authorship with him.
In a later letter, she continues to be very complimentary, acknowledging
that her book would not have been as worthwhile without his contributions" (119). I agree that, while Mourning Dove was obviously surprised
at the extent of McWhorter's changes and additions to her draft, she
may well have been pleased, at least to some degree, and she was acknowledging shared authorship with him. Yet her intentions, even if
positive, do not erase the fact that McWhorter did appropriate her 1914
draft of the text. Rather than focusing on authorial intention, itself always another in the series of interpretations we make of texts, as the key
to the ethical dimensions of this writing process, I am suggesting we
look at Mourning Dove and McWhorter as collaborators, a move that
lets them remain friends—for surely they were—and still allows us to
examine the relationship as one that is riddled with power negotiations,
not the least of which are McWhorter's exploitation of Mourning Dove
and her complex agreement to it.

4. Letter from Mourning Dove to McWhorter dated 24 February
1916. Quoted in Bernardin, 489.

5. For the most complete description of Mourning Dove's relation-

ship with her various editors, see Alanna Kathleen Brown, "Looking through the Glass Darkly: The Editorialized Mourning Dove."

6. Even more names emerge when we examine other texts surrounding Mourning Dove and McWhorter. As we see in the first epigraph to this chapter, Mourning Dove often fondly referred to McWhorter as "Big Foot" in her letters, and she went by Christine Quintasket and her married names, Crystal McLeod and Mrs. Fred Galler. Bernardin reports that Mourning Dove "had used interchangeably the names 'Cogewea' and 'Agnes' in the manuscript [of *Cogewea*]" and that McWhorter found the "use of two names . . . 'too confusing' to readers" and removed the name "Agnes" (497).

7. Mourning Dove, *Mourning Dove: A Salishan Autobiography*, ed. Jay Miller. In his introduction to what he has titled her autobiography, Miller points out that Mourning Dove, distressed over an accusation that she did not write *Cogewea* and instead only allowed her name to be affixed to a white man's work, was "determined she would do something on her own and this autobiography is the outcome" (xii). But despite his acknowledgment of Mourning Dove's determination to prove her literary abilities, Miller contradicts his statement of her desires when he claims that "it is clear that she intended her efforts to be edited" (xxxiii). In what can only strike me as a dismally predictable case of history repeating itself, Mourning Dove's autobiography is edited by a man who has carefully "imposed consistency" by rewriting every sentence to make the finished text conform to the conventions of Standard English and by including editorial additions to ultimately produce, as Miller says, "my sense of her work" (xxxiii).

8. Bernardin also makes this point when she notes that "in its fusion of Okanogan orality and mainstream plots and genres, *Cogewea* manages simultaneously to intervene in dominant constructions of Indian identity and to validate Okanogan culture and make it accessible to an outside reader. Working as cultural translator, Mourning Dove appropriated literary forms in order to reshape the discourse surrounding Indians in the early twentieth century" (490).

9. For a fuller discussion of the various editorial relationships that Mourning Dove entered into, see Brown, "Looking through the Glass Darkly: The Editorialized Mourning Dove." Bernardin also notes that Mourning Dove's authorship was questioned after the publication of *Cogewea* and speculates that her involvement in tribal politics made her vulnerable to such public challenges (495, 507 n. 20).

10. See Brown, "Looking through the Glass Darkly: The Editorialized Mourning Dove."

11. The effort to separate collaborators' contributions to a given text

is so common as to appear "natural" in a discipline that validates only singly authored texts. Lunsford and Ede quip: "Our interest in collaboration grew directly out of our personal experience as long-time friends and co-authors, piqued by our surprised realization that co-authorship was not valued in our own Departments of English. At the same time, we did not associate that devaluation of a mode which seemed important and productive to us with the phallologocentric nature of the academy; we were merely irritated" ("Rhetoric in a New Key: Women and Collaboration" 234).

12. Speculating about why Mourning Dove "permitted McWhorter such an obvious presence in her text," Donovan suggests that it is possible that "his editorial intrusion, which readers today find so annoying, did not appear unusual to her. . . . And just as her parents had difficulty accepting the Western construction of land as property, perhaps Mourning Dove had difficulty accepting the equally Western construction of intellectual property created and owned solely by an individual" (117).

13. For another example of sophisticated resistance to ethnographers, this time from African American culture, see Zora Neale Hurston's introduction to *Mules and Men*, in which she states: "We do not say to our questioner, 'Get out of here!' We smile and tell him or her something that satisfies the white person because, knowing so little about us, he doesn't know what he is missing. . . . The Negro offers a feather-bed resistance. That is, we let the probe enter, but it never comes out. It gets smothered under a lot of laughter and pleasantries" (18).

14. From a letter from McWhorter to Mourning Dove dated 29 November 1915. Quoted in Brown, "Legacy Profile: Mourning Dove (Humishuma) 1888–1936," 58.

4. MARY AUSTIN, I-MARY, AND MARY-BY-HERSELF

1. In grateful recognition of the collaborative relationship that exists between a writer and her editor, I wish to thank Melody Graulich for her suggestion that I think about Austin's uses of prior texts in her autobiography.

2. See Woodmansee, 279–92.

3. See London, chap. 2, "Something Obscurely Repellent: The Resistance to Double Writing," 63–90, for a thorough overview of feminist approaches to collaboration. While London focuses primarily on collaborative pairings in which women consciously wrote together, rather than the more expansive and (often) metaphorical approach to collaboration I take here, her review of collaboration within feminist criticism and theory is provocative and useful.

4. See Austin's roman à clef, *A Woman of Genius*, for her fullest description of the contradictions for and costs to women who pursue their

artistic talent. Although fictionalized, the novel is based on Austin's life, a point Nancy Porter makes in her afterword to *A Woman of Genius*.

5. An examination of Austin's handwritten revisions to the manuscript of *Earth Horizon* bears out the deliberateness with which she created and maintained the shifting subjectivity represented by the personae Mary, I-Mary, and Mary-by-herself. The manuscript, which is located in box 51 of the Austin collection at the Henry E. Huntington Library, shows Austin at times carefully replacing third-person referents such as "she" with "I-Mary," for example, or replacing "me" with the more distant "the child," even when the surrounding sentences or paragraphs retain first- or third-person phrasing.

6. This contempt is sometimes expressed in critics' linkage of Austin's behavior, when either seemingly or obviously influenced by Native American culture, with her personal appearance. Early in Austin scholarship, satiric comments on Austin's personal appearance, sexual life, and sense of spiritual authority abound, almost as if critics could not consider her writing without emphasizing her appearance and behavior. In her own time, D. H. Lawrence, who was among a group of writers Austin knew in New Mexico, satirized her appearance and beliefs in his unpublished play *Altitudes*. More recent criticism also mocks Austin's appearance and beliefs: Justin Kaplan's biography of Lincoln Steffens notes Austin's weight and adds, "She wore long priestess robes and was given to meditating in a tree house." Quoted in Austin, *Stories from the Country of Lost Borders*, xviii. Even when critics avoid linking Native American issues with personal appearance and behavior, Austin's physical departure from Anglo-American cultural norms of female beauty frequently receive commentary. Karen Langlois reminds us that Austin "was not in the classic image of the American beauty. Sallow and slender as a girl, inclined to dumpiness as an adult, she was once described as looking like Teddy Roosevelt in skirts" ("Mary Austin and Lincoln Steffens" 359). Finally, in her biography of Austin, *Mary Austin: Song of a Maverick*, Esther Lanigan Stineman claims that "although she greatly admired beauty, Austin did not possess it herself" (2).

7. See Klimasmith, 21–23.

5. COLLABORATION AND CONTRADICTION
IN THE WESTERN MEMOIR

1. As Sarris points out, whether stories are orally or textually based, they are meaningful collaborative interactions. As such, this text, like Sarris's, is a story that simultaneously describes and investigates collaborative interactions and, in collaboration with its readers, produces them.

2. See Peter Jaszi, who shows that " 'folkloric works,' for example,

are corporate productions which have no identifiable author(s), and their continual re-production through transmission within a cultural group makes it difficult to locate the moment at which any hypothesized individual can have made an 'original,' 'authorial' contribution" (38 n. 37).

3. See Blew, *Bone Deep in Landscape: Essays on Writing, Reading, and Place.*

6. "HER FUTURE AND MY PAST"

1. The attack to which Stegner refers is Mary Ellen Williams Walsh's article *"Angle of Repose* and the Writings of Mary Hallock Foote: A Source Study," 184–209. Collections of Foote's letters are housed at the Stanford University Library. The Huntington Library owns a photocopied set of the letters.

2. Melody Graulich argues that, in *Angle of Repose*, Stegner "is an insightful and pioneering feminist critic" (246), noting as well that he was the first to attempt to recover Foote's reputation by including her short fiction in a 1958 anthology (243). See Graulich, "Book Learning: *Angle of Repose* as Literary History." I do not dispute Graulich's reading entirely; however, "feminist" is an increasingly contested term, and the politics of Stegner's feminism in this unacknowledged instance of collaboration is my concern and leads me to a more dubious evaluation of Stegner as "feminist." I tend to agree with Krista Comer's evaluation that Stegner was not a feminist because he "did not hold the fundamental feminist conviction that women are oppressed" (*Landscaping the New West* 55).

3. Walsh's essay is both the most fully documented and the most adamantly critical of Stegner's use of Foote's papers. Melody Graulich, Audrey Peterson, William Abrahams, Rodman Paul, and Richard Etulain, while readily acknowledging Stegner's reliance on Foote's writing, do not foreground that reliance as particularly problematic. Most critics tacitly accept Stegner's term *borrowings* to describe his use of Foote's writing.

4. Moreover, collaboration studies often reveal the context of support that is frequently erased in such a vision of isolation: financial or emotional support, frequently provided by institutions, families, spouses, partners, and mentors; the history of ideas to which the author responds, even unintentionally; or even the range of other skilled individuals who are required in order to produce a text.

5. See Caroll Smith-Rosenberg, "The Female World of Love and Ritual: Relations between Women in Nineteenth-Century America."

6. Despite Walsh's dogged argument otherwise, in my reading,

Foote's original letters to Helena De Kay Gilder keep questions of possible lesbianism open in several ways. I agree with Walsh that the "language in Foote's letters is quite typical of that used between women friends in the Nineteenth-Century" (209 n. 11). However, the commonness of such sentimental and affectionate, even passionate, language neither confirms nor denies the possibility of deeper female attraction and bonding, whether emotional or physical. Moreover, as contemporary scholars have shown, homosexuality as we currently understand it was a concept constructed in the late nineteenth century, and even today there is no agreement on exactly what constitutes lesbian identity and behavior. All of this means that even if Foote's feelings for and behavior toward Gilder were what we might today describe as lesbian, it is unlikely she would have experienced those feelings or that behavior as meeting that definition. In short, there are numerous theoretical and practical problems that arise when impressing a contemporary construct of sexuality onto a past context when no such construct existed.

7. Letter from Mary Hallock Foote to Helena De Kay Gilder dated 6 March 1887. Cited in Graulich, "Legacy Profile," 51.

8. My thanks to Christie Hill Smith for pointing out the ways in which Foote's life exceeds any definition of a "nesting woman."

WORKS CITED

Abrahams, William. "The Real Thing." *Critical Essays on Wallace Stegner*. Ed. Anthony Arthur. Boston: Hall, 1982. 31–33.

Ahearn, Kerry. "*The Big Rock Candy Mountain* and *Angle of Repose*: Trial and Culmination." *Critical Essays on Wallace Stegner*. Ed. Anthony Arthur. Boston: Hall, 1982. 109–23.

Allen, Paula Gunn. *The Sacred Hoop: Recovering the Feminine in American Indian Tradition*. Rev. ed. Boston: Beacon, 1992.

Allmendinger, Blake. *Ten Most Wanted: The New Western Literature*. New York: Routledge, 1998.

Ammons, Elizabeth. *Conflicting Stories*. New York: Oxford UP, 1991.

Austin, Mary. *The American Rhythm: Studies and Reexpressions of Amerindian Songs*. Boston: Houghton, 1930.

———. *Earth Horizon*. Cambridge, Mass.: Riverside, 1932.

———. "Regionalism in American Fiction." *Beyond Borders: The Selected Essays of Mary Austin*. Ed. Reuben J. Ellis. Carbondale: Southern Illinois UP, 1996. 130–40.

———. *Stories from the Country of Lost Borders*. Ed. Marjorie Pryse. New Brunswick: Rutgers UP, 1987. Rpt. of *Lost Borders*. 1909.

———. *A Woman of Genius*. Garden City, N.Y.: Doubleday, 1912. Rpt. Old Westbury, N.Y.: Feminist, 1985.

Bakhtin, Mikhail M. *The Dialogic Imagination*. Ed. Michael Holquist. Trans. Carly Emerson and Michael Holquist. Austin: U of Texas P, 1981.

Barthes, Roland. "The Death of the Author." *Image-Music-Text*. Trans. Stephen Heath. New York: Hill, 1977. 142–48.

Baym, Nina. "Melodramas of Beset Manhood: How Theories of American Fiction Exclude Women Authors." *The New Feminist Criticism*. New York: Pantheon, 1985. 63–80.

Beidler, Peter G. "Review. *The Crown of Columbus*." *Studies in American Indian Literatures (SAIL)*. 3/4 (1991): 47–50.

Bernardin, Susan K. "Mixed Messages: Authority and Authorship in Mourning Dove's *Cogewea, The Half-Blood: A Depiction of the*

Great Montana Cattle Range." *American Literature* 67.3 (1995): 487–509.

Bhabha, Homi K. "Introduction: Locations of Culture." *The Location of Culture*. London: Routledge, 1994. 1–18.

Blew, Mary Clearman. *All But the Waltz*. New York: Penguin, 1991.

———. *Balsamroot: A Memoir*. New York: Penguin, 1994. Rpt. Norman: U of Oklahoma P, 2001.

———. *Bone Deep in Landscape: Essays on Writing, Reading, and Place*. Norman: U of Oklahoma P, 1999.

———. *Sister Coyote: Montana Stories*. New York: Lyons, 2000.

Bonetti, Kay. "An Interview with Louise Erdrich and Michael Dorris." *Missouri Review* 11.2 (1998): 79–99.

Breinig, Helmbrecht. "(Hi)storytelling as Deconstruction and Seduction: The Columbus Novels of Stephen Marlowe and Michael Dorris/Louise Erdrich." *Historiographic Metafiction in Modern American and Canadian Literature*. Ed. Bernd Engler and Kurt Muller. Paderborn: Ferdinand Schoningh, 1994. 325–46.

Brown, Alanna Kathleen. "Legacy Profile: Mourning Dove (Humis-huma) (1888–1936)." *Legacy* 6.1 (1989): 51–58.

———. "Looking through the Glass Darkly: The Editorialized Mourning Dove." *New Voices in Native American Literary Criticism*. Ed. Arnold Krupat. Washington DC: Smithsonian Institution P, 1993. 274–90.

———. "Mourning Dove's Canadian Recovery Years, 1917–1919." *Native Writers and Canadian Writing*. Ed. W. H. New. Vancouver: UBC, 1990. 113–22.

———. "Mourning Dove's Voice in *Cogewea*." *Wicazo SA Review* 4.2 (1988): 2–15.

Bruchac, Joseph. "Whatever Is Really Yours: An Interview with Louise Erdrich." *Survival This Way: Interviews with American Indian Poets*. Ed. Joseph Bruchac. Tucson: U of Arizona P, 1987. 73–86. Rpt. in *Conversations with Louise Erdrich and Michael Dorris*. Ed. Allan Chavkin and Nancy Feyl Chavkin. Jackson: U of Mississippi P, 1994. 94–104.

Caldwell, Gail. "Writers and Partners." *Boston Globe* 26 Sept. 1986: 15. Rpt. in *Conversations with Louise Erdrich and Michael Dorris*. Ed. Allan Chavkin and Nancy Feyl Chavkin. Jackson: U of Mississippi P, 1994. 64–69.

Carby, Hazel. "The Politics of Fiction, Anthropology, and the Folk: Zora Neale Hurston." Ed. Michael Awkward. *New Essays on Their Eyes Were Watching God*. New York: Cambridge UP, 1990. 71–93.

Cawelti, John G. *The Six-Gun Mystique.* 2nd ed. Bowling Green, Ohio: Bowling Green State U Popular P, 1984.

Chadwich, Whitney, and Isabelle de Courtivron, eds. *Significant Others: Creativity and Intimate Partnership.* London: Thames and Hudson, 1993.

Chavkin, Nancy Feyl, and Allan Chavkin. "An Interview with Louise Erdrich." Ed. Allan Chavkin and Nancy Feyl Chavkin. *Conversations with Louise Erdrich and Michael Dorris.* Jackson: U of Mississippi P, 1994. 220–53.

———. "An Interview with Michael Dorris." Ed. Allan Chavkin and Nancy Feyl Chavkin. *Interviews with Louise Erdrich and Michael Dorris.* Jackson: U of Mississippi P, 1994. 184–219.

Clarke, Joni Adamson. "Why Bears Are Good to Think and Theory Doesn't Have to Be Murder: Transformation and Oral Tradition in Louise Erdrich's *Tracks.*" *Studies in American Indian Literatures (SAIL)* 4.1 (1992): 28–48.

Coltelli, Laura. "Louise Erdrich and Michael Dorris." *Winged Words: American Indian Writers Speak.* By Laura Coltelli. Lincoln: U of Nebraska P, 1990. 41–52. Rpt. in *Conversations with Louise Erdrich and Michael Dorris.* Ed. Allan Chavkin and Nancy Feyl Chavkin. Jackson: U of Mississippi P, 1994. 19–29.

Comer, Krista. *Landscaping the New West: The Politics of Space in Contemporary Women's Writing.* Durham: U of North Carolina P, 1999.

———. "Literature, Gender Studies, and the New Western History." *Arizona Quarterly* 53.2 (1997): 99–134.

Cryer, Dan. "A Novel Arrangement." *Newsday* 30 Nov. 1986: 19–23. Rpt. in *Conversations with Louise Erdrich and Michael Dorris.* Ed. Allan Chavkin and Nancy Feyl Chavkin. Jackson: U of Mississippi P, 1994. 80–85.

Doig, Ivan. *Heart Earth: A Memoir.* New York: Penguin, 1994.

———. *This House of Sky: Landscapes of a Western Mind.* San Diego: Harcourt Brace, 1978. Preface, 1992.

Donovan, Kathleen M. *Feminist Readings of Native American Literature: Coming to Voice.* Tucson: U of Arizona P, 1998.

Dorris, Michael. *Cloud Chamber.* New York: Simon & Schuster, 1997.

———. *A Yellow Raft in Blue Water.* New York: Warner, 1987.

Dorris, Michael, and Louise Erdrich. *The Crown of Columbus.* New York: HarperCollins, 1991.

Elbrecht, Joyce, and Lydia Fakundiny. "Scenes from a Collaboration: Or Becoming Jael B. Juba." *Tulsa Studies in Women's Literature* 13.2 (1994): 241–57.

Elson, John. "1+1<2." *Time* 29 Apr. 1991: 76.

Erdrich, Louise. *The Antelope Wife*. New York: HarperCollins, 1998.

———. *The Beet Queen*. New York: Bantam, 1986.

———. *The Bingo Palace*. New York: HarperCollins, 1994.

———. *The Last Report on the Miracles at Little No Horse*. New York: HarperCollins, 2001.

———. *Love Medicine*. New York: Bantam, 1984.

———. *Tales of Burning Love*. New York: HarperCollins, 1996.

———. *Tracks*. New York: Harper & Row, 1988.

Foote, Mary Hallock. *A Victorian Gentlewoman in the Far West: The Reminiscences of Mary Hallock Foote*. Ed. Rodman W. Paul. San Marino, Calif.: Huntington Library, 1972.

Foster, Douglas. "Double Vision: An Interview with the Authors." *Mother Jones* 16.3 (1991): 26, 78–80. Rpt. in *Conversations with Louise Erdrich and Michael Dorris*. Ed. Allan Chavkin and Nancy Feyl Chavkin. Jackson: U of Mississippi P, 1994. 168–72.

Foucault, Michel. "What Is an Author?" *Textual Strategies: Perspectives in Poststructuralist Criticism*. Ed. José Harari. Ithaca: Cornell UP, 1979. 141–60.

Gilbert, Sandra M., and Susan Gubar. *The Madwoman in the Attic: The Woman Writer and the Nineteenth-Century Literary Imagination*. New Haven: Yale UP, 1979.

Gracia, J. E. "Can There Be Texts without Historical Authors?" *American Philosophical Quarterly* 31 (1994): 245–53. Cited in Gilbert Larochelle, "From Kant to Foucault: What Remains of the Author in Postmodernism?" *Perspectives on Plagiarism and Intellectual Property in a Postmodern World*. Ed. Lise Buranen and Alice M. Roy. Albany: State U of New York P, 1999. 121–30.

Grantham, Shelby. "Intimate Collaboration or 'A Novel Partnership.'" *Dartmouth Alumni* (March 1985): 43–47. Rpt. in *Conversations with Louise Erdrich and Michael Dorris*. Ed. Allan Chavkin and Nancy Feyl Chavkin. Jackson: U of Mississippi P, 1994. 10–18.

Graulich, Melody. "Book Learning: *Angle of Repose* as Literary History." *Wallace Stegner, Man and Writer*. Ed. Charles E. Rankin. Albuquerque: U of New Mexico P, 1996. 231–53.

———. "The Guides to Conduct That a Tradition Offers: Wallace Stegner's *Angle of Repose*." *South Dakota Review* 23.4 (1985): 87–106.

———. "Legacy Profile: Mary Hallock Foote (1847–1938)." *Legacy* 3.2 (1986): 43–52.

Green, Rayna. *That's What She Said: Contemporary Poetry and Fiction by Native American Women*. Bloomington: Indiana UP, 1984.

Halbert, Debora. "Poaching and Plagiarizing: Property, Plagiarism, and Feminist Futures." *Perspectives on Plagiarism and Intellectual Property in a Postmodern World*. Ed. Lise Buranen and Alice M. Roy. Albany: State U of New York P, 1999. 111–20.

Henige, David. "To Read Is to Misread, To Write Is to Miswrite: Las Casas as Transcriber." *Amerindian Images and the Legacy of Columbus*. Ed. René Jara and Nicholas Spadaccini. Minneapolis: U of Minnesota P, 1992. 198–229.

Hepworth, James R. *Stealing Glances: Three Interviews with Wallace Stegner*. Albuquerque: U of New Mexico P, 1998.

Hirschfeld, Heather. "Early Modern Collaboration and Theories of Authorship." *PMLA* 116.3 (2001): 609–22.

Howard, Rebecca Moore. "The New Abolitionism Comes to Plagiarism." *Perspectives on Plagiarism and Intellectual Property in a Postmodern World*. Ed. Lise Buranen and Alice M. Roy. Albany: State U of New York, 1999. 87–95.

Hoy, Helen. "A Second View." *Studies in American Indian Literatures (SAIL)* 3/4 (1991): 50–55.

Huey, Michael. "Two Native American Voices." *Christian Science Monitor* 2 March 1989. Rpt. in *Conversations with Louise Erdrich and Michael Dorris*. Ed. Allan Chavkin and Nancy Feyl Chavkin. Jackson: U of Mississippi P, 1994. 122–27.

Hurston, Zora Neale. *Mules and Men*. Philadelphia: Lippincott, 1935. Rpt. New York: Negro Universities P, 1969.

———. *Their Eyes Were Watching God*. Philadelphia: Lippincott, 1937. Rpt. New York: Harper & Row, 1990.

Hutcheon, Linda, and Michael Hutcheon. " 'All Concord's Born of Contraries': Marital Methodologies." *Tulsa Studies in Women's Literature* 14.1 (1995): 59–64.

Inge, M. Thomas. "Collaboration and Concepts of Authorship." *PMLA* 116.3 (2001): 623–30.

Jara, René, and Nicholas Spadaccini. "The Construction of a Colonial Imaginary: Columbus's Signature." Introduction. *Amerindian Images and the Legacy of Columbus*. Ed. René Jara and Nicholas Spadaccini. Minneapolis: U of Minnesota P, 1992. 1–95.

Jaszi, Peter. "On the Author Effect: Contemporary Copyright and Collective Creativity." *The Construction of Authorship: Textual Appropriation in Law and Literature*. Ed. Martha Woodmansee and Peter Jaszi. Durham: Duke UP, 1994. 29–56.

Jauss, Hans Robert. "The Alterity and Modernity of Medieval Literature." *New Literary History* 10 (1979): 181–229.

Johnson, Barbara. *The Feminist Difference: Literature, Psychoanalysis, Race, and Gender.* Cambridge: Harvard UP, 1998.

Kaplan, Carey, and Ellen Cronan Rose. "Strange Bedfellows: Feminist Collaboration." *Signs* 18.3 (1993): 547–61.

Kitler, Friedrich A. *Discourse Networks: 1800/1900.* Trans. Michael Metteer. Stanford: Stanford UP, 1990.

Kittredge, William. *Hole in the Sky: A Memoir.* New York: Knopf, 1992. Rpt. New York: Vintage, 1993.

Klimasmith, Betsy. "Storytellers, Story-Sellers: Artists, Muses, and Exploitation in the Work of Mary Austin." *Southwestern American Literature* 20.2 (1993): 21–33.

Koestenbaum, Wayne. *Double Talk: The Erotics of Male Literary Collaboration.* New York: Routledge, 1989.

Kolodny, Annette. "Letting Go Our Grand Obsessions: Notes toward a New Literary History of the American Frontiers." *American Literature* 64.1 (1992): 1–18.

Kristeva, Julia. *Desire in Language: A Semiotic Approach to Literature and Art.* Ed. Leon S. Roudiez. Trans. Alice Jardine, Thomas Gora, and Leon Roudiez. New York: Columbia UP, 1980.

Krupat, Arnold. "An Approach to Native American Texts." *Critical Essays on Native American Literature.* Ed. Andrew Widget. Boston: Hall, 1985. 116–31.

Laird, Holly A. " 'A Hand Spills from the Book's Threshold': Coauthorship's Readers." *PMLA* 116.2 (2001): 344–53.

———. *Women Coauthors.* Chicago: U of Illinois P, 2000.

Laird, Holly, ed. *On Collaborations: Part I.* Spec. issue of *Tulsa Studies in Women's Literature* 13.2 (1994): 231–426.

———. *On Collaborations: Part II.* Spec. issue of *Tulsa Studies in Women's Literature* 14.1 (1995): 7–212.

Langlois, Karen S. "Marketing the American Indian: Mary Austin and the Business of Writing." *A Living of Words: American Women in Print Culture.* Ed. Susan Albertine. Knoxville: U of Tennessee P, 1995. 151–68.

———. "Mary Austin and Lincoln Steffens." *Huntington Library Quarterly* 49 (1986): 357–81.

Leonardi, Susan J., and Rebecca A. Pope. "(Co)Labored Li(v)es; or, Love's Labors Queered." *PMLA* 116.3 (2001): 631–37.

Limerick, Patricia Nelson. *The Legacy of Conquest: The Unbroken Past of the American West.* New York: Norton, 1987.

London, Bette. *Writing Double: Women's Literary Partnerships*. Ithaca: Cornell UP, 1999.

Lorde, Audre. "Uses of the Erotic: The Erotic as Power." *Sister Outsider*. Freedom, Calif.: Crossing, 1984. 53–59.

Lunsford, Andrea, and Lisa Ede. "Collaboration and Concepts of Authorship." *PMLA* 116.2 (2001): 354–69.

———. "Rhetoric in a New Key: Women and Collaboration." *Rhetoric Review* 8.2 (1990): 234–41.

———. *Singular Texts/Plural Authors: Perspectives on Collaborative Writing*. Carbondale: Southern Illinois UP, 1990.

———. "Why Write . . . Together?" *Rhetoric Review* 1 (1983): 57–68.

———. "Why Write . . . Together: A Research Update." *Rhetoric Review* 5 (1986): 71–84.

Maclean, Norman. *A River Runs through It and Other Stories*. Chicago: U of Chicago P, 1976.

Masten, Jeffrey. *Textual Intercourse: Collaboration, Authorship, and Sexualities in Renaissance Drama*. Cambridge: Cambridge UP, 1997.

Miller, Jay. "Mourning Dove: The Author as Cultural Mediator." *Being and Becoming Indian: Biographical Studies of Native American Frontiers*. Ed. James A. Clifton. Chicago: Dorsey, 1989. 160–82.

Mitchell, Lee Clark. *Westerns: Making the Man in Fiction and Film*. Chicago: U of Chicago P, 1996.

Mourning Dove (Humishuma). *Cogewea, the Half-Blood: A Depiction of the Great Montana Cattle Range*. Boston: Four Seas, 1927. Rpt. Lincoln: U of Nebraska P, 1981.

———. *Mourning Dove: A Salishan Autobiography*. Ed. Jay Miller. Lincoln: U of Nebraska P, 1990.

Moyers, Bill. "Louise Erdrich and Michael Dorris." *A World of Ideas*. Ed. Bill Moyers. New York: Doubleday, 1989. 460–69. Rpt. in *Conversations with Louise Erdrich and Michael Dorris*. Ed. Allan Chavkin and Nancy Feyl Chavkin. Jackson: U of Mississippi P, 1994. 138–50.

Passaro, Vince. "Tales from a Literary Marriage." *New York Times Magazine* 21 Apr. 1991: 34–36, 38–39, 42–43, 76. Rpt. in *Conversations with Louise Erdrich and Michael Dorris*. Ed. Allan Chavkin and Nancy Feyl Chavkin. Jackson: U of Mississippi P, 1994. 157–67.

Paul, Rodman, ed. "Biographical Note." *A Victorian Gentlewoman in the Far West: The Reminiscences of Mary Hallock Foote*. By Mary

Hallock Foote. San Marino, Calif.: Huntington Library, 1972. 401–04.

Peterson, Audrey C. "Narrative Voice in Wallace Stegner's *Angle of Repose.*" *Critical Essays on Wallace Stegner.* Ed. Anthony Arthur. Boston: Hall, 1982. 176–83.

Pollit, Katha. "A New Assault on Feminism." *Nation* 26 (March 1990): 416–17.

Pratt, Mary Louise. "Arts of the Contact Zone." *Professions 1991*: 33–40.

Said, Edward W. *Beginnings: Intention and Method.* New York: Basic, 1975. Rpt. New York: Columbia UP, 1985.

———. *Orientalism.* New York: Pantheon, 1978.

Sarris, Greg. *Keeping Slug Woman Alive: A Holistic Approach to American Indian Texts.* Berkeley: U of California P, 1993.

Schumacher, Michael. "Louise Erdrich and Michael Dorris: A Marriage of Minds." *Writer's Digest* June 1991: 28–31, 59. Rpt. in *Conversations with Louise Erdrich and Michael Dorris.* Ed. Allan Chavkin and Nancy Feyl Chavkin. Jackson: U of Mississippi P, 1994. 173–83.

Smith, Sidonie. "Resisting the Gaze of Embodiment: Women's Autobiography in the Nineteenth Century." *American Women's Autobiography: Fea(s)ts of Memory.* Ed. Margo Culley. Madison: U of Wisconsin P, 1992. 75–110.

Smith, Sidonie, and Julia Watson, eds. *De/Colonizing the Subject: The Politics of Gender in Women's Autobiography.* Minnesota: U of Minnesota P, 1992.

Smith-Rosenberg, Caroll. "The Female World of Love and Ritual: Relations between Women in Nineteenth-Century America." *Signs* 1 (1975): 1–29.

Stearns, Laurie. "Copy Wrong: Plagiarism, Process, Property, and the Law." *Perspectives on Plagiarism and Intellectual Property in a Postmodern World.* Ed. Lise Buranen and Alice M. Roy. Albany: State U of New York, 1999. 5–17.

Stegner, Wallace. *Angle of Repose.* New York: Doubleday, 1971. Rpt. New York: Penguin, 1992.

———. *The Big Rock Candy Mountain.* New York: Doubleday, 1943. Rpt. New York: Penguin, 1991.

———. *The Sound of Mountain Water: The Changing American West.* New York: Doubleday, 1969. Rpt. New York: Penguin, 1997.

Stegner, Wallace, and Richard W. Etulain. *Stegner: Conversations on History and Literature.* Reno: U of Nevada P, 1990.

Stillinger, Jack. *Multiple Authorship and the Myth of Solitary Genius.* New York: Oxford UP, 1991.

Stineman, Esther Lanigan. *Mary Austin: Song of a Maverick.* New Haven, Conn.: Yale UP, 1989.

Stokes, Geoffrey. "Behind Every Great Woman . . . ? Louise Erdrich's True-Life Adventures." *Voice Literary Supplement* 48 (1 September 1986): 7–9. Rpt. in *Conversations with Louise Erdrich and Michael Dorris.* Ed. Allan Chavkin and Nancy Feyl Chavkin. Jackson: U of Mississippi P, 1994. 54–63.

Swain, Tim. "Touching Words: Helen Keller, Plagiarism, Authorship." *The Construction of Authorship: Textual Appropriation in Law and Literature.* Ed. Martha Woodmansee and Peter Jaszi. Durham: Duke UP, 1994. 57–100.

Swearingen, C. Jan. "Originality, Authenticity, Imitation, and Plagiarism: Augustine's Chinese Cousins." *Perspectives on Plagiarism and Intellectual Property in a Postmodern World.* Ed. Lise Buranen and Alice M. Roy. Albany: State U of New York, 1999. 19–30.

Tompkins, Jane. *West of Everything: The Inner Life of Westerns.* New York: Oxford UP, 1992.

Trueheart, Charles. "Marriage for Better or Words." *Washington Post* 19 Oct. 1988: B1, B8–B9. Rpt. in *Conversations with Louise Erdrich and Michael Dorris.* Ed. Allan Chavkin and Nancy Feyl Chavkin. Jackson: U of Mississippi P, 1994. 115–21.

Turner, Frederick Jackson. "The Significance of the Frontier in American History." In *Rereading Frederick Jackson Turner: "The Significance of the Frontier in American History" and Other Essays.* New York: Henry Holt, 1995. 31–60.

Walsh, Mary Ellen Williams. "*Angle of Repose* and the Writings of Mary Hallock Foote: A Source Study." *Critical Essays on Wallace Stegner.* Ed. Anthony Arthur. Boston: Hall, 1982. 184–209.

Warrior, Robert Allen. "Columbus Fiction: The Real Treasure." *Christianity and Crisis* 51.18 (1991): 393–94.

William Shakespeare's Romeo + Juliet. Dir. Baz Luhrmann. Perf. Leonardo DiCaprio, Clarie Danes, and Brian Dennehy. Twentieth Century Fox, 1996

Wong, Hertha D. "An Interview with Louise Erdrich and Michael Dorris." *North Dakota Quarterly* 55.1 (1987): 196–218. Rpt. in *Conversations with Louise Erdrich and Michael Dorris.* Ed. Allan Chavkin and Nancy Feyl Chavkin. Jackson: U of Mississippi P, 1994. 30–53.

Woodmansee, Martha. "On the Author Effect: Recovering Collectivity." *Cardozo Arts and Entertainment Law Journal* 10 (1992): 279–92.

Woodmansee, Martha, and Peter Jaszi, eds. *The Construction of Authorship: Textual Appropriation in Law and Literature.* Durham: Duke UP, 1994.

Woolf, Virginia. *A Room of One's Own.* New York: Harcourt, Brace, Jovanovitch, 1929.

Wordsworth, William. "Essay, Supplementary to the Preface." *The Prose Works of William Wordsworth.* Ed. W. J. B. Owen and Jane Worthington Smyser. Vol. 3. Oxford: Clarendon, 1974. 62–84.

Wright, Will. *Six Guns and Society: A Structural Study of the Western.* Berkeley: U of California P, 1975.

Zamora, Margarita. "Reading in the Margins of Columbus." *Amerindian Images and the Legacy of Columbus.* Ed. René Jara and Nicholas Spadaccini. Minneapolis: U of Minnesota P, 1992. 183–97.

INDEX

49; and memory, 124–25; and the New West, 121, 127; and nostalgia, 121–23, 126–27, 130; and the Old West, 121, 127; and oral history, 124–25; and racial privilege, 128–29; and representations of African Americans, 128–29; and representations of family, 140; and representations of Native Americans, 129–30; and rural folk, 126–27; and self-representations, 121–22; and silence, 149; and stereotypes, 125–26; and storytelling, 118; and voice, 124–25, 128, 130, 148–49; and women's stories, 123–24

Tompkins, Jane, 12, 189 n.11

Trueheart, Charles, 37, 38, 40, 51, 192 n.3

Turner, Frederick Jackson, xxv, xxvii, 26; "The Significance of the Frontier in American History," xxv, xxvii, 26

Twain, Mark, 18, 191 n.9

Walsh, Mary Ellen Williams, 161–63, 175–79, 198 n.1 n.3 n.6, 199 n.6

Warner, Susan, 11

Warrior, Robert Allen, 193 n.6

Watson, Julia: and Sidonie Smith, 101

the West: as contact zone, xxxi–

xxxii; definitions of, xxiv–xxvi, 150; and landscape, xxvi, 94; and national identity, xxvi–xxix; and nostalgia, xxviii; as salvation, 146

western American literature: canon of, xxiv, xxix, xxx, 188 n.7 n.8; and collaboration, xxxi, 185; as contact zone, xxxii; definitions of, xxiv–xxvi, xxx, 26–27; and "difference," 25–26; and gender, 189 n.8; and individual authorship, xxxi; and landscape, 26–27; and literary theory, xxx–xxxi; and regionalism, xxx–xxxi, xxxii, 27–30; and the Western, 189 n.11

Western Literature Association (WLA), xxix, xl

women writers, 11; excluded from authorship, 11–13; expectations regarding, 93

Wong, Hertha D., 35, 36, 192 n.3

Woodmansee, Martha, 8, 101, 196 n.2; and Peter Jaszi, xvii, 190 n.6

Woolf, Virginia, 98

Wordsworth, William, 10; and Coleridge, xvii–xviii, 2, 5; and Dorothy Wordsworth, 2

Wright, Will, 189 n.11

writing together. *See* collaboration: definitions of

Zamora, Margarita, 31

9 780803 218345